LINCOLN'S

LADY

SPYMASTER

ALSO BY GERRI WILLIS

Home Rich: Increasing the Value of the Biggest Investment of Your Life

*Rich Is Not a Four-Letter Word: How to Survive Obamacare, Trump Wall
Street, Kick-Start Your Retirement, and Achieve Financial Success*

LINCOLN'S LADY SPYMASTER

The UNTOLD STORY of the ABOLITIONIST SOUTHERN BELLE WHO HELPED WIN the CIVIL WAR

GERRI WILLIS

HARPER

An Imprint of HarperCollinsPublishers

HarperCollins books may be purchased for educational, business, or sales promotional use. For information, please email the Special Markets Department at SPsales@harpercollins.com.

FIRST EDITION

Designed by Nancy Singer
Title page art © Andrew Howe;© Getty Images

Library of Congress Cataloging-in-Publication Data

Names: Willis, Gerri author
Title: Lincoln's lady spymaster: the untold story of the abolitionist
Southern belle who helped win the Civil War / Gerri Willis.
Other titles: Untold story of the abolitionist Southern belle who helped in the Civil War
Description: First edition. | New York, NY: Harper, 2025.
Identifiers: LCCN 2024049892 (print) | LCCN 2024049893 (ebook) | ISBN
9780063333659 hardcover | ISBN 9780063333666 ebook
Subjects: LCSH: Van Lew, Elizabeth L., 1818–1900 | United States—History—
Civil War, 1861–1865—Secret service | Women spies—Virginia—Richmond. | Spies—
Virginia—Richmond. | Unionists (United States Civil War)—Virginia—Richmond—
Biography. | Richmond (Va.)—History—Civil War, 1861–1865 | LCGFT: Biographies
Classification: LCC E608.V34 W55 2025 (print) | LCC E608.V34 (ebook) |
DDC 973.7/85—dc23/eng
LC record available at https://lccn.loc.gov/2024049892
LC ebook record available at https://lccn.loc.gov/2024049893ISBN 978-0-06-333365-9

25 26 27 28 29 LBC 5 4 3 2 1

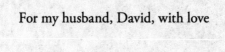
For my husband, David, with love

I HAVE NEVER STUDIED THE ART OF PAYING

COMPLIMENTS TO WOMEN; BUT I MUST SAY

THAT IF ALL THAT HAS BEEN SAID BY ORATORS

AND POETS SINCE THE CREATION OF THE WORLD

IN PRAISE OF WOMEN WERE APPLIED TO THE

WOMEN OF AMERICA, IT WOULD NOT DO THEM

JUSTICE FOR THEIR CONDUCT DURING THIS WAR.

I WILL CLOSE BY SAYING, GOD BLESS THE

WOMEN OF AMERICA!

—Abraham Lincoln,
remarks at the Sanitary Fair
in Washington, D.C.,
March 18, 1864

CONTENTS

❧ ❧

KEY CHARACTERS

IN RICHMOND

ON CHURCH HILL

Elizabeth Van Lew

Eliza Van Lew, her mother

John Van Lew, her father

John Newton Van Lew, her
    brother

Anna Van Lew, her sister

Mary Van Lew, her sister-in-law

Annie Van Lew, her niece

Eliza Van Lew, her niece

William Roane, slave

RICHMOND SPY RING

William Rowley

F.W.E. Lohmann

Sam Ruth

Mary Jane Richards

Philip Cashmeyer

Abby Green

Erasmus Ross

Robert Ford

Thomas McNiven

Charles Palmer

William Roane

Arnold B. Holmes

IN RICHMOND'S CAPITOL SQUARE

Jefferson Davis, Confederate
    president

Varina Davis, Confederate first
    lady

Secretary of War James A. Seddon

Attorney General Judah P.
    Benjamin, later secretary
    of war

xii ✦ KEY CHARACTERS

Secretary of Treasury Christopher
Memminger

Richmond mayor Joseph Mayo

CONFEDERATE MILITARY LEADERSHIP

General Robert E. Lee

Braxton Bragg, Davis's chief
military advisor

General Jubal Early

ELSEWHERE IN RICHMOND

PRISON COMMANDERS, GUARDS

Brigadier General John H. Winder

Richard R. "Dick" Turner

Lieutenant David H. Todd

Captain George C. Gibbs

Lieutenant Thomas Pratt Turner

Captain Alexander C. Godwin

RICHMOND JAIL PRISONERS

William Henry Hurlbert, *New
York Times* editor

William H. Lounsberry

Colonel Abel Streight

Colonel Thomas Ellwood Rose

Major A. G. Hamilton

Calvin Huson Jr.

CONFEDERATE SPIES AND OPERATIVES

Rose O'Neal Greenhow

Frank Stringfellow

Jacob Thomson

Clement C. Clay

Lieutenant Bennett Young

Thomas H. Hines

IN WASHINGTON

Abraham Lincoln, president

Mary Todd Lincoln, first lady

Secretary of State William Seward

Secretary of War Edwin Stanton

General Winfield Scott

Rear Admiral John Dahlgren

UNION MILITARY LEADERSHIP

General Ulysses S. Grant

Brevet Brigadier General George Sharpe, BMI chief

General George McClellan

General George Meade

General Benjamin Franklin Butler

General Isaac J. Wistar

Alfred Pleasanton, commander of Army of the Potomac Cavalry Corps

Marsena Patrick, Army's provost marshal

General Godfrey Weitzel, Union administrator of Richmond after the city fell

IN THE UNION RAID ON RICHMOND

Ulric Dahlgren

Brigadier General Hugh Judson Kilpatrick

George Armstrong Custer

Martin Robinson, free black and Union guide hung on Dahlgren's order

COVINGTON, KENTUCKY

Jesse Grant

Hannah Grant

MISSOURI

Julia Dent

Colonel Frederick Dent

Ellen Dent

UNION SPIES

Kate Warne

Allan Pinkerton

Timothy Webster, first spy executed since Nathan Hale

Lafayette Baker

Hattie Lawton

Milton Cline

BOOTH, HIS CONSPIRATORS

John Wilkes Booth

Samuel B. Arnold

Michael O'Laughlen

Dr. Samuel Mudd

Dr. William McQueen

Thomas Harbin

John H. Surratt

George A. Atzerodt

Thomas A. Jones

David E. Herold

Lewis Powell

AT HARPERS FERRY

John Brown, radical abolitionist

Edmund Ruffin, fire-eater

AT FORT SUMTER, SOUTH CAROLINA

General P.G.T. Beauregard

Major Robert Anderson

INTRODUCTION

This book began in the strange and unsettling days of the COVID pandemic. It's difficult in hindsight to remember just how unnerving those years were. Many of the young women I worked with were terrified. For me, lockdowns meant more time with family and less time spent commuting. For young women, the pandemic felt like a death sentence. Their social lives abruptly ended. They were isolated. One young woman I knew started having panic attacks. I wanted to introduce them to women who had beaten back challenges and defied the odds. American history is full of women like that.

It was during those years I discovered Elizabeth Van Lew, a Richmond belle who spied for the Union during the Civil War. I had never considered writing about the Civil War though I had read many brilliantly researched histories about the conflict. But as I read more about Van Lew and the war, I was drawn to the metamorphosis of women during the period. American women, both black and white, fought in the Civil War in ways I never dreamed possible. In the antebellum era, the United States mimicked the customs and habits of Victorian England. Women ran the household; men dominated the public sphere. Roles were specific and enforced. Hard to imagine now, but in those years, American women could be arrested or fined for simply wearing pants on the street. The war would begin to change all of that.

As men left home for the battlefield between 1861 and 1865, some women took over the jobs they left behind: working in factories; managing farms, businesses, and, in the South, slaves. In time, they would become essential to the war's prosecution. Men may have dominated the nursing profession during the antebellum years, but during the war, women took those jobs, first in hospitals and later on the battlefield, wielding the remedies their grandmothers had taught them. When the federal government set up the U.S. Sanitary Commission to collect charitable donations for the care of Union soldiers, an army of women raised more than $400 million. Phoebe Pember served as a matron at the nation's largest military medical center at the time, Richmond's Chimborazo Hospital. It treated 75,000 patients over the course of the war. Women physicians were rare, but Dr. Mary Edwards Walker was a surgeon who treated soldiers on the front lines.

On the battlefield, women took many roles. Harriet Tubman is known for her work freeing slaves as a conductor on the Underground Railroad. But she also led the Combahee River Raid on South Carolina coastal plantations in 1863, a military expedition for the Union that resulted in freedom for seven hundred slaves.

In fact, hundreds of women served on the battlefield as soldiers, wearing uniforms and passing as men. Some were patriots; others couldn't bear to be separated from their husbands, brothers, and fathers. Detection was rare because many male soldiers were young with high-pitched voices and a lack of facial hair. When one woman soldier was asked why she fought dressed as a man, she responded, "Nobody told us we couldn't." There were no gang showers or entry physicals that would have exposed their secret. Plus, nobody expected to see women wearing pants, especially the pants of a soldier's uniform.[1]

The newfound freedoms for women were tailor-made for Elizabeth Van Lew, a wealthy Richmond belle whose family was well regarded despite their Northern roots. Had the war never happened, she might have lived her life doing good works and assisting the poor. But the war opened the door to a world she had never considered, and she didn't hesitate to seize the opportunity. Her first actions as a committed Unionist were to help federal soldiers held prisoner in the Confederate capital. As the war ground on, she took more and more risks, developing a spy ring that provided General Ulysses S. Grant with some of the most critical intelligence of the war. Her reports helped the Northern commanders determine the timing of the war's final critical assault, each of her missives painting a detailed picture of the Rebel capital and the strength and location of Confederate army forces.

In the end, Elizabeth Van Lew forced me to tell her story. At first I didn't want to. There were other subjects, more well known, who demanded my attention. Belle Boyd was a seventeen-year-old Rebel in skirts who shot a Yankee soldier because she didn't like the way he spoke to her mother. In pictures, she wore most of her hair pinned up, with one long light brown corkscrew curl cascading along her bosom. Her friends called her the fastest woman in Virginia. But Boyd's career was short, and her shadow didn't extend very far.

More accomplished than Boyd as a spy, Rose O'Neal Greenhow was unofficially connected to most of official Washington. Her late-night meetings in the back parlor of her home just blocks from the White House were the stuff of D.C. gossip legend. Wild Rose's visitors were a who's who of the power structure. Senators, secessionists, abolitionists, congressmen, and even diplomats came calling. Her biggest claim to fame was providing critical information to Confederates that allowed them to whup the Yankees at the First Battle of Manassas. The loss was a major embarrassment for Union forces. In her pictures, Rose looks severe. Her dark hair is parted in the center; her lips never curl in a smile. Unfortunately, her story ended even before the war did. She drowned in the Atlantic Ocean trying to escape Union forces, weighed down by the gold she had sewn into her dress.

In the end, I kept coming back to Elizabeth. While never enjoying the celebrity of other, better-known spies, she had a far greater impact on historical events. She was a victim of her own success. Generally the best spies are the ones you've never heard of. In addition, what we do know about her life presents a mystery: Why did she stay in Richmond, not only during the war but also after, when she could have fled to the admiration and support of the North?

Her transformation was impressive. She began the war as a naive lady of genteel manners and a sweet disposition and morphed into a courageous wartime spymaster. Plus, she maintained a diary throughout the war, where she spilled her most intimate thoughts, sharing how she got scared, nervous, and angry. I could understand how she felt. She felt real to me. I started the book during the pandemic hoping to inspire young women fearful of the world that developed during the lockdowns. But over the months of writing *Lincoln's Lady Spymaster*, I've come to understand she is *my* mentor. Her persistence, courage, and dedication to a cause have come to inspire me.

During the final days of composing *Lincoln's Lady Spymaster*, I wrote about the struggle of Elizabeth's last years and the disdain with which her Richmond neighbors regarded her even in her final days. Sometimes I imagined I heard the rustle of her black silk dress behind me in my office. Her presence, even now, is powerful. For me, she still lives, and I am grateful for that.

LINCOLN'S

LADY

SPYMASTER

1

A KINDRED SPIRIT

On Church Hill, once Richmond, Virginia's preeminent neighborhood, a small figure with hunched shoulders proceeds on foot along Grace Street, unsteady but determined. The dusty hem of her old-fashioned black silk dress scours the walk. Wisps of gray hair escape her vintage hairdo. Behind her, a group of children follow, threatening and taunting her. "Crazy Bet!" they yell. "Crazy Bet!" Sadly, their parents encourage such behavior. She attempts to bat them away, swinging her hand behind her.

Elizabeth Van Lew shudders and makes the turn up the walk to her dilapidated mansion, with its peeling paint and cracked stucco. *Maybe I do look crazy,* she thinks to herself. After all, the Civil War ended more than three decades ago, yet she still wears her hoop skirt, a relic of that era. She no longer needs the corset to cinch her bodice. She is really quite skinny.

The fact is, her years as a Union spymaster during the war destroyed her family's fortune. No one forced her to do it. She was the one who gave her money away to desperate Union soldiers on the run and slaves seeking freedom in those years. It was her decision to bankroll prison breakouts and hand cash to suffering Richmond families. Now, in the first years of the twentieth century, her future is dim; her hometown, the former capital of the Confederacy, is rebounding due to a Lost Cause mythology suffusing the entire country. The pain of war and indignity of slavery have been set aside to glorify the past. Survivors of General Robert E. Lee's army and the Ladies' Lee Monument Association have come together to celebrate the life of the Confederate war general. To Elizabeth's horror, in May of 1890 they erect a sixty-foot statue commemorating Lee. According to newspaper accounts, ten thousand people push the four wagons carrying the monument from the railroad to its location in one of the city's soon-to-be best neighborhoods. To Elizabeth, it seems everybody is back to normal except her.

Elizabeth's neighbors agree she isn't normal. They think she is crazy. Many hate her. Even after all these years, she is still a traitor to them. No invitations to dinner or parties come to the Church Hill mansion, and not many visitors. A few loyal servants keep her company.

She walks into the house, the large wooden door creaking on its hinges as she passes silently through it. The eighteen-foot-wide hallway that had once admitted Supreme Court justices and European opera stars is now empty and dusty, the wood floors in need of waxing. It leads all the way to the back of the house, where the back lawn falls away to the river. The garden is badly neglected. The entryway echoes hollowly, reflecting the fact that so many of her personal possessions and those of her family are gone. She has given them away to the needy or sold them to stave off her poverty and pay the bills stacking up on her desk in the library.

She heads there now, running her hand over the fireplace columns, pulling back the heads of the lions, where she had once hidden stolen Confederate secrets bound for Union generals' eyes. Oh, the thrill and the excitement of it all! Running her circle of agents, commanding them to her bidding, advising the leadership—the actual leadership—of the Union military! No ball or garden party compared to the feeling of being a player in the greatest conflict in American history.

On the walls of the study and parlor are the pictures of the men she came to idolize, some to love. There is a picture of the Virginia politician and family friend John Minor Botts, a slaveholder who, like Elizabeth, fought to keep the Union from shattering. A drawing of him from his youth makes him look like a poet of the Romantic era, but the photo in Elizabeth's house shows Botts with a more careworn face, his jaw set in defiance. There is a small framed photo of Ulysses S. Grant as a war hero dressed in his general's uniform, slightly unkempt, his eyebrows furrowed over bright blue eyes. The photo is signed by Grant, inscribed to "Miss Van Lew." The third of Elizabeth's watchful guards is no less than the sixteenth president, Abraham Lincoln. He appears in the form of a bust on a table in the library.

The war seems so long ago to her now: its privations, and her work as a spymaster. Elizabeth knows, like anyone fully informed about espionage, that the spies you've heard about aren't likely to have been the best or most effective. Sure, the teenage Belle Boyd, who was said to have supplied Stonewall Jackson with secrets she extracted from smitten Union soldiers, was famous, and Rose Greenhow was practically a legend for her D.C. salon, which was frequented by some of the nation's top political and military leaders, who sometimes, after a drink or two, shared details they shouldn't have. But the best agents, Elizabeth knew, were the ones that disappeared completely with no trace, just as she had.

Of course, *spy* was a word that Elizabeth never accepted. She was no spy; she was simply one of the few truly loyal hearts in Richmond during those years. She was a loyalist through and through. But she also firmly believed, with an intensity usually reserved for religious converts, that Virginia couldn't have gone on as it was. Slavery was wrong. Its brutality infected not just those held captive, but all of society. The bullying tactics of plantation owners, a minority, to intimidate loyal Virginians into acquiescing to their secession plans was wrong. They had subverted democracy. She could still feel it now, a white-hot anger at what Virginia, her dear and beautiful Virginia, had become under the slave system.

Yet when the war began, she didn't run. Others of her class and wealth had packed their bags and headed north to safety and a new start. But Elizabeth couldn't. She still wasn't quite sure why. Maybe that would have been the better choice. Had she opted to go, maybe her beloved mother, Eliza, would have lived longer. Perhaps her family would even now be alive and living together in Philadelphia, her brother, John, and sister, Anna, by her side. Perhaps her beloved Mary Jane Richards would have remained with her instead of traipsing off to New York to teach for the Freedmen's Bureau, her generous efforts barely rewarded. And what would have happened to the blond and handsome Ulric Dahlgren? Without her, he might have lived instead of dying with a bullet to the back.

She knew, of course, that she had been privileged to stay and fight. What had Edgar Allan Poe, a favorite guest of this house, written? "Never to suffer would have been never to have been blessed." It was true. The war, hard as it had been, was the work of her life, containing all her high points and many of her low ones. It transformed her from a serious but directionless young woman into an iron-willed spymaster. She had begun by employing what she had learned as a Southern belle. She knew how to set men at ease and how to appeal to their vanity. She put together a diverse team of agents, her own Black servants, German business owners, and others sympathetic to the Union cause. She bribed Confederate officers for information, and the details were put on scraps of paper stashed in secret compartments in the heels of her servants' shoes or sewn into their clothing. Troop movements, rumors, and Richmond's precarious economy all became topics. As the war drew to its final days, she sent critical information to allow Grant to perfectly time his final assault. Her work had been essential to his and the Union's success.

She makes her way to the dining room, remembering the "Starvation Dinner" nights, when the rest of Richmond was fasting to support the men on the battlefield. She laughs to herself, remembering how she and her spy ring met here on those days for the most elaborate meal Elizabeth's kitchen could prepare. The laughter, the singing, and the story telling were all conducted behind closed curtains. Rebels were never far away during those dangerous days.

The strains, the stress, the anxiety of it all came flooding back to her. The late nights worrying about whether her agents would make it back from an assignment. The knock at the door heralding the arrival of Confederate detectives here to drag her away. She is too old for all this now. She heads briskly to the top floor to make one last stop.

As she walks along the third-floor hallway, her footsteps echo. Here at the end of the hall is her hideaway. The bureau that hid the hole in the wall is gone, but the opening remains. Visitors, lured by the home's history and the possibility of seeing a ghost, still come to see the hideaway. She peers in, remembering the frightened faces of those who had hidden inside, so many years ago. How she wished they all could have made it out safely. The memories are all that remains of those days. It was worth it, after all.

Now it's time for her to go, to be on her way. She hears the voices of the regular intruders, the workmen trying to turn this vast and empty building into something useful. She knows she is scaring them. She doesn't care. She may be only a ghost, but she deserves a little fun. After all, how could such a formidable woman disappear simply because she is dead? In the basement, the outline of her figure appears against basement walls, sending workers running. "I done hear Miss Lizzie walkin' 'bout," one says. "I knowed all 'long she was here."[1]

The myth of Crazy Bet—her ghost and her wanderings—was the stuff of legend on Church Hill and throughout Richmond. No small number of misbehaving children were set straight by threats of being sent to Miss Lizzie. As the years passed, the legend persisted and even grew.

In 1943, so the legend goes, one Richmond woman taking a walk on Church Hill with her young son felt a cat brush against her leg. Suddenly, cats were all around her. And then the woman remembered Elizabeth Van Lew was said to have had dozens of cats. Before she could react, she heard a rustle of fabric. She turned and saw Elizabeth, wearing a black dress just as she did in life. The hat on her head was held in place by ribbons. The face below was wizened like dried fruit, the voice crisp. "We must get these flowers through the lines at once for General

Grant's breakfast table in the morning." And then, with a rustle, the ghost was gone.[2]

The Elizabeth Van Lew of the ghost stories was only a myth. But it had a way of keeping Elizabeth from getting her true recognition. Painting the spy as crazy and unreasonable had a way of diminishing her contributions.

Ninety-four years after the Civil War, Edwin C. Fishel, himself a former spy active during World War II, uncovered a roomful of documents at the National Archives tied with red tape and unopened since the war between the states ended. They were the records of the Army of the Potomac's Bureau of Military Information (BMI), the spooks of the Union. One name among many kept popping up in the BMI records: Elizabeth Van Lew. As Fishel wrote, "The most productive espionage operation of the Civil War, on either side, that has ever been documented was the service performed by Richmond's Unionist underground." And that underground was run by Elizabeth.[3]

What follows is no ghost tale. This is the real and true story of Elizabeth Van Lew, Lincoln's lady spymaster.

2

✦•✦

SOUTHERN BELLES

The South loves its traditions, and few are better known than that of the Southern belle. During the years before the Civil War, young women from the region's elite families were introduced to society, following the elaborate rituals of Southern culture. The strictures of Victorian society were many, but that didn't mean debutantes couldn't have fun. In fact, it would have been hard not to. The period between the end of childhood and marriage was a time when a young Southern woman possessed more freedom than at any other point. She spent her time dancing, chatting, and flirting, teasing young men who might make suitable partners and socializing with her girlfriends and relatives. Luncheons, dinners, and balls were held in her honor. For sheltered young women, it was all pretty head-spinning.

The elaborate costumes worn by debutantes in the antebellum South reflected their idealized image held by the society of the day. Candy-colored ball gowns made of silk, satin, and even velvet, were common, the neckline plunging or off the shoulder. Lace insets, embroidery, or beadwork defined the bodice. The focal point, of course, was the waist. In the style of the time, it was cinched by corsets with whalebone inserts for structure and pulled tight with silk laces. Leaning over to pick up something off the ground was nearly impossible, a restriction that allowed the savvy belle to engage a possible suitor's attention for assistance. The skirt was full and bell-shaped, held in place by layers of petticoats or crinolines. At its widest, the skirt could measure five feet, nearly as wide as the young woman was tall. Girls typically didn't wear makeup, but they did wear their hair in elegant styles, pinned to the head or allowed to flow loose in curls down the back of the head. The whole effect was of a beautiful hourglass, although the costume was heavy and limited the wearer's movement. As a result, women walked with mincing, delicate steps that made them appear to float across a ballroom.

The Southern belle wore these costumes to balls and cotillions, when during her mid- to late-teen years she was formally introduced by her parents and family into society. The dresses and the parties were intended to emphasize the wearer's beauty and modesty, as well as her good manners and mild temperament, and most important, her suitability for the marriage market. These rituals both celebrated the traditions of the region's elite class and made for its continuance. Unions between belles and their fiancés were expected to cement and grow family fortunes. For that reason, elite families in the South's cities, like Richmond, also practiced the traditions of "coming out," just as their rural cousins did on plantations.

War would change everything, of course. But decades before she worked as a spymaster, Elizabeth was a belle. She would have participated in the rituals of being presented to Richmond's tight-knit society by her parents, who were skillful social climbers transplanted from the North. As a girl, Elizabeth would have vacationed at Virginia's mountain springs in the summer, danced at parties, and flirted just as the other girls did. In many ways, the teenage Elizabeth fit the Southern belle tradition like a glove. Quick-witted and sociable, she was dainty and pretty, with dark blond hair swept up in a chignon, from which curls fell nearly to her shoulders. Her bright blue eyes were set in a narrow face. Her mother had taught her the manners prized by Southern culture. She could set a guest at ease quickly and entertain them with lively conversation. Her letters of that era reveal a young woman with a flirtatious and fun nature. It's easy to imagine the young Elizabeth captivating gentleman callers.

Plus, she had an advantage not all young women, not even all debutantes, could claim. She was rich. Her father, John Van Lew, was an ambitious New Yorker from Long Island who ran a successful hardware business at a time Richmond was growing and expanding. His client roster, which included Thomas Jefferson and the University of Virginia, connected him to Virginia's storied history, a past venerated by that generation's conservatives. The family's life centered on a three-story brick and stucco mansion that John Van Lew bought on Church Hill, Richmond's most prestigious neighborhood. It was there that Elizabeth, the eldest of three children, spent most of her life.

There was just one problem. While Elizabeth had many of the qualities prized by Southern culture in their debutantes, she was neither meek nor mild. She had opinions and ideas that didn't fit the social ideals of the time, and she wasn't shy about voicing them. "From the time I knew right and wrong, it was my sad privilege to differ," Elizabeth wrote, on "many things from the perceived opinions and principles" of Richmond society. This was true, but a tremendous understatement. She argued with her father and acknowledged her contrariness in her diary, writing she was "quick in feeling and ready to resent what seemed to me wrong."[1]

It wasn't just her family members who received her barbs. When war threatened and young women advocated for secession, Elizabeth was withering in her criticism. They were "unknowing and unreflecting" with "an almost universal want of national patriotism." In her view, the men were worse: bloodthirsty, eager for all Union people to be "driven into the streets and slaughtered." It doesn't escape her scrutiny that the few remaining Unionist men were afraid to voice their views. While they hung back, Elizabeth was determined to find a way to have hers heard.[2]

Elizabeth was also generous to a fault and felt things deeply. Even as a young woman, she visited the slums in Richmond, bringing food and other necessities to those who lived there. Over the course of her life, she would give away most of her fortune to those she deemed needy.

It's difficult to reconcile her big heart with her quarrelsome nature, but both qualities could be found in Elizabeth Van Lew and both were necessary for the work she would do during the war.

Unlike most other debutantes, however, she never married. Her family has said she fell in love with a young man, but he died before they could walk down the aisle. She may never have recovered from the loss. But it's just as likely that she simply didn't see any benefit to marriage. She was not eager to surrender the freedom she had achieved on Church Hill. In her diary she comes across as a willful woman who liked to make up her own mind and pursue her own goals. She was not a good candidate for marriage in an era in which women were expected to hand over all their assets to their husband and obey his wishes. The $10,000 her father, John Van Lew, left her after his death, a handsome sum at the time, was hers to spend as she wanted. Her father had made sure of that. The money gave her options she wouldn't have had otherwise. In her own home, her parents enjoyed a more egalitarian marriage that may have made other relationships seem lacking by comparison. She wrote in her diary that she was "thankful for the memory of one true marriage," that of her parents. She may have also felt a keen responsibility to her family. After her father died in 1847, perhaps she wanted to personally make sure they were looked after and cared for, an obligation that would have been difficult to fulfill as a married woman.[3]

Elizabeth was most influenced by her mother, Eliza, also a Northerner, but one with deep connections to the country's origins. Elizabeth's later Unionist sentiments were likely shaped by the rich civic pride that her family could claim in the nation's founding. Eliza's father, Hilary Baker, had served in the Continental Army during the Revolutionary War. He was a member of the Pennsylvania Constitutional Convention of 1789 and 1790, which produced the nation's government charter, establishing individual liberties and limiting government by establishing a system of checks and balances for its three branches.

His service to the city of Philadelphia was famous. Elizabeth heard the stories again and again as a small child. When yellow fever swept

Philadelphia in 1798, most of the well-heeled residents evacuated the city to stay safe. Not only did Baker stay, but he also commissioned the first uniformed police force to watch over the city and protect it from looting and vandalism. He eventually succumbed to the disease, and the tale of how Elizabeth's mother, baby Eliza, was taken to his side and touched her father's brow as he died was legend in the Baker family.

But Elizabeth would inherit another part of her grandfather's legacy besides his strong leadership in a crisis. Baker was one of the first members of the Pennsylvania Abolition Society, a powerful antislavery organization that he remained a member of his entire life. It counted both Blacks and whites as members. Founding father Benjamin Franklin served as its president and, at the society's request, petitioned Congress to ban slavery in 1790. (That petition failed.) Elizabeth's mother likely shared all this family history with her during her childhood, though Eliza would have little guessed how strongly it would inspire her child.

During the antebellum years, most young women who were members of the social elite in Richmond were educated at nearby private all-girl schools that celebrated Southern culture. In the decades before the Civil War, Richmond city fathers were eager not to expose their children to what they believed were the uncivil and corrupting influences of the North. According to the founders of one such school, "The originators of this effort desired that the daughters of the South should be educated at the South and under the refining influences of Southern society." But Elizabeth's Northern-born parents didn't send their daughter to such a school. Instead, in her early teens she was packed off to Philadelphia to receive a formal education, most likely at the school her mother had attended. While her peers were being taught loyalty to the South, Elizabeth undertook a very different course of study. Much of her education took place outside the classroom. She would have witnessed political ferment firsthand in the city. Moral reform societies helped promote antislavery feeling. Her grandfather's abolitionist society was still functioning and, in fact, served as a model for many similar reform societies operating in the city at the time.[4]

While in Philadelphia, Elizabeth would have been careful to keep up her attendance at church. She was raised an Episcopalian, growing up in a society church barely a block from her home. Her diary contains references to Christ and the Almighty, and she describes falling to her knees to pray. She writes how Christian charity drove her to carry out her good works, but she was not opposed to a mystic interpretation of God's action in history. In describing her lifelong struggle with the people of Richmond, she recalled the words of William Roane, a Black man who, she wrote, "called us owners." He had quoted the Bible, a warning in the Book of Daniel about the downfall of the "king of the South." In retrospect, she saw this as an omen from God. The man had told her that her whole world was doomed. "They shall fall down slain. That is the fulfillment of prophecy."

Everyone seemed to see conflict coming, like a burgeoning storm. In 1856, Robert E. Lee wrote to his wife: "Slavery as an institution is a moral & political evil in any Country." If abolition was to occur quickly, he acknowledged, "it must occur through the agency of a civil and servile war," an outcome he found odious and ungodly. Unlike William Roane, who foresaw apocalyptic action and judgment, Lee preferred a Providence slow and deliberate, bringing about emancipation after a great length of time (and, needless to say, without any sacrifice required on the part of Robert E. Lee).

Politics and faith were intertwined for Richmonders. The white clapboard church Elizabeth attended her entire life, St. John's Episcopal, was an institution favored by many of the city's elite and had an important past. Founded just seven years after the city of Richmond, it served as a backdrop for the Second Virginia Convention, whose members debated how to respond to Great Britain's heavy-handed taxes and repression of Boston colonists. On March 23, 1775, its windows were flung open so that colonists crowding the church's hilltop grounds could hear the fiery proceedings. Patrick Henry delivered a rallying cry that would not be forgotten. Responding to arguments that colonists should resist taking up arms, Henry said, paraphrasing an Old Testament prophecy, "Peace,

and markets. Stories of slave uprisings, real and imagined, were common. The dailies' coffers were lined with proceeds from ads purchased by traders promoting slave markets, and others bought by owners seeking slaves who had run away. Some slave markets were held in the city's best hotels. Owning slaves was a prerequisite to entry into the city's elite classes and best neighborhoods. Some city councilmen traded slaves. Even the most liberal-minded of politicians didn't advocate freeing slaves; they spoke only of limiting the practice of slavery.

This was the entrenched system Elizabeth grew up in. She would have known a great deal about the slave trade. Wall Street and Lumpkin's jail were only a few blocks from Church Hill, and while she doesn't describe witnessing the trade in her diary, she could not have avoided observing the horrors of slavery on the street, where Black men, women, and children sometimes faced physical punishment by their masters. To the tenderhearted Elizabeth, such sights were unbearable. Even listening to slaves singing in tobacco factories as they worked could send Elizabeth into tears. A Van Lew visitor, Swedish author Frederika Bremer, recorded such a scene, describing Elizabeth as compassionate and good-hearted. A similar experience was recorded by her cousin, Anna Whitlock, who remembered Elizabeth's tale about a visit to Hot Springs, a popular resort three days north of Richmond. There, Elizabeth met and talked with a slave trader who told her a story she would never forget. The trader described a mother and a baby on the auction block who were separated and sold to different masters. When the mother was separated from her baby, the mother's heart literally broke and she fell dead. The anger and anguish young Elizabeth felt on hearing that story would last a lifetime.

But what made Elizabeth different was not her sensitivity, but the fact that she had the gumption and vision to act on it. When her father died in September of 1843, she swung into action to chip away at the unjust foundation of the world she lived in. Within a few decades, she'd swapped her chisel for dynamite. As much as she loved her world, always calling Richmonders "our people," she would be the one who helped bring it crashing down.

After the death of her husband, Eliza became even more committed to her own father's abolitionist beliefs, and her daughter was with her every step of the way. Eliza and Elizabeth ensured that a favorite slave of theirs, a young girl named Mary Jane Richards, was baptized at St. John's. Eliza also sold property at below-market prices to a pair of free Black women. These may sound like small decisions, but in Southern culture they would have been considered at odds with convention and suspect as Southern nationalism sentiment grew.

Just as Elizabeth didn't fit the stereotype of the Southern belle, so Richmond wasn't a bucolic, sleepy Southern town. Times were changing. The city was an odd combination of the industrialized North and the rural South. On her long rambles through the city, Elizabeth would have seen smokestacks sitting atop factories along the James River, belching exhaust and coal smoke, which blended into a potent haze. And she would have been familiar with the city's stink, which was caused by bird dung shipped thousands of miles from Peru, offloaded at Richmond, and bought by Virginia tobacco farmers, who said its application tripled the yields of their farms. While Elizabeth's hometown had been built on the riches from Virginia's tobacco fields, the city fathers recognized that tobacco production was labor intensive and its profitability limited. By the 1850s, antebellum Richmond was looking for more lucrative endeavors. That meant only one thing—modernization. New industries sprouted along the James River: industrial-scale milling; sophisticated ironworks; cooperages; naileries; cotton and woolen manufacturing. Elizabeth's father's business would have supported the expansion. By the end of the 1850s, the city increasingly resembled its Northern counterparts: gritty, industrial, and dangerous.[10]

All these developments would make the city an important powerhouse in the coming war. Richmond had been home to mills powered by the James River since its founding, but Gallego Flour Mills, opened in 1790 by Spaniard Joseph Gallego, was a colossus. Generations of managers had expanded its operations. By 1859, the operation was housed in a nine-story redbrick production facility that sat astride the James River, and Gallego managers scoured maps to find the most efficient sea routes to new markets in South America. In the years before the Civil War, Gallego flour was recognized internationally.

A short twenty-minute walk from the mill, Tredegar Iron Works was the South's most important iron producer. It fed the development of the region's railroads, producing locomotives, spikes, and car wheels.[11] Its sprawling five-acre site in the heart of Richmond employed more than seven hundred people, where "the roar of hundreds of fires, the clanging of hammers, machinery boring, turning, cutting, rolling thousands of sheets of iron," wrote the *Richmond Dispatch,* were "almost deafening, a music all its own."

As the 1850s drew to a close, Elizabeth's hometown had transformed itself into an economic dynamo. Its industries drew workers from all over the world for jobs. German, Irish, and British immigrants provided the specialized skills required by the new businesses. The city's population swelled to its largest on record until that time, 37,910, a third of which was enslaved and more than a tenth foreign born.

While the city more and more resembled the industrial North rather than the South, Richmond elites prided themselves on their Southern roots and traditions. On the eve of the Civil War, most Richmond residents would have considered the city a modern one. But the changing times seemed to entrench the attitudes of Virginia's aristocracy. Foreseeing the end of their empire, an old-world system in a new world full of unfulfilled promises, Southern elites clung all the more desperately to tradition.

It is perhaps because of those traditions that a young actor just getting his feet as a performer moved to the city. In 1859, John Wilkes Booth apprenticed at the Marshall Theater, barely twenty blocks from Elizabeth's Church Hill home. He was young on the boards and just learning what it would take to be a success, but he fell in love with Richmond and would later describe it as a place he was reborn. Would the two have passed each other on the street? Would Elizabeth have attended one of his performances? Likely we will never know. But in the coming months, the two would both be swept up in the story of a firebrand whose actions would shock the nation and serve as a matchstick for the war. The actions of radical abolitionist John Brown would begin to weave together the story lines of Elizabeth Van Lew and John Wilkes Booth.

꽃 꽃

PEACE, PEACE, BUT THERE IS NO PEACE

NOVEMBER 19, 1859

All Richmond was in turmoil. People swarmed the governor's mansion on Capitol Hill, where the city's mayor had scrambled atop the portico. He screamed out the latest news and rumors from Harpers Ferry, a small mountain town 165 miles north of the capital. Seventeen days had passed since the radical abolitionist John Brown had been sentenced to hang for his crimes in the once-bucolic town.

After dark on October 16, 1859, John Brown nearly started the Civil War on his own in the mountain town of Harpers Ferry, seizing the federal armory there with just eighteen men. The one watchman guarding the complex was easily overwhelmed. Brown thought he was leading a slave revolt, but nobody followed him. Seventeen people died in the raid, including a free Black man, who was fatally shot. The whole escapade was an abject failure, but the event seized the imagination of anxious Southerners. If America had thought the moment of decision could be put off any longer, Harpers Ferry put the lie to that dream.

In Richmond, the threat of violence still hung in the air.

The pandemonium was stilled by the sounds of the bell in the tower in Capitol Square. Six bursts, followed by a pause, and then six more bursts.

The signal was unmistakable. Governor Henry Wise was calling the city's militias to duty. Hundreds of men responded. They rushed to the Broad Street train depot, grabbing guns and cartridge boxes of ammunition. They wrestled on their military jackets. Mothers, wives, and sisters looked on, some crying, others wondering if this was the start of a greater conflict.

John Wilkes Booth burst into the Marshall Theater, grabbing his coat, his face bright with excitement. "I'm off to the wars," he announced to the stagehands sitting nearby. He ran back onto Broad Street and headed for the depot. Already, his friends with the Richmond Grays militia were boarding. They were resplendent, wearing distinctive gray jackets with black edging. Booth, his handsome face upturned, called up to them, begging to be allowed onto the train. His demanding apprenticeship at the Marshall had precluded joining the Grays, but he was friends with many of its members all the same, attending their frequent outings and parties, watching them drill in city squares. Though this mission was for militiamen only, Booth was insistent; he wanted to be included. He wouldn't be turned away from such an exciting mission. Soon a jacket and hat were thrown from one of the train's windows, and the actor was invited to join.[1]

Booth had come to the city the previous year. He was twenty-one, with a charming personality that could occasionally turn dark. What was most notable about him at that time was his beauty. His black hair fell in ringlets about his face; his skin was porcelain. He was athletic from years of outdoor exercise in the rural Maryland countryside where he had grown up. In short, he was nothing like the angry and bitter assassin of Lincoln he would become six years later. Instead, most people who met him loved him. Young and eager to impress audiences and friends, he craved camaraderie and intimacy. But mostly he just wanted to be famous.

His father was a famous British actor named Junius Brutus Booth, a favorite of American audiences, particularly in Shakespearean roles. But Junius had warned his son against following in his footsteps and judged John incapable of succeeding onstage. The younger Booth persisted anyway, coming to Richmond, where he hoped to burnish his talent and boost his confidence. The city's active social scene and its politics, too, fit him like a glove. Friends recalled he was well accepted in the city and politically at home. One remembered him as "always an intense Southerner in all his feelings and thoughts."

He was in nearly every way a contrast to Brown, the subject of Richmond's outrage, who was a member of a small national abolitionist movement to bring an end to slavery. While Booth was young and fresh-faced, Brown, at fifty-six, was leathery and wrinkled; his body lean and tall. His political cause, abolitionism, was anathema to Booth, who favored slavery and the South's ascendency. The old abolitionist, his silver hair and beard making him look like a woodcutting of Moses parting the Red Sea, was hoping that his violent actions would provoke a reconsideration of slavery. In fact, it only hardened the views of voices on either side of the argument. It's one of the ironies of history that Brown's theatricality resonated even with his political enemies. War represented, for glory-hungry young men, a stage upon which they could give a historic performance.

But Brown didn't fit in with other abolitionists, either. Most abolitionists of the day pursued their goals by peaceful means. The founders of the movement were Quakers and evangelical Christians. They didn't advocate violence and hoped to change public attitudes by circulating petitions and writing about the scourge of slavery in newspapers. They assisted slaves escaping bondage traveling the Underground Railroad to freedom. This was the sort of abolitionism that Elizabeth favored. She and her mother had pursued a slow but steady effort to free their own slaves, though they were constrained by two things. First, John Van Lew's will explicitly barred them from freeing or selling their slaves. Second, Virginia law made it illegal for newly freed slaves to remain in Richmond. This was a practical barrier for many slaves who had lived in Richmond for years and had families in the city. Like many conservatives in Virginia, Elizabeth wanted the practice of slavery ended, but she didn't want its end forced on the Commonwealth by outside forces. She longed for the state to take action on its own. That would prove a wish too ambitious to be fulfilled.

Brown's violent streak had brought him to national attention in 1855, when hundreds of pro- and antislavery advocates flooded into Kansas to influence whether the state's status would be as a free or a slave state. Brown moved there, joining six of his sons to fight the extension of slavery. While deeply religious, adhering to a strict Calvinist dogma, he was willing to subvert Christian teachings against murder to fulfill his abolitionist beliefs. In short, he believed it was right and righteous to murder those who stood in the way of freeing slaves. On the night of May 24–25, 1856, he led a small band of radicals that did just that. Summoning a volunteer force that included five of his sons and three associates, over two days Brown led an orgy of killing of proslavery men in Franklin County, Kansas, in what came to be known as the Pottawatomie Massacre. Under Brown's order, they struck after dark on May 24, dragging husbands and sons from their beds and hacking them with cutlasses, leaving their mangled and dead bodies strewn outside their homes. Brown alone decided who lived and who died as they moved from cabin to cabin, leaving wives and children sobbing in the darkness. Brown claimed afterward that he personally took no lives. The killings at Pottawatomie Creek marked the beginning of the bloodletting of the era called Bleeding Kansas, a four-year period of violent guerrilla warfare. Brown never admitted responsibility and was never prosecuted for his role, which some characterize as the opening shot in the Civil War.[2]

While the Pottawatomie Massacre fueled anxiety throughout the South, what he did next in Virginia stoked the fires of secession directly with the people most likely to decide to break up the Union. The abolitionist had spun together a plan cultivated from his studies of guerrilla warfare and slave revolts and inspired by this New Testament passage (Hebrews 9:22): "without the shedding of blood, there is no remission of sin." His idea was to instigate a slave rebellion in the mountains of

Virginia. There, following the ridgelines, he and his band would encourage thousands of slaves to rise and join his insurrection. Harpers Ferry was a logical starting point for such a revolt. Located on a neck of land at the confluence of the Shenandoah and Potomac Rivers in the Blue Ridge Mountains, the town was the site of a large federal armory and rifle works where several hundred people manufactured arms for the U.S. Army. The town was built on a steep slope with narrow streets winding up and down the hills. Brown knew the operation was lightly guarded. [3]

He began by renting a wooden farmhouse outside Harpers Ferry from which to stage his operations, making plans and gathering forces and ammunition. After dark on October 16, 1859, he and the eighteen men he had recruited crept into Harpers Ferry, seizing the armory. The surprise couldn't have been more complete. Just one watchman guarded the entire complex, and he was easily overwhelmed by Brown's gang. Next they barricaded the railroad and fatally shot the baggagemaster, a free Black man, ironically the first casualty in Brown's war for freedom. Word was circulated in the neighborhood among slaves to induce their participation in the raid, and Brown and his men took several hostages, including a great-grandnephew of George Washington.

Locals began firing on Brown and his men the next morning as nearby militias converged to protect the town. Brown set up to make a stand from a thick-walled firehouse. Despite that cover, that afternoon, eight of his men were killed, including two of his sons. The fatalities also included three townsmen. Seven of Brown's raiders ran off. Rushing to assist Harpers Ferry that night was a company of U.S. Marines, led by a man who would become a household name, Robert E. Lee, who would later lead the Army of Northern Virginia.

That night, the Marines retook the firehouse from Brown. Without firing a single shot, they battered in the door and killed two of the raiders, capturing the others, and losing but one man. Brown was taken unharmed, save for a wound made by an officer's dress sword. His quixotic raid was over barely thirty-six hours after it had started.

Virginia officials were immediately worried that public sentiment was so high that Brown might be lynched if they did not act quickly. Virginia governor Henry Wise ordered Brown moved to Charles Town, West Virginia, where a grand jury was already in session just eight miles away. Within a week of his capture, Brown was on trial, charged with treason, murder, and fomenting insurrection. He was convicted and sentenced to hang in short order, on December 2.

But that was just the beginning of the trouble. Brown's raid would further drive a wedge between the North and the South. Everyone appeared to be certain of their opinion, whether for or against abolition. In the North, antislavery newspapers initially characterized Brown's actions as "misguided, wild, and apparently insane," as the *Worcester Spy* did, but that view in the North gave way to approval and even a canonization of Brown. It was Brown himself, speaking eloquently on his own behalf, that fired the engines of a reappraisal. He said famously, "Now, if it is deemed necessary that I should forfeit my life for the furtherance of the ends of justice, and mingle my blood further with the blood of my children and with the blood of millions in this slave country whose rights are disregarded by wicked, cruel, and unjust enactments, I say, let it be done."[4]

A who's who from the literary world and the pulpit offered statements of support for Brown, including essayist and poet Ralph Waldo Emerson, reformer and clergyman Henry Ward Beecher, and poet Henry Wadsworth Longfellow. Beecher, whose sister Harriet Beecher Stowe wrote *Uncle Tom's Cabin,* wanted to see Brown hanged for no reason other than turning him into a martyr around which antislavery forces could rally. In a sermon, Beecher declared, "Let no man pray that Brown be spared!"[5]

Southern newspapers called for Brown's execution, damning the raid as an act of war and labeling Brown's insurrectionist band murderers. Some editorial writers saw war on the horizon. The *Richmond Inquirer* said this: "The Harpers Ferry invasion has advanced the cause of Disunion more than any other event that has happened since the formation of the Government."

Southern reaction moved from outrage to hysteria when the details of Brown's plan for freeing slaves throughout the South were revealed. Brown's maps of seven states denoted counties where slaves outnumbered whites. The sites were marked with crosses. Horrified Southerners saw themselves in the crosshairs.

Many came to believe that Brown wasn't acting alone or even, as he was, with a small band of Northern abolitionists for support, but ascribed the plot to either fanatical Republicans or simply all Northerners. *The Federal Union* of Milledgeville, Georgia, opined that the insurrection was "a premeditated attempt of Abolitionist Fanatics to overthrow the Government and emancipate the slaves."

Proslavery forces in Richmond, meanwhile, worried that the commonwealth's long stretches of border with Pennsylvania and Ohio might be breached by revenge-seeking abolitionists. Who could tell if Brown was just the start of a wave of abolitionists coming to free slaves? Should they brace for a slave uprising? The anxiety rippled all the way from Harpers Ferry to Church Hill. Elizabeth recorded the fears swirling around in Richmond in her diary: "There were rumors the whole North was coming. Thousands of men marching in battle array to overwhelm us. The alarm bell would be rung; the tramp of armed men could be heard through the night, and no time was given the people for a sane breath and a perception of the truth."

Only feelings of anger outweighed fear, Elizabeth wrote. "Our people required blood, the blood of all who were of the [John] Brown party. They thirsted for it; they cried out for it. It was not enough that one old man should die." [6]

Meanwhile, Booth and the other men from Richmond didn't arrive in Charles Town until the next evening, clouds threatening rain. Charles Town treated the men with respect. And in a surprising twist, Booth, though he had no formal military training, became central to the activity, working in the regimental quartermaster office and ordering food for the hundreds of men called there from every part of the state. He also served as sentry, guarding the jail where Brown was being held. All the while, tensions were high as everyone braced for what might come next. An assassin? An armed party of abolitionists? Since the troops were green, false alarms were common. A horse was nearly shot to death by just such an anxious militiaman. The city was full of cannons and cavalry patrols, the days starting with drums beating reveille. Charles Town was under military law.

Booth thrived. Not only did he take a leadership role, but given such a captive and bored audience, he also performed, reciting Shakespeare to troops around the campfire or in the soldiers' barracks. Eventually he began performing for larger crowds at a local church. And he was fascinated by Brown. Even though Booth was an avowed proslaver whose worldview was widely different from Brown's, he asked to meet with the fire-and-brimstone abolitionist and was granted an audience on the eve of Brown's execution by the sheriff. The two sat and visited for a short period in Brown's cell, leaving Booth, like so many people who met Brown, with a grudging admiration for the abolitionist radical. In a letter to his sister, Booth described him as a brave old man. There is no record of what was said in the encounter. But one can imagine the two, sitting opposite each other. Booth's smooth, handsome face and compact muscular body were a contrast to Brown's weathered countenance and lean silhouette. And yet, in their own ways, both were consummate showmen.[7]

The next day, Booth joined the Grays, whose assignment was to guard the gallows, which stood on a rise, in a large meadow. The morning started quietly without the bugle sounding reveille or even troops saluting one another as they made their way to the meadow. In brilliant red shirts, Virginia Military Institute cadets stood in formation at the foot of the gallows, the Grays to their left, only thirty feet away.

Appearing perfectly composed, Brown was led from his jail cell to a wagon that contained his coffin. As he rode to the gallows, he remarked on the beauty of the Blue Ridge Mountains, the weather setting up for a fine day, the mountains wrapped in a haze.

On the scaffold, Brown appeared calm, thanking the sheriff for his help, but saying nothing more; he issued no sermon on slavery, no chastisement for his handling. His feet were tied together and a white linen hood was draped over his face. Ten minutes later a hatchet cut a rope holding the trapdoor, and he briefly struggled as his body fell. And then the struggling stopped.

Booth, who had been watching closely, grew pale and, turning to a friend, said he felt faint, adding he would like a "good, stiff whiskey." The young actor kept a piece of the wood from Brown's coffin for the rest of his short life.[8]

Booth's initial admiration of Brown's dedication and personal resolve faded. The next year he wrote: "While I live, I shall think with joy upon the day when I saw the sun go down upon one traitor less in this land," he wrote in 1860. But the image of Brown dangling from a hangman's scaffold was one he would never forget.

What Brown had proven to the young actor, however, was that a single person could challenge the status quo. Staging his protest in the heart of Dixie, the old abolitionist played on the deepest fears of slave-holding Southerners, that their enslaved people would rise up and reclaim their freedom. Charles Town was a classroom for the young actor. And the main lesson he learned was this: Audacity could change history.

4

❧ ⬧ ❧

ELIZABETH VS. THE FIRE-EATERS

The divisions had hardened. Harpers Ferry made it clear that there were two sides. Was compromise possible? Could war be avoided? If not, every American would face a choice, including Elizabeth. For her, devotion to the Union was a given. But what would resistance look like? Who would she follow? She found it intolerable to march in lockstep with the decadent, oppressive aristocracy into which she had been born. But she knew the John Browns of the world hadn't truly reckoned the cost of the whirlwind they were unleashing.

She had to keep hoping there was another way. An Illinoisan, Abraham Lincoln, had won the Republican nomination for president, a shock to Southern advocates of disunion, known as disunionists or secessionists. Self-educated and ambitious, the fifty-one-year-old had cannily avoided taking sides on the national slavery debate. Instead, despite his own misgivings about slavery, he had carved out a careful compromise position based on his exhaustive research on the thirty-nine signers of the Constitution. A slim majority of those men, twenty-one, had voted at least once for the restriction of slavery in national territories. The speech in which Lincoln described his findings, the Cooper Union Address, is still regarded as one of his most important.[1]

Staking out a politically successful position on slavery was hard.

Previous politicians had ended their careers by embracing abolitionist ideas. Lincoln didn't want to do that. He was only getting started. Still, Southern disunionists didn't trust him, despite Lincoln's more measured position. How the Railsplitter, as he was nicknamed, would govern was an open question. Many believed he would be a party hack, likely to be ruled by politicians and vested interests more powerful than he.

One of the best-known early secessionists, Edmund Ruffin, described Lincoln as "inferior in ability and reputation." Though he was no supporter of the Union, Ruffin believed other better-known candidates would more easily galvanize the South against the North. And that is just what he wanted to see happen.

Slaveholders and farmers alike saw the Republican Party, which they described as the Black Republican Party, as bent on destroying the South's way of life. Newspaper reports of slave insurrections and abolitionist invaders stoked a general atmosphere of paranoia. Disunionists blamed the Republican Party for John Brown's raid, reasoning that no single man could have wreaked such havoc on his own. They were, of course, wrong. But Lincoln, as the head of the party, came in for the most opprobrium.

As much as John Brown's raid had stoked Southern fears, people in the South did what most folks do when their way of life is challenged. They returned to habits they found reassuring. And so during that summer of 1860, the elite went on vacation. Like much of the South's aristocracy, Elizabeth and her mother made the trip to White Sulphur Springs in the mountains of Virginia 157 miles west of Richmond, anticipating an escape from the miserable humidity and heat of the city. But Elizabeth didn't see this vacation as a retreat from reality. She saw it as a last chance at diplomatic intervention. She was about to marshal every aristocratic tool in her domestic tool kit to try and stop this war before it started.

At White Sulphur Springs, Elizabeth, now a lady of social prominence, met Edmund Ruffin, an owner of dozens of slaves and two plantations outside Richmond along the James River. The two lost in conversation amid the charming clapboard cottages and crowds of visitors would have made for an interesting sight. Ruffin's white hair, which fell just below his shoulders, made him instantly recognizable. He was one of the country's most fanatical secessionists, restlessly traveling throughout the South advocating disunion even if it necessitated a war. The so-called fire-eater told all who would listen that the North's dominance and bilking of the region's cotton wealth through high tariffs would only get worse if the South stayed part of the Union. Time was running out. Each Western territory added to the Union as a state chipped away at the South's political power in the Senate.

While Ruffin had enlisted in the armed services during the War of 1812, he never saw action, and had spent the years since farming and making a name for himself in the emerging practice of soil science. But this didn't seem to be enough for the father of eleven. Animated by Brown's raid on Harpers Ferry, Ruffin had rushed to attend the abolitionist's hanging, but was arrested as a "suspicious character." Realizing only those in uniform would be allowed to attend, Ruffin finagled his way in with some Virginia Military Institute cadets, wearing a borrowed overcoat and carrying a musket. And now he was a one-man dissent machine spreading unrest and high emotion wherever he went. His conversational style, animated and emphatic, would have contrasted dramatically with Elizabeth's composed demeanor.

But if she thought Ruffin or others of his set might be open to persuasion, she was quickly disabused. It became clear that the fire-eaters were a lost cause. Still, she sensed that the silent majority was dominated by Unionist beliefs. She wasn't alone.

Even if she was calm on the outside, Elizabeth's diary reveals her inner turmoil during that visit: "The dissolution and reconstruction of the Union was daily talk at the Springs. People were, if anything, more morbid than ever on the subject of slavery."

White Sulphur Springs was a backdrop conducive to amplifying this mood, celebrating as it did the South and its institutions. At the resort, visitors were insulated in a world of privilege and reassurance.

The cottages where many of the elite stayed were arrayed in rows and named for Southern states, such as the Alabama, the Carolina, and the Louisiana. On breaks from taking the healing waters, the upper class indulged in rich delicacies. The kitchen staff slaughtered 22 sheep and 300 chickens a day and brewed 115 gallons of coffee twice a day. A military company from Richmond added an aggressive backdrop to the talk of secession, marching and drilling relentlessly and filling the tranquil mountain haven with bombastic martial music. One can imagine the Southern anthem "Dixie" played again and again, lending the blue-green hills of Virginia a nostalgic grandeur.

The air was charged with emotion. Elizabeth heard threats of violence. "About slavery, I heard a number of the Virginia legislature say that anyone speaking against it or doubting its divinity ought to be hung," she wrote. "Yes, hung, as certainly and truly as he would be for murder."

To her dismay, the people that Elizabeth would have expected to challenge the growing secessionist orthodoxy chose to say nothing, fearing the escalating rhetoric of fire-eaters. An unusual exception was the Van Lews' family friend, John Minor Botts. The former congressional legislator and outspoken Union advocate refused to be silenced.

"Muzzles were made for dogs," he said, adding, "And no press and no party can put a muzzle on my mouth as long as I value my freedom."[2] But he was virtually alone in making his pro-Union sentiments public. One state senator confided to Elizabeth that "members of the [state] senate did not dare to speak as they thought and felt, that they were afraid." She assured him his confidence was safe with her. But she felt rising grief at the inaction of Southern Unionists. Would the pride and foolhardiness of secessionists receive no satisfactory answer from loyal Americans?

Even as she tried to hide her rising anxiety, Elizabeth must have wondered what she should do. She couldn't vote. Women wouldn't be allowed to vote for another sixty years. Anyway, casting a ballot would do nothing to combat the very real threats being made to families of

Yankee heritage, like hers, living in the South. In some states they were tarred and feathered. There were even lynchings. Many Northern-born Richmond residents pulled up stakes and left the South in those years. Elizabeth wouldn't do that.[3]

She felt torn. She believed she had an obligation to all living under the Church Hill mansion roof, free and slave alike. And her loyalty extended to her family's adopted city, where her father had worked so hard to elevate his family. Elizabeth had to choose sides. In her view, both the fire-eaters and John Brown were too extreme. The Union must be preserved, that much she knew. And so, like Botts, her first impulse was to support the Union. She might not be able to vote, but she decided she would learn to fight.

After Elizabeth left White Sulphur Springs, the election season got under way in earnest. The stakes for Southerners were high because they were about to lose the political clout they had enjoyed for decades. The proslavery Democratic Party had managed to keep nearly complete control of both houses of Congress since 1833. A win by Lincoln would sweep the Democratic Party from power, and with it, the hold on federal posts, which had been occupied by proslavery forces for decades. As a result, the election was more hotly contested than any in recent memory. It was also unusual. First, the candidates didn't campaign. Presidential candidates were expected to remain silent, their message taken to the electorate by other party leaders. Second, the election was unique among American presidential races because there were essentially two separate contests: one in the North, where Lincoln and his former debating rival, Stephen A. Douglas, a Democrat, squared off; and a second in the South, where Tennessean John Bell of the Constitutional Union Party, a successor to the Whig Party, and states' rights advocate and Democrat John C. Breckenridge, vied for power. The reason for this split was the deep antagonism between the two regions. Republicans, for example, didn't even appear on the ticket in ten Southern states, where they risked being tarred and feathered or worse.

To be clear, Virginia conservatives—the Whigs and the Unionists—wouldn't have voted for Lincoln even if they had the opportunity. The Van Lew family, like other Whigs, wanted to elect the Tennessean John Bell, a slave owner who, like Lincoln, didn't support expanding slavery into the new territories but, unlike Lincoln, believed that the Constitution protected slavery, a view he hoped would attract border-state voters.[4]

Viewed through the perfect hindsight of history, John Bell's compromise position was doomed. Supporting the status quo—the Constitution and the existing slave system—without endorsing the wave of support for slavery's expansion appeared pointless to Southerners facing political disenfranchisement. Weren't such compromises just effectively handing power to Northern abolitionists?

An old friend of the Van Lew family, John Minor Botts, who had served in the U.S. House of Representatives and was a well-known Whig, would find out how unpopular such an approach was. In a stance that would draw fire from states' rights advocates, Botts disdained Breckenridge's secessionist talk, but he was equally critical of abolitionists in the North and promised to act against Lincoln if, as president, he threatened slavery. Critics accused him of indecisiveness. Botts's standing would slowly sink with that of his fellow Unionists.

Lincoln's election on November 6, 1860, shook the foundations of the South. Not only did Bell lose, winning just three states narrowly, including Virginia, but Breckenridge failed, too. The South was shut out of the White House at a time that expansion of the Union through the creation of new states was diluting the power of the South in Washington. Southern leaders keenly felt this diminishing power.

Lincoln received little support in the upper South, since he wasn't even on the ballot in many states. And he received just 40 percent of the national popular vote, making the election difficult to swallow for Southerners. But in the electoral college, Lincoln overwhelmed his opponents with 180 votes.[5]

The 1860 presidential election forced Southern Unionists to confront just how far apart their views were from the country's electoral majority. The divide that had previously existed mainly in the editorial pages and the mouths of radical speakers became real.

The impact was swift. South Carolina seceded six weeks later, on December 20, 1860, citing unfair taxation and a federal government that overrode state sovereignty, especially when it came to slavery. The *Charleston Mercury*'s extra edition on that day, famously headlined, "Union Is Dissolved," crystallized the rationale this way: "The issue before the country is the extinction of slavery. The southern states are now in the crisis of their fate; and if we read aright the signs of the times, nothing is needed for our deliverance but that the ball of revolution to be set in motion." [6]

Six states followed Charleston's lead in short order. On January 9, 1861, Mississippi adopted an ordinance similar to South Carolina's. Florida followed the next day and Alabama the day after that. By February 1, Georgia, Louisiana, and Texas had seceded, and three days later, Montgomery, Alabama, was chosen as the capital of the Confederate States of America.

By the standards set by the country's dissolution of its ties with England during the Revolution, the South's carving away was conducted at lightning speed. The Continental Congress had debated for fourteen months before declaring American independence in 1776. It took a further two years to write the U.S. Constitution and put a new government in operation. The Confederate States of America was organized within just three months of Lincoln's election. [7]

Secession was a reality. But would war follow? The nation was in a standoff, and much depended on the decision of the most populous Southern state. Virginia aristocrats weren't about to be forced into war by South Carolina or any other state. They were committed to their own sovereignty. Moreover, they believed the rest of the country was watching to see what they would do. But the state's situation was perilous. Virginia sat in the middle of any conflict that might evolve, bordering both Washington and the South. The threat was existential. Faced with those high stakes, Unionists like Elizabeth, who were in a majority at that time in Virginia, supported a peace commission that could develop a compromise between dissenting states and Northern ones. After all, Lincoln was new to national politics and unsophisticated. The wise old guard from a venerable state such as Virginia could surely wrest a compromise from him. They sent former president John Tyler to chair the proceedings.

Meanwhile, in Richmond, a Secession Convention convened on February 13, 1861, meeting at the Mechanics' Institute at the foot of Capitol Hill, only blocks from Elizabeth's home on Church Hill. Pro-Union and pro-secession factions could each claim thirty members. They were evenly divided, but both were minority views. Most of the delegates were undecided.

Overshadowing the talk at the convention was a conflict brewing four hundred miles to the south, just off the coast of South Carolina. There, the disposition of a lightly guarded fort was being fiercely debated. Fort Sumter sat on a man-made granite island, an installation that had drawn little attention until the tensions between the North and the South hit fever pitch. The South maintained that the fort should naturally be the property of South Carolina. Even some in the North agreed. Others believed the fort was more properly the property of the Union.

Despite the brewing conflict in South Carolina and the agitation in the streets of Richmond, the first vote by the secession delegates on whether the Commonwealth should secede overwhelmingly failed by a vote of 88 to 45.

Virginians were not yet ready to rend the Union. The convention president wrote home exultantly to his wife that the secessionists were "without the slightest hope of success."

THE KNIGHTS OF THE GOLDEN CIRCLE

If slumbering Baltimoreans had awoken and looked out their windows that February night, they would have seen an odd sight—a train car being pulled through the dark streets. But even more unusual was the carriage's contents.

A hundred miles away, the carriage had been booked by a serious young woman who'd told the conductor she needed extra space for her invalid brother. She'd boarded with the man she said was her brother, hidden under a slouchy hat and a blanket.

Her "brother," in fact, was Abraham Lincoln.

There was a plot afoot to murder President-Elect Lincoln even before he assumed office in March 1861. Not that Lincoln believed this was a real threat. Despite the flood of hate mail he'd received since his election, his secretary said Lincoln had shrugged it off. It wasn't logical, he thought, or charitable, so why would anyone do it? But the country was gripped by unreason and hate.

The newly elected Lincoln was in Springfield, Illinois, when he received the news of his election. His planned trip to the inauguration in Washington had been well publicized, a move of great interest to Lincoln's enemies.

The president of the Philadelphia, Wilmington and Baltimore

Railroad had received a tip from a female philanthropist and advocate for the mentally ill, Dorothea Dix, who had overheard concerning conversations during her work in Southern hospitals. She claimed that a radical group of states' rights advocates were planning to swarm and kill Lincoln as he passed through Baltimore on his way to his swearing-in ceremony in the capital.[1] Baltimore was a town dominated by secessionists; hatred of the Union there had grown exponentially since his election. By some accounts, 15,000 men would assist in ending Lincoln's life, making the assassination look like a riot that grew out of control. The police department was said to be complicit with the plan.[2]

The railroad president employed the celebrated Allan Pinkerton, the owner of the detective agency that bore his name, who would dispatch his fleet of detectives to investigate. They got to work infiltrating groups of Confederate sympathizers, including a white supremacist secret society called the Knights of the Golden Circle. The group was built on the dream of forging a new country formed from the American Southern states and large portions of Central and South America—a slave empire called "the golden circle."

John Wilkes Booth, who must have been delighted by the society's grandiose agenda, joined the group in 1859. Multiple members of James Buchanan's administration were Knights, including Buchanan's secretary of war, secretary of the treasury, and vice president, John Breckenridge. In Baltimore, Pinkerton went undercover in the group. Having connected with a leader, he found himself in a saloon with fifteen aspiring assassins who drew straws for who would receive the privilege of killing the "Black Republican" Lincoln. In addition to witnessing this murderous plotting, Pinkerton overheard the Baltimore police commissioner hinting that he wouldn't protect Lincoln on his route through the city.[3]

Alarmed by this intelligence, Pinkerton devised a strategy to change Lincoln's travel plans, moving his trip earlier than the plotters expected from Philadelphia to Baltimore and on to Washington. In the nineteenth century, traveling by train required customers to change trains by taking carriages between depots, which were at different locations.

For Lincoln, it meant exposure in a hostile city. But Pinkerton's plan held promise, if and only if he could keep it closely held, because any leak could jeopardize Lincoln. One of those inside the plot to save Lincoln was the nation's first female detective, Kate Warne, twenty-eight.

Just five years earlier, Warne had convinced a skeptical Pinkerton that despite her gender, she could be a valuable addition to the staff. Not only did she manage to convince him to hire her, but her ease of manner and reliability caused Pinkerton to form an entire women-only unit of detectives.

Her participation was especially important this cold February night because of her ability to blend unnoticed into any scene. In fact, only days before, she had posed as a Southern belle complete with an Alabama accent, an elaborate gown, and a telltale cockade, a black and white brooch worn by women true to the Confederate cause. Her assignment was to befriend Southern ladies in town to gather intel on the plot. Her success and that of several other agents convinced Pinkerton of the need to move immediately to save Lincoln.[4]

Kate was tasked with protecting Lincoln from Philadelphia, where he boarded the train, to Baltimore. The president-elect was delivered to the train station by Pinkerton and Lincoln's massive bodyguard, Ward Hill Lamon. Lincoln emerged from the shadows wearing a loose coat, a shawl, and a felt hat pulled low on his brow. The depot was deserted. The three walked briskly to a train car containing sleeping berths, where Warne awaited. She had bribed a railroad agent to hold the berths for her and still had to fend off customers eager for sleep.

Convincing Lincoln that the plot was serious took some doing. To him, the cloak-and-dagger adventure seemed ridiculous, and as they smuggled him onto the carriage in Philadelphia, he was cracking jokes. No one else felt like joking. Kate, who had been involved in infiltrating secessionist groups in Baltimore for the last week, knew all too well that the threat was real.

Lincoln laid down awkwardly, the berth too short for his long legs. The agents closed the curtains covering his bed and sat down to wait.

Warne couldn't help but think about the possibility of secessionists getting wind of Lincoln's move, sabotaging the railroad line, jumping aboard the train, and rushing in to kill the president-elect. She squeezed the small barrel of her handgun.

And as the hours passed and she grew weary, still Warne stayed awake.

By 3:15 a.m., the train was within the city limits of Baltimore and, not long after, it rolled into President Street Station. Finally they were in Baltimore. Warne would have peered through the train windows. Was there an angry crowd awaiting them? In fact, there were no people at all. Warne had performed her role and now had to move on to her next one, monitoring the radical secessionists and the team of Pinkerton agents still in place. Lincoln gave her a warm farewell and thanked her for her vigilance. The car was transferred to another train and made the rest of the trip to Washington safely.

Years later, when Pinkerton devised a logo to identify his agency, he chose an open eye, with the words *We never sleep* below it.

Lincoln arrived in D.C. to a fraught national situation. Seven states had already left the Union. Was it inevitable that the rest would as well? And even as the country teetered on the brink of war, the Union's new president hadn't yet assumed office. During the four-month-long interregnum between Lincoln's election in November and his assumption of office in March, plots and intrigue prevailed. Washington was at its core a Southern city, and many residents were hostile to the new president. Federal military officers favoring the South smuggled government guns and ammunition south, and Washington residents worried that secessionists might try to take over before the new government could get up and running. Buchanan's secretary of war, a Knight of the Golden Circle, was later indicted because of suspicions that he'd intentionally oversupplied federal forts in the South, anticipating the matériel's seizure by secessionists.

Richmond newspapers fanned the flames of fear by demanding that Maryland and Virginia take steps to block Lincoln's inauguration.

A House committee on treason was formed to probe the rumors of a possible coup by Southern forces.[5]

The president-elect's arrival in Washington ten days before his inauguration was unheralded. He was not met by marching bands or delegations of congressional leadership. In Washington, no one knew of the attempt against Lincoln's life, and he was criticized for sneaking into the city.

The inauspicious arrival foreshadowed the chaotic first months of Lincoln's administration. In a divided country, with an untested leader, everyone was looking to find a foothold in the new world. Lincoln would prevail, proving himself a steely leader of courage and insight, but first he'd have to face down powerful voices who opposed his agenda.

In Richmond, Elizabeth faced the same decisions, even as she felt her public influence slipping away. How could she fight for the Union when her entire society was gripped by war fever? Having encountered fire-eaters personally, she—like Dorothea Dix and Kate Warne—also understood something Lincoln did not: The secessionists would not be dissuaded by diplomacy.

She must have eagerly awaited Lincoln's opening moves. Inauguration Day, March 4, dawned rainy and unpleasant. And during the morning hours, visitors streamed by the thousands to Pennsylvania Avenue to witness Lincoln's installation. His inauguration speech would be immensely important. On that rainy morning, the city of Washington, D.C., was heavily guarded by 2,000 army soldiers, including cavalry and sharpshooters perched atop buildings along the route the new president would pass. The skies cleared by the time Lincoln strode to a small table from which he would deliver his long-awaited inaugural speech at the East Portico of the U.S. Capitol, its dome yet to be finished. Lincoln himself had written the text, but it had been heavily edited by his onetime rival for the presidency, William Seward, a former New York governor and senator and Lincoln's choice for secretary of state in his new cabinet.

Seward would become an extremely important member of Lincoln's administration. One friend later described him as possessing a "slouching slender figure; a head like a wise macaw; a beaked nose; shaggy eyebrows; unorderly hair and clothes; hoarse voice; offhand manner; free talk; and perpetual cigar." For Seward, a consummate politician, "the political had become nature, and no one could tell which was the mask and which the features. At table, among friends, Mr. Seward threw off restraint, or seemed to throw it off, in reality, while in the world he threw it off, like a politician, for effect."⁶

Lincoln's speech is remembered today for its conclusion, an appeal for peace, asking Americans to summon "the mystic chords of memory" and listen to "the better angels of our nature." But in it, Lincoln made two important statements that would guide the early days of his administration.

First, he pledged to "hold, occupy and possess the properties falling to the federal government." And second, Lincoln prophetically placed the fate of the Union in the hands of the seceding Southerners. "In *your* hands, my dissatisfied fellow countrymen, and not in *mine,* is the momentous issue of civil war. The government will not assail *you.* You can have no conflict, without being yourselves the aggressors."

Lincoln, dressed in a shiny new black suit, his high voice piercing the heavy Washington atmosphere, placed his hand on a Bible and was sworn in as the sixteenth president by Chief Justice Roger B. Taney, the man who had led the Supreme Court in ruling that Blacks were not citizens in the *Dred Scott* decision.

Though Lincoln had worked hard to make the text of his speech conciliatory to the South, secessionists despised it. Disunionists heard the inaugural speech as a call to war, not peace—thanks to just a few short words. Lincoln described the movement to break away as "the essence of anarchy," not exactly the pacifying tone Southerners had expected. Worse, Lincoln's statement that he would hold and occupy the property belonging to the Union left no ambiguity about his views on federal properties like Fort Sumter in Charleston Harbor. The properties had been the focus of intense interest because their status within separatist Southern states was uncertain and ambiguous. Lincoln made clear he would not surrender the federal outposts.

Against that backdrop, Virginia's secession convention continued its debating, with Lincoln's resolve strengthening the grievances of disunionists. For Elizabeth, everything seemed to hang in the balance that spring: the prospect of war; her safety and that of her family and friends. Desperate to see firsthand the deliberations at the convention, she accepted an invitation to attend.

It might come as a surprise to modern readers, but the conversations were dominated by women's voices. Elizabeth was shocked by the vociferous anger of female supporters of secession. In a surge of excitement and regional pride, they had become the strongest advocates of war. Like other ladies of social standing, Elizabeth was courted by both sides to show support. The men fought for women's' approval because women were seen as important moral arbiters. And rather than counseling prudence or restraint, Richmond's hoopskirted belles were overwhelmingly in favor of this new revolution. Elizabeth's brother, John, found himself at odds with his secessionist wife. Family dinners grew strained.

And it wasn't just in Richmond where women's voices were heard more loudly and more often. Seward put it this way: "The men are all in the army and the women are the devils." Mary Greenhow Lee, Rose Greenhow's sister-in-law, said: "This is surely the day of women's power; the men are afraid to do, or say, anything, and leave it all to us." It was a sign of what was to come.

Elizabeth likely listened to the proceedings in the state's general assembly chambers in Richmond's state capitol building, where the secession convention had moved. Designed by Thomas Jefferson, the imposing neoclassical building and its grounds covered fourteen acres atop one of the city's seven hills. Inside the building, Elizabeth could see the secessionists gaining ascendancy, noting in her diary how they grew "bold and more imprudently daring." An astute observer of human nature, she believed secessionists were gaining strength, in part, because Southerners simply didn't want to be told what to do by Washington.

"The doctrine of secession seemed to gratify an innate feeling of pride." And they had a power base that couldn't be ignored. "Drunk with . . . license, our Southern leaders firmly believed in the power of cotton to rule the world," Elizabeth wrote. "It had clothed and fed them, was it not necessary to cloth and feed all nations!"[7]

It was becoming clear to her that Virginia was on the precipice of joining the rest of the South in taking a step which it couldn't easily retract: secession. Even if former Unionists wouldn't resist the strengthening Confederacy, Elizabeth would. On this she couldn't compromise.

And just as secessionists gained ground, Unionists retreated. Elizabeth described one of her heroes, former president John Tyler, a Union advocate, "With his voice raised for heaven, almost crying, and saying that he had 'no influence and was only by courtesy permitted on the floor'" of the convention. Surely Elizabeth was beginning to understand that waiting for the old-line Whigs and Unionists to confront secessionists was a fool's game. New leadership was desperately needed. Perhaps even *her* efforts were needed to guide the city in a different direction.

Back in Washington, Lincoln faced his first day as president. More than likely, he followed his lifelong habit of rising early and taking a short walk before getting to the desk. Lincoln's office was nondescript. The furniture was all hand-me-downs from previous presidents. His desk was a mahogany table standing between two windows that afforded views of the unfinished Washington Monument and the red-roofed Smithsonian. But Lincoln wasn't taking in the views on his first morning in office. The very first thing placed in the new president's hands was a letter from the commanding officer of Fort Sumter. Major Robert Anderson was leading a tiny contingent of federal troops—just eighty-four, some of them musicians—occupying the Union fort in Charleston's harbor, where they were surrounded by thousands of Confederate soldiers armed and ready to defend the city. Anderson's letter described the shortages of provisions, estimating they would be exhausted in four to six weeks. Anderson and his men desperately needed food and supplies. But the major, a veteran of the War with Mexico, estimated that supplying the fort would take a massive effort, "no less than 20,000 good and well-disciplined men."[8] It's notable there weren't 20,000 men in the entire U.S. army at the time.

For Lincoln, the challenge was immense. The situation was made more difficult by the fact that his predecessor, James Buchanan, in an effort to ensure peace, had made an agreement with the South Carolina governor not to reinforce the harbor's federal garrison if South Carolina didn't attack it. What to do? On the one hand, Lincoln had promised the South that his government would not start a war; on the other hand, he had promised that he would take control of properties of the federal government. Fort Sumter, a shambling stone and masonry fort designed and built by the U.S. Army Corps of Engineers and paid for with federal dollars, qualified as just that. Rescuing Anderson and his men from a location on a man-made granite island in the middle of Charleston Harbor appeared impossible for Lincoln without breaking his word, a perilous move for a new president facing a nation on the brink.

If expectations are everything, it's notable that many Charlestonians *and* Washingtonians alike believed Sumter would be handed over to the Confederacy without a shot being fired. Certainly, that's what Buchanan expected. Many in the North advocated such a policy as a way of keeping border states, like Virginia, in the Union. And as a practical matter, it was impossible to reinforce Sumter. The fort was surrounded by hostile batteries constructed by the secessionists. But Lincoln wasn't about to make such a decision lightly.

First, he turned to the éminence grise of American military matters, General Winfield Scott, a legendary soldier who had valiantly led American forces to victory in the war with Mexico. Now seventy-four years of age and weighing 300 pounds, the old general was past his prime, but he was still respected. Should the men's rations be reinforced? asked Lincoln. Should more soldiers be sent to assist them?

Scott was definitive. "I now see no alternative but a surrender . . . as . . . we cannot send the third of the men in several months to give them relief . . . Evacuation seems almost inevitable."[9] Lincoln's cabinet concurred.

Lincoln didn't stop his fact-finding mission. The new president's deliberation was seen by many as waffling to delay a decision. But Lincoln didn't bow to public pressure to make haste. Taking Scott's advice to evacuate Sumter would mean abandoning his presidential authority right away. Seeking other informed opinions, he turned to Gustavus Fox, a former navy officer with a plan to resupply Sumter under the cover of darkness using two tugboats and a steamer loaded with troops. Lincoln presented Fox's plan to his cabinet, but only one member endorsed the idea. The rest, rallied by Seward, Lincoln's secretary of state, advised against resupplying Sumter. Seward wasn't the only one of Lincoln's electoral opponents appointed to the new cabinet, which meant the new president faced a tough job getting them all on his side.

The clock was ticking on Lincoln's decision. The forces on Sumter would be bereft of supplies by April 15, and Charleston was unanimous in its sentiment for the South. Unionism was dead in the South Carolina city.

Seward, still smarting from being electorally defeated by a cornpone lawyer from who knows where, thought the path forward was obvious. The president's apparent indecision looked like a power vacuum—and a personal opportunity. Washington was at its core a Southern city, and many residents were hostile to the new president. Seward plotted behind the president's back to resolve the crisis without a war. He reassured a Southern commission visiting Washington that it was only a matter of time until the garrison was officially turned over to the South. Claiming to speak for the president, Seward met in mid-March with the commission and two U.S. Supreme Court justices attempting to defuse the situation and prevent war. Seward told the panel that not only would Sumter be abandoned by Union forces, but that it would be turned over to secessionist hands in five days. "Before the letter reaches [Jefferson] Davis, the fort [Sumter] will be abandoned." [10]

The press picked up the story the following day, possibly from the overconfident Seward himself, reporting the evacuation as not only a fait accompli but also, somewhat outrageously, as Lincoln's decision. Seward had come to view himself as a critical part of the administration, describing his role to outsiders as a prime minister, a man who ran things behind the scenes while Lincoln was a figurehead. But Lincoln did not see things that way. When he saw the story, the president was astonished. He had made no such firm decision.

Lincoln acted. He disabused Seward of his misconceptions about the power of his office. Whatever passed between them seemed to both cut Seward down to size and persuade Lincoln of the latter's new loyalty.

With Seward now in line, it was time for the president to get his cabinet on board. On March 28, Scott sent a memo to Lincoln that galvanized the president.

That night, Lincoln and his wife, Mary, hosted their first state dinner at the White House. The president regaled those attending with an endless number of entertaining stories. Before the dinner was over, however, Lincoln's lightheartedness evaporated when he summoned his cabinet into a separate room, where he revealed the new Scott memo. It was a strange missive that spoke more to the veteran soldier's desire for peace than his current political insight. The old general wrote the president that he favored evacuating not only Sumter but also Fort Pickens, a Pensacola, Florida, federal fort that, like Sumter, secessionist forces were eager to take over. According to Scott, the move would "instantly soothe and give confidence to the eight remaining slave-holding states under pressure by secessionist forces."[11]

Members were astonished at Scott's boldness in making political prognostications in addition to military ones. It became obvious to them what Lincoln had already suspected—Scott's guidance on this point was not good. Lincoln had proven his good judgment and won his cabinet's trust. The next day, the cabinet met again, and Lincoln presented the additional intelligence he had gathered from Fox alongside Scott's advice. Lincoln had made up his mind. By this point, he saw Sumter as more than just a federal fort; it was a symbol of the union. Giving up Sumter, in fact, might legitimize the South rather than stabilize the Union. He wrote: "I am decided; my course is fixed, my path is blazed. The Union and the Constitution shall be preserved, and the laws enforced at every and all hazards. I expect the people to sustain me. They have never yet forsaken any true man."[12]

This time, the cabinet voted in favor of resupplying both Sumter and Pickens by a vote of six to three.

Though he had taken weeks to determine how to move forward, and just as important, what fundamental beliefs would guide his decisions, Lincoln was now decided on a course. In his inaugural speech, he had committed himself to not firing the first shot in any civil war. He would stick with that idea. However, it was one thing to insist that federal property remain in the hands of the government, but to start a war over the status of a handful of forts could be perceived as irresponsible. If the Confederates fired the first shots, Lincoln could claim his actions were defensive, rather than offensive. Determined to place the onus on Southern leaders to act, Lincoln decided not to surprise the Southern leadership with his actions. The president made clear his intent to secessionist leadership in South Carolina ahead of time. He sent a messenger to the state's governor, Francis W. Pickens, with a clear communication that ships had left New York City, intended only to resupply Sumter, not attack the positions of the secessionists. The president promised that "if such attempt be not resisted, no effort to throw in men, arms or ammunition will be made."[13] In this way, Lincoln provoked the newly forming Southern Confederacy but forced them to make the first move. The president had backed the South into a corner.

And Jefferson Davis was more than happy to oblige. Pickens wired the Confederate government, and its president, Jefferson Davis, in Montgomery. Davis, who had served as both a U.S. representative and senator, had long been Capitol Hill's most ardent advocate of Southern rights. He helped pass a law that repealed limits on slavery in the Kansas and Missouri territories, leaving the decision to the popular vote. The Kansas-Nebraska Act of 1854 not only contributed to the demise of the Whig Party and the rise of the Republicans, but also led to an increase in civil violence, drawing in radicals like John Brown.

It didn't take Davis's cabinet long to decide to fire on Sumter, and only one member voted no. Since many had attended West Point or served in the Mexican-American War, it was not unusual for commanders to find themselves facing former classmates and brothers-in-arms across a battlefield. So it was at Sumter. General P.G.T. Beauregard, a former student of Anderson's at West Point and the dashing leader of the growing Southern force in Charleston Harbor, was given authority to shell the fort. There was just one caveat: First Beauregard had to ask Anderson for an evacuation date. Anderson declined to evacuate.

At 4:30 a.m. on April 12, the Confederates attacked Fort Sumter. A single signal shell arced over the harbor, hitting its apex and exploding like a Fourth of July firework, scattering red and gold sparkles, just before hitting the fort. A huge boom echoed across the bay. Wealthy Charlestonians gathered on rooftops to watch the spectacle, reclining on rugs, their picnic baskets at hand. The single signal shell was followed with a bombardment, each Confederate battery firing in secession, forty-three guns going off at two-minute intervals. Ruffin, the man Elizabeth had spoken with at White Sulphur Springs, had managed to get himself appointed as an honorary member of the South Carolinian Palmetto Regiment. The white-haired grandfather fired one of the South's massive columbiad cannons and was widely—though mistakenly—credited with firing the first shot of the war, thereafter. The South's forces were overwhelming. Some 9,000 Confederate soldiers had streamed in from all over the South to be part of the first battle of the Civil War. Artillery batteries were positioned around the harbor, encircling Sumter. Well aware of his extreme disadvantage, Anderson ordered his men to hide in the bowels of Sumter.

They did not return fire until the following morning. When they did, the Charleston crowd cheered. Lincoln's relief fleet finally appeared at the mouth of the harbor that afternoon, but because the battle was under way, the ships couldn't move in to assist Sumter. Union forces were forced to evacuate the fort at 1:00 p.m. April 13, thirty-four hours after the battle had begun.

The news of Sumter's fall, communicated by the chatter of telegraphs, spread quickly. Ironically, the battle was celebrated in both the North and the South. The North was galvanized by the example of Anderson and his men. When Lincoln called for 75,000 volunteers to fight the South, states overwhelmingly responded.

Elizabeth's world had changed forever. Unbeknownst to her, the group of men whose lives and destinies would intertwine with hers were making their first decisive choices in a war that would span a continent. How would they serve?

A little-known veteran of the Mexican-American War, Ulysses S. Grant had experienced little success in the war's aftermath. He had moved to the plantation of his wife, Julia Dent Grant's, family near St. Louis, Missouri, attempting to carve out a role for himself as a farmer, but failed.

Fittingly, the ill-fated property was called Hardscrabble. Next, he moved his family to Galena, Illinois, where he went to work for his brother's leather goods store as a clerk. That too, was a bust for the thirty-eight-year-old. As the details of the crisis in Charleston Harbor unfolded, Grant found himself the center of attention. Customers came from nearby towns in Wisconsin, Minnesota, and Iowa to hear the veteran talk about the burgeoning conflict. The conversations would continue into the early morning hours.

When Lincoln called for volunteers to serve as Union soldiers, the city of Galena was awash in patriotism. A meeting was called at the local courthouse to enlist a regiment. All of Galena attended, forcing the city's businesses to shut down in the excitement. Grant found himself running the meeting and turned down an offer to serve as captain of a Galena regiment, but he knew, even then, what his future would hold, telling his brother he thought he ought to go back into service. "I never went into that leather store after our meeting to put up a package or do other business," he later wrote. His first command was as colonel of the 21st Illinois Infantry, but promotions would come fast and furious. Months later, he would be appointed brigadier general, and by September, he was given command of the District of Southeast Missouri.

In the meantime, a Southern gentleman paced his room, holding a resignation letter, racked with indecision.[14] Finally he steeled himself. The Union's most capable soldier, the man who had commanded the forces that captured John Brown, resigned from the Army, declining Lincoln's offer to lead Union forces. The loss of Robert E. Lee left a hole in Union military leadership for months.

While William Seward's disagreements with Lincoln would continue, he would also become one of his staunchest allies and closest friends. "Conferences between Mr. Seward and Mr. Lincoln were almost of daily occurrence," one journalist wrote later. "These conferences were generally held at the White House, to and from which Mr. Seward went and came with the easy familiarity of a household intimate," while Lincoln would "walk over to the State Department, in the daytime, or to Mr. Seward's house, in the evening."[15]

Another future ally of Lincoln's, Edwin Stanton, also found himself galvanized by Sumter. Having served as Buchanan's secretary of state, he witnessed the disarray of the federal government in the months-long period before Lincoln's inauguration and secretly advised some of the nation's highest-profile politicians, like Seward, of the crisis developing in the leadership vacuum. Stanton's paranoia wasn't without basis. In fact a congressional investigation identified two hundred federal employees who were Southern sympathizers and ideal for Rebel recruitment as espionage agents.[16]

Stanton funneled information to the treason committee about Buchanan's secretary of the navy and his failure to secure the federal navy yard in Pensacola, Florida. When Buchanan waffled on whether he was willing to resupply Anderson's small band in the Charleston Harbor, Stanton, who was serving as the president's secretary of state at the time, argued that Sumter had to be defended. He directly challenged Buchanan, saying that if he surrendered, his reputation would be that of Benedict Arnold, the traitorous American general who secretly conspired to turn over West Point to the British. When Buchanan didn't follow his advice, Stanton leaked information from cabinet meetings showing the president as a weak leader. The defiant and opinionated Stanton would become Lincoln's secretary of war, an appointment particularly surprising since, as a private counsel in a big patent infringement case during the war, he had snubbed the country lawyer and even described him as a "long-armed ape."[17]

Grant would later make great strides in strengthening America's burgeoning intelligence network. He understood that wars were won and lost on information. The man who would come to run Lincoln's most valuable spy ring and the nation's first intelligence operation, George H. Sharpe, was working as an attorney in the Hudson Valley in New York when the first shots of the war were fired. He immediately abandoned his successful career and raised a regiment, the 120th New York Volunteer Infantry, commanding it during the early days of the war.

In Richmond, the news of Sumter's fall was met with celebration. Residents poured into the streets, forming a spontaneous parade down Main Street accompanied by a band and waving the flag of the Confederacy. The *Richmond Dispatch* described the crowd as offering "one of the wildest, most enthusiastic and irrepressible expressions of heartfelt and exuberant joy." By the time the crowd reached Tredegar Iron Works, there were 3,000 people gathered, and a band played "La Marseillaise." One speaker drew ecstatic cheers when he noted that the cannons that breached Sumter's walls had been produced at Tredegar. The crowd hoisted the stars and bars there and then moved on to the Fayette Artillery, where they grabbed guns and dragged them to Capitol Square and fired them in a salute.[18]

Later that evening, the crowd marched to the governor's mansion and called out to John Letcher, who had tried to find some alternative to the brewing conflict. As the band played "Dixie," the crowd chanted

Letcher's name to draw him out of the mansion. The governor came out, issued a few noncommittal sentences, and quickly withdrew. Hours later, the crowd hoisted the Confederate flag over the state capitol building.

Officially, Virginia had not yet seceded. But that was soon to change. Richmond's secession convention was now backed into a corner. Virginia's choices were slim: Either join Lincoln's Union and fight her sister Southern states or ally with the Confederacy and risk becoming a battlefield for the next several years. Secessionists on the floor of the convention seized their advantage. In a dramatic speech in which he flashed a horse pistol as he spoke, former governor Henry Wise said he had set the "wheels of revolution" against the U.S. government in motion and that a Virginia militia under his control was already seizing the Harpers Ferry armory that John Brown had briefly taken only months ago. He said his forces were preparing to seize the Gosport navy yard at Norfolk. His speech had the impact he had hoped for: The second and final vote on secession succeeded, 88 to 55. After eight weeks of debate, Virginia delegates had made their choice. Virginia voters would follow in short order.

For the Confederacy, Virginia's entry was critical. Her population was greater than any other Southern state. And she brought critical industrial resources. Virginia's industrial capacity was nearly as great as all the Southern states combined. Tredegar Iron Works was the only plant in the South that could produce heavy ordnance.

Virginia's status as the predominant Southern state was confirmed when the Confederate capital was moved to Richmond from Montgomery, Alabama. Many Southerners believed that with Virginia in the fray, the Confederacy could win the war.

Elizabeth suddenly found herself at the center of the most powerful city in the Confederacy. The war was being determined by decisions made in the houses of her friends and neighbors.

Upon seeing the Confederate flag hoisted the day of the vote above the capitol, which she described as the "flag of treason," she wrote she felt energized. "I never did remember a feeling of more calm determination and high resolve for endurance over me than at that moment." The uncertainty was over. The goal was clear.

In Baltimore, a secessionist mob attacked the 6th Massachusetts Regiment, which was traveling toward Washington by train, with knives and guns. Four soldiers and nine civilians died.[19] Secessionists then cut telegraph wires in Baltimore and demolished the railroad bridges surrounding the city.

The Baltimore attack on soldiers dissolved Elizabeth's cool reserve. "War in all its reality is upon us," Van Lew wrote. She described the anger in Richmond's streets, recalling "one man, whose eyes flared with the red light of hate." The sight was "awful to see, to feel, to face."[20]

That night another parade celebrating the commonwealth's secession filled the streets. Elizabeth's description of the scene was vivid.

That night I went to the bottom of the garden to view the torchlight procession. Such a sight! The multitude, the mob, the whooping, the tin pan music and the fierceness of a surging, swelling revolution. This I witnessed . . . The threats, the scowls, the frowns of an infuriated community; who can write of them? I have had brave men shake their fingers in my face and say terrible things. We had threats of being driven away, threats of fire and threats of death. Surely there was a madness upon the people. Some wished all Union people could be driven into the street and slaughtered. Some proposed the hanging of all persons of northern birth, no matter how long they had been in the South.

From that moment, Elizabeth knew she would have to hide her most heartfelt convictions. "Mobs went to private houses to hang the true of heart," she wrote. "Loyalty was now called treason, and cursed. If you spoke in your parlor or chamber, to your next of heart, you whispered."

But if the time for words was over, the time for action had begun. Elizabeth might not be able to pick up a gun, but she knew she had a powerful advantage. No one would suspect a Southern belle.

6

❦ ❧

AIDING AND GIVING COMFORT . . .
TO THE ENEMY

Henry Wilson sighed. If only she weren't a Southerner.

The woman with the dark, glittering eyes didn't seem at home in her black silks, her lively and intelligent conversation at odds with her widow weeds. Her salon, elegant and refined, filled with a who's who of Washington dignitaries and sophisticates, seemed a world away from the unfolding bloody conflict, which was exactly why so many found it a welcome escape. Across the room, he saw William Seward, a bit unsteady on his feet, deep in conversation with another high-ranking official.

In those surroundings, one was easily tempted to complain about the sad state of the Union army, the subject of many meetings of the Senate Committee on Military Affairs that Senator Henry Wilson chaired.

The beautiful dark-haired Rose Greenhow was always eager to listen, and anyway, he was so tired—Rose's company was a salve in these busy times. If only he weren't married . . . [1]

To say that the Union's first efforts in the war were unimpressive in the wake of Fort Sumter is to understate its general incompetency. Soldiers were green, and their commanders were aging or untested.

Aware of the enemy's lack of preparation, Richmond society was bursting with confidence. Already the city was surrounded by armed

Rebel camps. Elizabeth could hear the strains of martial music daily, reveille in the morning and taps at night. "Our papers assured us of a great victory," she wrote.[2] Maybe, just maybe, they were right. Though she made light of claims that one Rebel could whip 500 Yankees, it would have been difficult to escape the notion that Southern men who lived day to day in the saddle and shot the night's dinner or hunted for amusement would be bested by men with little or no exposure to anything but the inside of a Northern factory. In fact, the task the Union had set out to accomplish was daunting. While Confederate forces could engage in a strategy of attrition, federal forces would have to subdue 750,000 square miles of Confederate territory, an enormous swath of land twice the size of the original thirteen American colonies, to succeed.[3] It was a huge task, weighing heavily on the mind of men like Henry Wilson.

Not long after speaking to Wilson, the comely Southern widow Rose Greenhow summoned her friend, Betty Duvall, a dark-haired, blue-eyed sixteen-year-old beauty who would look perfectly simple and enchanting as a farm girl. Who would suspect her?

With detailed military intelligence concealed in an enciphered message on her person, Betty set off cross-country, passing the fresh-faced Union boys camped outside Washington, hitching rides on farm carts, and stopping at a friend's plantation before continuing on to Manassas, where P.G.T. Beauregard's Confederate forces waited. At Fairfax County Courthouse, Betty met General Milledge Bonham, informing him she had vital information about the planned Union attack. Recognizing her from his days in high society, Bonham was astonished that she'd made the trek through enemy lines. The general said: "She took out her tucking comb and let fall the longest and most beautiful roll of hair I have ever seen. She took then from the back of her head, where it had been safely tied, a small package, not larger than a silver dollar, sewed up in silk."[4]

The package contained information that Jefferson Davis would later credit with winning the first major battle of the Civil War.

What the Yankees called the first Battle of Bull Run took place just eighty miles from Richmond and on Washington's doorstep.

The North was as confident as the South. As the battle approached, New York newspaper editors became obsessed with subduing the South before the Confederate legislature could meet in Richmond. The *New-York Tribune* initiated the rally cry "Forward to Richmond," and other newspapers picked it up. Optimism ran so high in the Union capital that a group of congressional politicians and their friends followed the soldiers to the battlefield to watch what they were sure would be a huge victory. Henry Wilson arrived by carriage with sandwiches at the ready, eager to see the war that his political rhetoric had helped stoke unfold before him.

But while he may have been wrong about Fort Sumter, General Winfield Scott did correctly foresee that the war could not be won in a short and decisive victory. He understood all too well the rawness of his recruits. The Battle of Manassas, as the Confederates called it, proved him right. The battle was full of confusion, false starts, and valiant fighting. Neither side could claim their soldiers had extensive training, and the lack of preparation showed. Soldiers' uniforms were so similar that men fired on soldiers from their own side. Flags were also similar and difficult to distinguish on the battlefield. Federal forces attempted to flank Confederate positions by crossing Bull Run Creek but were turned back. The confusion snowballed and soon led to a rout, as federal forces fled in a panic, seeking the defenses of Washington, D.C. The South's win would keep federal forces from invading Virginia for months. But the price had been high. Four hundred Confederates were killed, 1,600 wounded. For the Union, 625 died or were mortally wounded and 950 were injured.

The naive sightseers only slowly realized what was happening. Members of Congress lost their cheerful confidence, and the regular citizens who'd turned up to witness history suddenly found themselves part of it. The Confederate advance was so swift that gray-clad soldiers actually caught up to fleeing Union politicians and turned the naive civil servants into prisoners of war. Events turned tragic for New York lawyer Calvin Huson Jr., who was captured by Rebel soldiers. Ironically, Huson was said to have planned to become governor of Virginia once the Union won the war. Now he would enter Richmond under a different guise, that of POW.

Early the next morning, Jefferson Davis's wife, Varina, visited the wives of the Confederate staff's command one by one. She told them which of their husbands had survived the grisly battle and which had died. Society lady Mary Chesnut had been sick and recalled Mrs. Davis coming in "so softly" that she didn't know she was there until she leaned over and kissed her on the cheek. "Your husband is all right," she whispered. Other women didn't receive the news they had prayed for.[5]

Henry Wilson could only flee, joining the panicked mob that pelted down the Centreville Road away from the battle. Thrown from his carriage, Wilson found himself without horse, servant, or sandwiches, and had to pathetically commandeer a stray army mule and galumph bareback to the capital. In subsequent days, he attempted to rewrite history, erasing his own support for the Bull Run attack, only to be mocked by newspapers for making "double quick time" to escape the battle.[6]

While many scholars believe it wasn't Wilson who slipped secrets to Rose Greenhow, but rather one of his clerks at the time, rumors ran rampant that Wilson was the mysterious "H" in the tranche of love letters later discovered in Greenhow's house.

Greenhow's exploits were made possible because she was already entrenched in elite circles as a Washington socialite. It couldn't have escaped Elizabeth's notice that she knew many in the Confederacy's leadership personally, and thus had the same access that Greenhow did. She had gone to church with them, attended balls and parties and dinners with them. She knew their parents and their homes. In short, she had the sort of inside information that would fill a spy's dossier to bursting. Surely she was in the perfect position to assist the Union. She began to explore just how she could use that information.

To determine just how well it was going for the Confederates, Elizabeth decided to conduct her own reconnaissance mission. After the first real clash of the war, the Battle of Big Bethel or Bethel Church, she walked the city's downtown streets to find out firsthand what was happening. The battle was fought on the Virginia Peninsula eight miles west of Hampton on June 10, 1861, barely seventy miles from Elizabeth's home on Church Hill. Ebullient Southern soldiers streamed into Richmond. Though seven federal regiments had marched overnight to attack a Confederate force less than half its size, the Union attack itself was hesitant and confused. The Rebels won a convincing victory with only a single battlefield death. The Union lost eighteen men. Though strictly Unionist in her sentiments, she felt sympathy for these young Rebels. On previous encounters, they had asked her for "ballard books" or hymnals, and she pitied them. But now with their first experience of battle behind them, they were changed. Eavesdropping on returning soldiers, she found them angry and belligerent. "I heard them tell how men had tossed the dead Yankees into pits, in a fashion as 'creatures too disgusting to touch.'" Women, too, were hardened. "Kill as many Yankees as you can for me," they'd say to soldiers. Some would call for Lincoln's head or an ear.[7]

The vehemence of their reactions stunned her. An idea began to form in her mind. If treatment of the Yankee war dead were that uncivil, what of the wounded? She began to consider what she and her mother could do to help. Just a month later, an opportunity would present itself.

The Battle of Big Bethel was a mere skirmish compared to the Battle of Manassas on July 21, 1861. Soon after the latter battle, Richmond was awash in wounded soldiers. Thousands of injured Confederate men streamed onto city streets, many hobbling, using their muskets as canes, while others were carried or held up by their comrades. Gunpowder, mud, and blood stained their weary faces. Again and again, funerals scored by the solemn "Dead March" from Handel's *Saul* echoed around the city. Richmond women wept as they watched horses with empty saddles being led along Capital Square. As the hours passed, trains unloaded pine box after pine box, the caskets of the dead. At the same time, a thousand Union prisoners of war arrived in the city; the vast majority were soldiers, but some were civilians who had gone to watch the battle unfold. Richmond officials, scrambling to react to the new situation, converted former tobacco factories downtown into makeshift prisons.

Helping the Union cause would start with helping Union soldiers, Elizabeth reasoned. She would offer to tend to Union officers and soldiers injured in the Manassas battle. It was risky. Richmond women were nursing Rebel injured, not federals. Even so, she headed for Ligon's Prison, one of the new jails recently opened in downtown Richmond at Main and 25th Streets. Elizabeth was accustomed to doing her charitable work in difficult circumstances and dangerous neighborhoods, but this was different. The officers in charge of the prisons might well sense her keen desire to help the Union cause. They might decide she was a traitor, and even at this early stage in the war, the penalty could be severe. Her heart pounded in her ears on the journey.

That day, she met with three Confederate officers. The first was Lieutenant David H. Todd, the brother-in-law of Mary Todd Lincoln, whose Kentucky family had been divided by the war. He ran Ligon's. "He took down my name," she recalled in her diary. "Looked at me in surprise, and said I was the first and only lady that had made any such application." She asked to see the prisoners. He turned her down flat.[8]

Deciding to continue to press her case, she went to see his boss, Confederate secretary of the treasury Christopher Memminger, whom she had once seen speak at a religious convention. In a one-on-one meeting, she begged Memminger to allow her access to the prisoners. He protested that the work wasn't appropriate for a lady, at such length that Elizabeth grew bored. The very suggestion that a lady would dirty her hands with the wounded was *shocking*. In any case, Yankees, he maintained, didn't deserve such levels of care. But this time Elizabeth was prepared. She changed her approach, reminding him of his speech and praising its message of Christian patience and love. Memminger softened. Pressing her advantage, she pivoted from faith to patriotism, describing how she believed it was imperative to the Confederate cause to begin "with charity to the thankless." In other words, the appropriate role for devout Rebels was to show generosity in the way they treated the enemy prisoners, especially the wounded. Chastened, Memminger assented and gave her a note to use as an introduction to the officer in charge of prisons.

She'd learned an important lesson. The most suspect of actions could be cloaked if she invoked her position and gender. Like Rose Greenhow, she knew men would underestimate her. On her third visit to the prison, she was readier than ever to take the chivalrous, oblivious soldiers unawares.

Brigadier General John H. Winder, the Confederate inspector general of military camps for Richmond, was sixty-one at the time but looked seventy, the edges of his mouth and eyes turned down. Winder's commanding feature was his snow-white hair, tufts of which framed his face, and white beard. His face showed the wear of a tough personal life, the death of a wife at a young age, and the loss of his father-in-law's plantation due to mismanagement. Having served all over the country in U.S. Army posts, he had reluctantly joined the Confederates. His military career had been successful, but even that had its price.

Going to his crowded office on Bank Street that summer day, Elizabeth would already have known much of this. She may have also known that the war had split his family. One son had joined the Confederate Army, while the other was an artillery captain for the Union. And she may have surmised that he tended to give deference to upper-class men and women. She played that role to the hilt, wearing her usual fine silk dress, gloves, and hat to the meeting. He was rumpled but polite. She decided to appeal to his vanity.

"After sitting a moment, I said to him, your hair would adorn the temple of Janus, it looks out of place here," she recalled in her diary. Would he reject the compliment and see it for what it was, an effort to manipulate him? No. Elizabeth's ability to quickly size up those whose cooperation she needed was decisive. The compliment bowled the old man over. When was the last time a beautiful lady had commented on his appearance?[9]

She told him she would like to visit the prisoners and bring them items that might ease their internment. Winder raised no objection, and instead turned to write a note she could show wardens to enter the prisons. "Miss Van Lew has permission to visit the prisoners and to send them books, luxuries, delicacies and what she may please." Elizabeth was ecstatic. "How joyful was I to be put in communication with what to me was the most sacred—Federal soldiers in prison and distress!"

Richmond had been generous in support of the Rebel wounded. The entire city had effectively become one large hospital, with individual homes opened to receive soldiers. Hundreds of Southern ladies attended these men. But Elizabeth and her mother were virtually alone in assisting the Union wounded. They carefully thought about what items would be useful to the men held prisoner and what they could manage to pass through prison guards.

On their first visit to Ligon's Prison on July 25, Elizabeth and her mother brought chicken soup and cornmeal gruel to the Union men, and ginger cakes and buttermilk to Todd, hoping to win his cooperation. Over the course of the next few days, they expanded their list of items, bringing books, bedding, and clothing to the men and secretly taking prisoners' letters to be mailed home.

All this charity served a surreptitious goal. She was learning how to obtain and smuggle information. Elizabeth discovered more ways to help, often calling on her status as a Southern lady to disguise her intent. Because prisoners had been stripped of their cash, she would send food in a custard dish that contained a false bottom for keeping food warm with boiling water. But she filled the space intended for hot water with rolled-up currency and messages from family. She also convinced physicians to send some of their Union patients to hospitals where Elizabeth could attend them directly. It's also likely that the Van Lews supplied bandages and other first aid, as the medical needs of the Union wounded took second place to those of the Rebels. In addition, she was building trust with Union officers—just the men to explain to her the ins and outs of martial intelligence. Slowly but surely, she was building a resistance movement—small, to be sure, but it would grow as the war ground on.

Conditions at Ligon's, though better than those in notably horrible prisons like Andersonville in Georgia, were still grim. Rats and vermin tortured the prisoners, who were forced to sleep on the floor without blankets or pillows for months. Bathing was out of the question.

Elizabeth's efforts didn't go unnoticed in Richmond social circles. One day, an invitation arrived from fellow Southern ladies requesting Elizabeth and her mother's presence at a gathering to sew shirts for Confederate soldiers. Elizabeth turned it down.

What might once have been an unnoticed social move suddenly had tremendous meaning. The information was deemed worthy of a story in the *Richmond Examiner*. On July 29, 1861, the paper noted:

> Two ladies, a mother and a daughter, living on Church Hill, have lately attracted public notice by their assiduous attention to the Yankee prisoners confined in this City. Whilst every true woman in this community has been busy making articles of comfort or necessity for our troops, or administering to the wants of the many hundreds of sick, who, far from their homes, which they left to defend our sacred soil, are fit subjects for our sympathy, these two women have been expending their opulent means in aiding and giving comfort to the miscreants who have invaded our sacred soil, bent on raping and murder, the desolation of our homes and sacred place, and the ruin and dishonor of our families.[10]

The *Richmond Dispatch* followed up, describing the Van Lew women as "Yankee offshoots" and people who should be "exposed and dealt with."[11]

It's likely that Elizabeth's entire social set knew exactly who the stories were describing. The two women prior to the war hadn't hidden their affinity for the Union; at that time, one didn't have to. But now things were different, and the fact that the *Dispatch* story ended by describing the Van Lew women as people who should be dealt with was purely and simply a threat on their lives.

For Elizabeth, it must have been a startling escalation of social hostilities. She now knew for a fact that her neighbors weren't simply judging her but plotting her destruction.

It was clear Elizabeth would have to do something to persuade all Richmond that she and her mother were loyal to the Confederate cause. But what could they do? Bowing to necessity, she began giving equal time to Confederate soldiers, visiting the hospitals where they were held and attending them with gifts of food just as she did the Union soldiers. But she didn't stop her work on behalf of the federal prisoners. When Calvin Huson, one of the Northern officials who had been taken prisoner at Manassas, became deathly ill with typhoid fever, Elizabeth and her mother took him in, housing him at their Church Hill home. Elizabeth told her neighbors she was extending simple Christian charity to a married father of five. Desperate to help him, she read medical books and brought in the prison physician trying to find a cure. They tried all manner of nineteenth-century remedies: anal injections of cold water; oil of turpentine enemas. Nothing worked. When Huson died, Elizabeth had him buried on Church Hill and even organized a funeral, though a quiet one with few attendees. [12]

News of the burial spread through her neighborhood. It didn't help that she had laid a bouquet of roses at the grave. Her situation grew more and more precarious. Complicating things was Elizabeth's sister-in-law. Mary Van Lew lived in the Church Hill mansion with her husband, John, Elizabeth's brother. Mary was pro-Confederacy and suspicious of Elizabeth's intentions. She was critical of the household's servants and sowed dissension among the family. Elizabeth had to be careful not to discuss her real feelings about the Confederacy before her.[13]

That month, as Elizabeth was walking alone through the city, as she often did, she sensed someone following behind her. She quickened her pace. So did her follower, who came in close, a hot voice whispering in her ear: "You dare to show sympathy for any of those prisoners. I would shoot them as I would blackbirds. And there is something on foot up against you now!"

He didn't make good on his threats, but the fact that he felt confident threatening one of the most prominent women in the city must have alarmed Elizabeth. She didn't know the man who threatened her. But she knew the next encounter would be worse. Assuming that as a member of the city's elite class she would be given assistance, she appealed to Jefferson Davis's office for help. The president was in a cabinet meeting, but she met his private secretary, who dodged responsibility, telling her to go to the mayor instead.

If the government wouldn't help her, she must—at least appear to—help the government. When her appeal for protection was ignored, Elizabeth did the next best thing. She volunteered to house the new chief of the tobacco factory prison complex, Captain George C. Gibbs and his family. The Van Lew mansion came to her rescue. "So perilous had our situation become that we took him and his family to live with us."[14] In her typical fashion, she went all out to convince Gibbs of her support, ordering the servants to set the table for the first dinner with their best china. The menu was elaborate. The Van Lews served their Confederate guests duck soup, chicken pie, sweetbreads with cauliflower, and fried artichokes. All of it was washed down with whiskey and champagne. Gibbs couldn't help but be delighted. And, Mary, normally a thorn in Elizabeth's side, spent the evening toasting Gibbs's every word and supporting his political views.

Ironically, it was Gibbs's tales, his tongue loosened by the Van Lews' alcohol, that gave Elizabeth new insight into the workings of the prisons. He was battling problems with drunkenness among his guards, who arrived at work intoxicated and then drank on the job. Eleven prisoners had escaped. Seeing that the entire system was corrupt and vulnerable wasn't difficult. Though Elizabeth didn't yet know it, she would later play a critical role in the largest and most famous prison escape in the Civil War. For now, these conversations did something important: They showed her exactly the type of person running Confederate prisons. She'd need to know that going forward.

Amid her campaign to ease the minds of her critics, Elizabeth stepped up her efforts to minister to the Union sick, expanding her efforts beyond officers to soldiers and civilians. She visited other facilities and sent her servants and slaves to deliver food and clothing to prisoners throughout the prison system that summer and fall.

Her efforts were paying off in other ways she might not have expected. Prisoners of war who overheard discussions of Rebel troop movements by guards and Confederate soldiers passed on the information to Elizabeth. The books she lent out would come back with secret notes and messages encoded in pinpricks. At this point she had no way to communicate with Union military leaders. She wrote up the information in reports she mailed unsolicited to Washington, but never heard anything back. She had a treasure trove of information, but how could she pass it on?

She lacked the aggressive civility of Confederate spy Rose Greenhow, one of the most celebrated socialites in antebellum Washington, D.C. The Maryland native and Washington resident was everything Elizabeth was not—outgoing, outspoken, comfortable with the limelight, and eager to exploit it. Greenhow's salon for powerful men in Washington was legendary. She was a powerful woman in her own right, with relationships with famous senators and administration officials. On the other hand, Rose was sloppy. Greenhow could count senators and diplomats among her most valued sources of intel, but her espionage was one of the worst-kept secrets in Washington. She had long-standing close relationships with senators Clement Claiborne Clay of Alabama and James M. Mason of Virginia as well as Vice President John C. Breckinridge. She had been outspoken in her support of the Confederacy before the war, and her surreptitious entertaining of Washington elite, always male, drew whispers. Even William Seward, who in the early days of the war was known to abuse alcohol and speak a little too freely at her salon, knew her well.[15] Those were also the days, however, when Seward commanded the nation's burgeoning intelligence service. That service was run by Allan Pinkerton, who had volunteered his and Kate Warne's services to General McClellan after Fort Sumter. Pinkerton was determined to arrest Greenhow. Such a coup would affirm to Lincoln his value to the administration. Pinkerton left no stone unturned.

In August of 1861, he cased Rose's home, just four blocks from the White House. The location was perfect for attracting the highly placed Union officials she charmed and gleaned information from. Standing on top of a fellow officer's shoulders, Pinkerton was able to see into Greenhow's home through a window as she met with a Union officer. When the officer left, Pinkerton chased him, but the officer ran into a provost marshal station and had the *detective* arrested. His attempt to arrest Greenhow was fumbled, but for just one day. He informed the War Department of what he had seen, and the next day Pinkerton was set free and *she* was arrested.

The payoff was huge. Union soldiers found a map of federal fortifications and other incriminating documents inside her home, where she initially was held under house arrest. Even so, she managed to continue sending reports to the Confederacy, smuggling notes out of her home, which became known as Fort Greenhow. She even snuck out a letter to Secretary of State William Seward demanding her freedom. It was reprinted in a Richmond newspaper. Flummoxed by their inability to constrain Greenhow, federal officials eventually sent her to Old Capitol Prison, the spy's irrepressible efforts finally earning her the same treatment that would have been afforded a man.

Greenhow's story and that of three other women spies caused both Union and Confederate leaders to reassess how they treated women charged with espionage. After all, if a single woman could uncover information that could help swing a key battle, why couldn't a Union spy do the same thing in Richmond?

Spooked by the highly publicized arrest of Rose, the Confederate establishment began to take action against threats on the home front. Two pieces of legislation were passed in short order in August 1861. The first was the Alien Enemies Act, which required men over the age of fourteen who were not citizens of a Confederate state to swear an oath of allegiance to the Rebel government. Elizabeth must have made note as she engaged in her daily practice of studying the city's newspapers for war headlines that the law didn't mention women. But the second wasn't so narrowly written. The Sequestration Act authorized the seizure of properties of the Confederacy's enemies, male or female. Did Elizabeth worry the family mansion could be at risk? She made no note of it in her diary. To anyone else, it might have felt like the walls were closing in for Unionists, but stubborn Elizabeth kept on going.

As the first year of the war ended, Elizabeth could take pride in the fact that her work was assisting the lives of Union soldiers held in Richmond. In fact, some said she had saved their lives. But she longed to do more. The question was *how*. Richmond newspapers celebrated the exploits of Rose Greenhow. Her intelligence about Union troop movements in advance of the Battle of Manassas supplied Beauregard with information he used to beat the Federal army. The fact that it took Pinkerton so long to catch her, and that other Unionist spies had failed in the lead-up to Bull Run, also showed how amateurish early intelligence efforts were. Elizabeth would have to invent her own organization from scratch.

The unusual nature of the Civil War, where combatants shared a single language and culture, members of the same families were often on opposite sides, and the border between the sides was indistinct and often porous, created a heightened atmosphere of paranoia and suspicion even in the highest offices.

So, as all the South braced for an onslaught by Union forces that spring, Davis took yet another step to punish anyone trying to dismantle the Confederacy from within. He suspended the writ of habeas corpus, the right of individuals to contest their confinement in a court of law.

In other words, if the government wanted to sideline or threaten a potential spy, they could simply throw that person in jail. Next, Davis put enforcement of martial law in the hands of a man Elizabeth knew well, Winder, the Rebel prison chief who had first allowed her to visit the prisoners.

Elizabeth had to be shocked at what came next. The white-haired man whom Elizabeth had charmed would later earn the title "the Dictator of Richmond." His first actions as administrator of martial law demonstrate why. Winder set in motion the arrest and imprisonment of Richmond men suspected of conspiring to overthrow the Confederate government in early March 1862. A total of twenty-eight men were jailed. Elizabeth's good friend and inspiration, Whig John Minor Botts, was snatched from his bed and imprisoned. Botts had been a social friend of the Van Lew family. Many of those arrested were workingmen and laborers. The best connected and wealthiest were able to make their way out in short order, but others languished for months behind bars. All, however, eventually made their way home.

The Richmond newspapers covered the details of the roundup, which Elizabeth would have carefully read. But there was a silver lining to the arrests, one that would help her in her work to assist the Union. What she had started with—a small informal group of people, including her, her mother, and the slaves and servants who worked for her—could now be expanded. She had names of fellow Unionist sympathizers. By penning these civilians together in prison, the Confederate government had exposed the Union sympathizers in Richmond . . . to one another. These were people Elizabeth might never have met otherwise. Farmers, German tradesmen, an ice dealer, and an import-export merchant. She could organize these men into a network of Unionist supporters inside the Confederacy. The South's effort to quash dissent had in fact provided the path to its organization.

❖ · ❖

IN THE CONFEDERATE WHITE HOUSE

Elizabeth knocked on Jefferson Davis's door and waited. Behind her the hustle and noise of downtown Richmond traffic continued as usual. Yet Elizabeth's visit was far from the normal social calls to the Confederate executive mansion that in later years would be called the Southern "White House."

Today, Elizabeth was calling on the president's wife. Though born in Louisiana, Varina Davis, like Elizabeth, had Northern roots. Varina Davis's grandfather, Richard Howell, had been governor of New Jersey. She was educated, outspoken, and controversial in Richmond social circles because of her boldness and her Yankee connections. Despite its name, the Davis home was light gray, not white, and steps from the Virginia state capitol. Situated at the top of a hill, the home had a columned portico at its rear that offered sweeping views of Capitol Square. Dressed in her best silk for visiting, Elizabeth was ushered from the small porch into a circular entry room by the Davises' longtime butler and slave, William Jackson.

As her eyes adjusted to the interior light, she noticed life-size statues of the Greek muses of comedy and tragedy, each holding a gas lamp. The home was impressive. It possessed a functioning water closet, a coveted innovation. Mahogany tables were scattered throughout. Underfoot, red carpeting patterned with white flowers and lime-green leaves stretched from wall to wall. Light fell on the scene from French doors that opened onto a view of the grounds. The entire effect was one of elaborate wealth, such as you might see in a titled French aristocrat's home or possibly in a high-end bordello. Paying for the upkeep of the building and its staff was a challenge for the Confederate Treasury.[1]

Varina Davis was already sitting in the elaborate drawing room, which was furnished with deep crimson rococo sofas and chairs. Elizabeth joined the First Lady, and sat with knees held daintily together, ankles crossed. She perched at the very edge of the divan, the only posture possible given the constrictions of her whalebone corset and crinoline petticoats.

The two likely exchanged pleasantries about the upcoming holiday season, and Elizabeth took her time getting to the reason for her visit. She had heard that the First Family was seeking a housemaid. Might she lend the Davises one of her slaves? The answer from Varina was a relieved yes.

Thus, legend has it, Elizabeth Van Lew's servant Mary Jane entered the service of Varina Davis in her household, the most protected sanctum of Rebeldom.

Though she could read and write, Mary left no record of her own about living alongside the Davis family, but according to the narrative that has developed over decades, she lived and worked on the Confederate White House grounds just like any other member of the Davises' extensive staff, housed in a separate building. Elizabeth's plan was for Mary Jane to establish herself as a reliable servant. In the meantime, Elizabeth recruited the seamstress of her neighbor and friend Eliza Carrington to serve as a go-between. Mary was to scour the desk of Jefferson Davis, memorizing the details of his letters and maps, and at night in her room transcribe the lot. She was then to hide the notes in the folds of one of Varina's dresses or sew it into a waistband. The next day, the dress would be picked up for repairs by Carrington's seamstress and taken to Church Hill, where the notes would be retrieved and given to Elizabeth. When Mary had information ready, she would place a red piece of clothing on a clothesline outside the house, a signal she needed a pickup. Alternatively, she could hand off her notes to fellow Union sympathizer Thomas McNiven, who ran a bakery not far from the White House, on his regular early morning deliveries.

The facts of the life of Mary Jane Richards are elusive. We're not even entirely sure of her name. Sometimes known as Mary Bowser, M. J. Denham, or Richmonia Richards, her various aliases and married names make her difficult to track in historical records. It doesn't help that accounts of her life are conflicting. But her story is irresistible to historians and their audiences alike.

Here is what we do know. Mary Jane was born a slave in the Van Lew household sometime between 1839 and 1841. Her parents' names are unknown. But even as a baby, Mary was a favorite of the household and Elizabeth treated her as a daughter. Elizabeth and her mother, Eliza, took the unusual step of having her baptized at St. John's Episcopal, the family church where much of Richmond society gathered every Sunday for services. White members of the segregated church were likely shocked. The move reveals just how much Elizabeth and her mother adored the young girl and how willing they were to endure social censure for their beliefs that slavery was wrong.

If the baptism was unusual, what Elizabeth did next was virtually unheard of. First, she freed Mary Jane sometime after Elizabeth's father, John Van Lew, died in September 1843, despite the fact his will was written to prevent Elizabeth from doing so. Presumably, Elizabeth ignored it. Moreover, Elizabeth paid for the girl to move north, likely to Princeton, New Jersey, for an education at the age of seven or eight. The path Elizabeth had set out for Mary, with or without the girl's consultation, mirrored her own. Elizabeth, too, had been sent away for education, but to Philadelphia. What Elizabeth had planned next for Mary was very different from the path Elizabeth had followed. The education Elizabeth had bought for Mary was training for a future Elizabeth had devised. She wanted the girl to pursue a life as a missionary, and she had just the spot for Mary to do such work. Elizabeth was a member of the American Colonization Society, a national and influential reform society that established a colony in Liberia, a West African territory, as a new home for Blacks from the United States before the war. The organization had the support of several famous Americans at the time, including Harriet Beecher Stowe, Henry Clay, and Abraham Lincoln, as well as Southern slave owners. Ultimately, this strange experiment was abandoned, but for a time slavery opponents saw it as the best route to gradual emancipation, while proslavery forces embraced it as a way to rid the country of free Blacks, whom they believed to be a source of social destabilization and slave uprisings. By choosing Liberia for Mary, Elizabeth was still operating within the norms of Richmond society, though inwardly she despised slavery.

And so after five years of schooling, on Christmas Eve in 1855, fourteen-year-old Mary was packed off to Liberia under the care of a white missionary. She was one of some 15,000 freeborn and formerly enslaved Blacks who attempted to make a home in the country located on the coast of West Africa. But the girl, like many who were similarly sent to Liberia, was deeply unhappy. Africans who were native to Liberia were hostile to the new arrivals. Disease was rampant, and sporadic warfare made living conditions dangerous. Mary toughed it out for nearly four years, with Elizabeth sending care packages. But then the young girl started pleading with Elizabeth by letter to bring her home to Virginia.

Returning to Virginia was no easy chore. First, Elizabeth had to repeatedly write to her ACS contacts for permission to allow Mary to leave, begging for her to come as soon as possible. "I do love the poor creature," she wrote.[2] Second, Mary's legal status coming back to the commonwealth was complicated. She wasn't supposed to return to Richmond, because Virginia law made it illegal for a black educated in the free states to return to the commonwealth. Arriving in Baltimore in March of 1860, she returned to Richmond nonetheless, possibly going directly to the Van Lew household. She was arrested soon after, charged with "perambulating the streets and claiming to be a free person of color" without having the usual certificate of freedom in her possession. The penalty Mary would have faced for being in Virginia as a free, educated black would have been re-enslavement. She was held in a city prison until Elizabeth's mother Eliza Van Lew bailed her out, claiming that Mary was her slave. Eliza paid a fine of ten dollars. [3]

Back in the Van Lew home, Mary became a part of Elizabeth's household staff and network. She attended Elizabeth as she walked alongside Libby Prison, their presence a signal to inmates of the possibility of escape. Even more important, Mary kept her ear to the ground, picking up gossip and rumors critical to the spy network, presumably much of it from the slave network. Household slaves tended to hear, or overhear, many of the secrets Rebels tried to keep. In a late diary entry dated May 14, 1864, Elizabeth described how she relied on Mary Jane for information. "When I open my eyes in the morning, I say to the servant, 'What news, Mary?' and my caterer never fails! Most generally our reliable news is gathered from negroes, and they certainly show wisdom, discretion and prudence which is wonderful!"[4]

Here's where Mary's history becomes murky. The version of her life that has captivated historians and history readers alike and made Mary famous was published in the June 1911 edition of *Harper's Weekly* and in the Richmond newspapers. Details were sourced to members of Elizabeth's family, much of it to Annie Hall, Van Lew's niece, who was nine years old at the time Mary Jane is said to have served in the Davises' household as a spy.

This version of Mary's life takes its start in the early winter of 1861, the war barely under way. Elizabeth heard that Jefferson Davis and his wife were looking for a servant for the Confederate White House. She decided that Mary, literate and educated with a prodigious memory, would make the perfect spy working undercover inside the home of the Davises, where she would be tasked with scanning the Confederate president's desk for information and eavesdropping on conversations among Rebel staff and generals. Just as Elizabeth had sent Mary to Liberia, now she sent her on what would have been one of the most dangerous of missions. What Mary thought of this plan is unknown. Were she to be found out, she would no doubt have faced a death sentence.

Like many former soldiers and spies, Mary went on the lecture circuit describing her war years to audiences in Manhattan and Brooklyn under a pseudonym, Richmonia Richards, even then concerned about repercussions from white racists. In her own words, she described her contribution to Van Lew's espionage efforts very differently from what Annie Hall described. She says that late in the war she entered the Confederate Senate when it was in secret session, hiding in a closet to pick up details about Confederate officers in Fredericksburg. She said her efforts assisted in their capture and the freeing of Union soldiers held captive. She also combed city streets compiling rumor and gossip from households across Richmond, a contribution that was critical to Elizabeth's reports to her Union handlers.[5]

As to whether she acted as a spy in the Confederate White House, Mary was quoted in *The Anglo-African,* a New York abolitionist newspaper, as saying that she did visit the White House, but only once. At a time when the Union was desperate for information about military plans, Mary entered the Davises' home pretending to be there to pick up the laundry. Ushered into Davis's office, she began poking around, looking at papers and opening cabinets. Davis walked in on her and asked what she was doing. Mary pretended to be what she was not, an unintelligent slave. Davis, imagining no other explanation, let her go.

If you visit the White House today, which is maintained in nearly identical condition as it was during the war, a guide will point out the small mahogany desk from which Mary is said to have stolen secrets. The desk sits just off the public rooms where Elizabeth would have met with Varina and offered Mary's services. It is a small room, called a snug, with a fireplace and a chaise longue next to it, where Davis, whose health was failing, was said to lie.[6] He had a larger office on the second floor, one big enough to house guests like his cabinet, members of the war department, and occasionally Rebel generals, but the snug was a favorite for writing correspondence. A single window lights the room and the desk. Above the desk hangs a framed picture of George Washington, Davis's hero. Sadly, there is no record of what information, if any, Mary managed to take from that desk.

Was Mary a spy in the Confederate White House? Though she did later describe herself as a "detective" during her Richmond war years, she never copped to spying in the White House. But it is worth remembering that Union sympathizers didn't consider themselves safe even after Lee surrendered at Appomattox Court House on April 9, 1865, and an end to hostilities was declared. Reprisals were common. Elizabeth, always savvy about potential threats, destroyed evidence of much of her work, worried about exposure of her spy ring after the war. For those reasons, Mary herself may have chosen not to speak publicly about all the details of her spy career or she may have destroyed evidence of her own work. We may never know the true details of what she described as her secret service to the Union.

What is clear is this: Whether Mary worked undercover in the highest Confederate sanctums, she was extraordinary. She was well educated, traveled the world, and worked with Elizabeth to destroy slavery, taking immense risks. Mary is a hero, though her exact role remains a mystery.

❯ ❮

INSIDE JOB

Erasmus Ross strutted about Libby Prison, ready for anything, wearing a pair of prominently displayed revolvers on each hip and carrying a large bowie knife. Two armed guards flanked the Libby clerk at every turn, even during roll call, which was Ross's responsibility. Overweight at a time when prisoners were starving, he abused and taunted Union men under his watch. He was young, just twenty-one, but despised by prisoners as a cruel martinet. When he summoned a prisoner to meet him alone, it was likely they would never return. The other Libby prison officers were similarly hated. Dick Turner was known for kicking dying prisoners whose only offense was lying on the prison floor. George Emack once held a gun to the head of a sick prisoner and threatened to pull the trigger if the man didn't get up. The prison attendants were generally young and ruthless.[1]

For some, the Civil War offered adventure and glory; for others, the chance to effect social change. Women like Elizabeth and Rose Greenhow discovered new outlets for their abilities.

But the chaos of war also offered opportunities for more unsavory ambitions. Often these cruelties were realized most dramatically in "hidden" places like prisons, where officers who hated their jobs were combined with underfed and resentful prisoners of war.

The most notorious prison in Richmond, later dubbed the second worst in the South after Andersonville, was Libby Prison. The prison had formerly been a ship chandlery and grocery warehouse. It was located at 20th and Cary Streets along the James River waterfront. Its Confederate designers congratulated themselves on painting the exterior of the first floor white, all the better to see—and shoot—any escapees. The three-story facility groaned under the weight of 4,000 Union men, most of them officers. Its commandant was a man worthy of a fairy tale collected by the Brothers Grimm. Lieutenant Thomas Pratt Turner ruled Libby with an iron fist, and at his direction a sign was posted on the stairs to inmate rooms that read: "Abandon hope, all ye who enter here!"[2]

Church Hill, Elizabeth's home, was a ten-minute walk away. Gradually the Confederates had come to understand she was doing more than just her Christian duty in attending Union POWs. The prison commandant, Archibald C. Godwin, warned her that she had been reported many times for her efforts assisting the enemy. In a diary entry for June 21, 1862, she recorded that a stranger came to her door offering intelligence. She was polite but turned him away, assessing the offer was a trap and that he had been sent by the Rebel government. She knew her actions were risky but refused to back off. "We have to be watchful and circumspect—wise as serpents—and harmless as doves, for truly the lions are seeking to devour us," she wrote in a June 21, 1862, diary entry.[3]

Responding to the Confederate crackdown, Elizabeth had quickly begun organizing and training a large group of Unionist sympathizers, some of whom she personally knew and others whose names appeared after they had been rounded up by the Rebel government. After the security sweep, it was she they naturally turned to as their unofficial leader. Among them, Charles Palmer was a wealthy import-export merchant and ardent Unionist, who, like Elizabeth, was committed to helping Union prisoners. He spent $30,000 of his own money to aid them. [4] Botts and Palmer helped put Elizabeth in touch with Unionists outside her social class who would become critical allies in helping to ferry Union prisoners and deliver needed aid. Grocer and restaurant owner

Frederick William Ernest Lohmann, also known as F.W.E. Lohmann, and his brother were loyal assistants to Elizabeth and her efforts. They were part of a small group of German immigrants who were opposed to slaveholding. F.W.E. helped prisoners and distributed Palmer's money to Unionist families in need. Though Confederate leadership sent him to Castle Thunder for a three-month imprisonment, he remained true to the Union cause.

Elizabeth's closest ally—a man she described as the "bravest of the brave" and "truest of the true"—was William S. Rowley, a transplanted New Yorker whose farm served as a staging area for some Unionist operations. Among his fans was Botts, who promoted him to Elizabeth. Rowley helped her provide safe houses for escapees and passes and disguises to travel north. In the Rowley household, resistance was a family affair. Rowley's fifteen-year-old son often went undercover as a courier for his dad and even helped sabotage a Confederate ammunition train.

Women in the ring were rare, but Abby Green, a friend of Elizabeth's, also helped the men at Libby and offered her own home as a safe house.

As Elizabeth organized her ring, the war was about to escalate dramatically. While Civil War battles raged across North America, including engagements as far west as the Arizona territory, the action, even when far afield, ultimately drove toward the twin cities, Washington and Richmond, one hundred miles apart.

If fall is the season of political campaigns, summer is the season for war. Better weather and firmer ground make it easier for generals to move their armies like chess pieces. In the sweltering summer heat of 1862, men marched and fought more and died more. Virginia was at the center of much of the action that came to be known as the Seven Days Battles, which would end up being a decisive turning point in attitude for both the Union and the Confederacy. They were the culmination of the Peninsula Campaign, the Union's attempt to bring the Confederacy to its knees by driving through Virginia to take Richmond. This was it—surely now that the Union had a real fighting army, they could bring this war to a swift and efficient end.

When the war had started, the Union had no army. The capital was a sitting duck for ambush by Confederate forces, which sat across the Potomac ready for attack. "Here we are in this city," Lincoln's secretary John Nicolay wrote his fiancée, "in charge of all the public buildings, property and archives, with only about 2,000 reliable men to defend it."[5]

General George McClellan had been just the man for the job—building, organizing, and arming the Army of the Potomac, earning the undying love of his men. What he didn't have—increasingly as the war dragged on—was the love of Abraham Lincoln. Lincoln wanted a fighter, not an organizer, and McClellan had repeatedly defied Lincoln's orders to move forward and take Richmond.

The first battle at Seven Pines, at the end of May 1862, took place barely five miles from Richmond, putting the city in danger. The battle ended in a bloody draw. McClellan, who was already ill, also found the carnage distressing, writing to his wife: "I am tired of the sickening sight of the battlefield, with its mangled corpses & poor suffering wounded! Victory has no charms for me when purchased at such cost."[6] Meanwhile, Confederate commander Joseph Johnston had been badly wounded.

The Union army sat for nearly a month, frozen by McClellan's hesitation. The Confederates, however, had a new commander. Robert E. Lee would not hesitate.

Elizabeth experienced the aftermath of the Battle of Seven Pines as a stressful pause. No one knew McClellan's mind or what Lee would be like as the new top general. The month-long lull set all of Richmond on edge.

What was next? Would the North directly attack Richmond? Lay a siege? As the hours ticked by, the anxiety rose in the homes and public spaces across the city. "How long is this to last?" wrote Elizabeth in her diary. "We are in hourly expectation of battle." The newspapers made things worse. Their pages were full of warnings about lusty and violent Yankee soldiers bent on assaulting Southern women at the first opportunity. Children were taught that Federal soldiers weren't human. Young ladies on the streets of the city carried parasols in one hand and purses containing a derringer or a bowie knife in the other.[7]

But in the Van Lew home, optimism reigned. Elizabeth's mother, Eliza, set about making up one of their bedrooms for General McClellan, assuming that Federal forces would soon take the city. Servants installed new curtains. The sheets were washed and ironed, the pillows fluffed, even a bath drawn as if the brooding mustachioed officer would sweep into their drawing room at any moment and demand shelter. Eliza's actions indicated more hope than military acumen. McClellan, his confidence shattered by the previous battle, did not appear.

Instead, Lee took the strategic initiative and attacked the Federal Army at the Battle of Oak Grove and then moved on to Mechanicsville, a small town six miles north of Richmond. Hundreds of Richmonders— men, women, and even children—clambered up the highest hills around the city to watch the unfolding battle.

Elizabeth was not to be left out. She and a close friend and neighbor from Church Hill, Eliza G. Carrington, rode northeast out of Richmond to visit their friend and fellow Unionist John Minor Botts, newly released from prison. Their trek that day to Botts's farm took them along the Mechanicsville Turnpike, in the direction of the fighting. Confederate soldiers were posted along the way. Elizabeth and her friends had to show government-issued passports to pass.

To that point, Elizabeth had mostly seen the effects of war, the broken bodies and the dead, but this was her first time in the presence of the thing itself. She found it unexpectedly thrilling. "Men riding and leading horses at full speed; the rattling of their gear, their canteens and arms; the rush of the poor beasts into and out of the pond at which they were watered. The dust, the cannons on the crop roads and fields, the ambulances, the long line of infantry awaiting orders."

When the group reached Botts's farmhouse, the family huddled inside, listening to the roar of artillery. The windows rattled. She could see the flash of shells exploding and hear the roar of muskets. "The rapid succession of guns was wonderful," she wrote.

The experience heightened her sense of the importance and glamour of her cause and inspired her. That night in her diary, she wrote: "No ball could ever have been so exciting as our ride this evening." The experience drove her to flights of poetry. "I realized the bright rush of life, the hurry of death on the battlefield."[8]

The failure of the Peninsula Campaign marked a vital moment in the war. Both sides realized that this war would not reach a speedy end, but would rather turn into a brutal war of attrition. Ironically, it was Robert E. Lee's success that also ensured Lincoln would solidify emancipation as a war goal. The war against the South couldn't be won with half measures.

Emancipation was the positive side of that coin; increasingly brutal tactics were the negative side. Modern warfare was here to stay. The officers who were able to adapt to this would be the ones who succeeded. In an atmosphere like this, espionage and "dirty war" tactics would flourish. Elizabeth realized that. So far, Elizabeth's actions had mostly been reactions to the situations on the ground as she found them. But now she was ready to put everything she owned on the line. Already, she had used the Church Hill mansion as a safe house for escaping slaves, but now she aimed to give shelter to Union officers and soldiers. And her efforts went beyond the military. When she worked to help free journalist William Henry Hurlbert, she unleashed through his pen a series of highly publicized articles that depicted in detail the conditions in prisons and the South more generally. Hurlbert, an editor for *The New York Times,* had been traveling the South in 1861 doing research for a series of articles. He interviewed the Confederate secretary of war Judah P. Benjamin in Richmond, and traveled to Charleston and Atlanta, where he was arrested as a spy and sent back to Richmond. After Hurlbert escaped with Elizabeth's help, his articles argued that the South was not unanimously in favor of the war, and that in fact Unionism was on the rise.[9]

Elizabeth had another powerful tool she could use to expand her influence: money. She had already tapped the $10,000 her father had given her. Proceeds from the family hardware store also went to assisting the Union cause. She used some of the money to help slave families stay together, buying family members who might otherwise be separated. She had given money to some of her own slaves as pay for their work and helped others escape to freedom in the North; the Van Lew butler and his family had benefited from such generosity. Now she wanted to use her money as a tool to outwit the Rebels. Some Blacks working inside the prison system went on her payroll to serve as guides to potential escapees and informants. She looked for like-minded Union sympathizers, many hiding their true loyalties, buried in the Confederate bureaucracy. Eventually she would find a few key allies, including a clerk in the attorney general's office, with access to information about troop strengths, and clerks in the navy and war departments. Some could be relied on to share information out of a sense of loyalty to the Union, but others wanted to be paid, especially as wartime inflation soared.

The Union's spy efforts to that point had been largely lacking. Officers, originating as they did from private life, had little training in the fundamentals of military organization and deployment, much less spying. Even West Point–trained officers had little exposure to the finer points of intelligence gathering, though they knew enough to hire their own operatives. General McClellan, for example, hired Allan Pinkerton, the Glasgow-born detective who prevented Lincoln from being assassinated on his way to his inauguration.

But the importance of gathering information in the field would become obvious. After all, how else could one find the enemy without some reconnaissance? Using cavalry to locate enemy lines and estimate enemy strength had been common for centuries. In the Civil War, both sides experimented with hot air balloons to similarly locate enemy positions. Unfortunately, they were easily shot down. Signal towers, which provided a vantage from which to view enemy positions, were common. Using flags or torches, signalmen sent messages using a wigwag code in which certain movements or positions represented letters and numbers. Messages could be quickly transmitted via relay stations set up in a network. The messages were read using telescopes or binoculars, sometimes by the enemy.

The biggest innovation was the telegraph, which came into prominence just as the Civil War was under way. Both sides used the telegraph extensively, though its effectiveness was hampered by the possibility that messages could be intercepted by the enemy and lines could be sabotaged.

Transmitting information was one thing, but gathering it in the first place required more expertise and effort. On the ground, information was gathered by hand. Spies and scouts largely deployed for sometimes days or months turned overheard conversations, stolen correspondence, and even newspaper stories into written or oral reports and were paid a handsome sum for their work. Spies employed by the Union earned $500 per mission, while scouts, who experienced less risk and were in enemy territory for less time, might earn $100 to $300. Even scout's pay was significantly higher than that of a private, and many soldiers turned to the business of espionage to make more money. Some were better intentioned than others.

Grant learned the hard way the importance of good intelligence on April 6, 1862, at the Battle of Shiloh. On that day, Confederate forces launched a surprise attack on Grant's forces that the general never expected. Thirteen thousand Union men were lost over the two days of the battle. Though Union forces were able to regroup and counterattack, the general's reliance on deserters for information on the Rebels' numbers and intent led him to discount their ability to mount a strong offensive. The deserters fed Grant's own belief that the enemy's morale was withering, and that weak leadership would make it impossible to mount an impressive attack. He was wrong on both counts. Grant wouldn't make the mistake again and would become the Army's foremost practitioner of the use of intelligence, developing a small group of sophisticated analysts who provided him with the detailed information he needed to win the war.[10]

Early in the war the Union struggled to get information from the Confederate capital. The fate of Timothy Webster, a thirty-nine-year-old Brit and Pinkerton's star agent, was a good case in point. In October 1861, Webster made three reconnaissance trips to Richmond, posing as a rich Southern arms buyer. He brought with him hundreds of letters from Baltimore secessionists to their Richmond friends and relatives, an effort to reinforce his cover as a Southern arms buyer. Each of the letters had already been read by Pinkerton's staff for useful intelligence.

On the first trip, he toured the city's defenses and even visited its ordnance department, where he counted the number of Enfield muskets[11] (there were 12,000) that had been smuggled through the blockade. After each trip, he returned to Washington to write his reports, mostly from his excellent memory of what he had witnessed. His confidence earned the Union plenty of intelligence as he visited military camps throughout Virginia, assessing the strength of Confederate forces and their arms.

But Webster, surprisingly, would never have gotten the access he needed to conduct such an intelligence sweep without the help of General Winder. The general, who didn't know Webster's true identity, unwittingly issued a pass allowing the spy to move freely. In exchange, he asked Webster to take a message to his son, who was serving for the Union in Washington. Winder wanted his son to return home to Richmond.

Webster's cover was blown when Pinkerton sent two more Union spies to Richmond to determine the status of his star agent. Winder found the men suspicious and had them arrested, and during their interrogation they fingered Webster. On April 25, 1862, a Richmond court declared Webster a spy and sentenced him to be hanged. While many spies were arrested, few had been executed. Accordingly, Lincoln's cabinet pressed for leniency, to no avail. Kate Warne had one of her female detectives, Hattie Lawton, pose as Webster's wife and appeal to First Lady Varina Davis for a lesser sentence. Varina refused to intervene. When guards came to take the spy from his cell at dawn on April 29 for hanging, Lawton fell to the floor, weeping.[12]

On April 29, 1862, Webster became the first spy to be executed since Nathan Hale during the Revolutionary War. Spectators crowded the scene to get a good view of the proceedings, which were held at a former parade ground called Camp Lee. On his first try, the hangman failed to tie the rope tightly around Webster's neck, and Webster's head slipped through, his body falling to the ground with a thud. As he was lifted back up the steps for a second attempt, Webster said, "I suffer a double death. Oh, you are going to choke me this time."[13] On the second try, the noose was wrenched tightly around Webster's neck. This time, the execution succeeded.

On Church Hill, Elizabeth shuddered. "Heartless murder" is how Elizabeth described the hanging in her diary.[14] As always, her first impulse was simply to provide comfort. And that day she went to Castle Thunder to ask permission for Hattie to stay at her home. Elizabeth did not know Hattie herself was a spy, her naiveté surprising. Elizabeth was denied her request, and Hattie spent a year in prison in Richmond until she was released in a prisoner exchange. But the experience served as a warning to Elizabeth and her ring.

Intelligence failures had also contributed to the failure of the Peninsula Campaign. Allan Pinkerton may have been a good detective, but he was a terrible spymaster. The main problem was that he was working for McClellan, who was committed to believing his opponent's army was bigger than his own. Wittingly or unwittingly looking to please the general, Pinkerton presented figures "made large" for safety's sake. McClellan then took even those exaggerated figures and inflated them to present to his superiors.

By the time of the Peninsula Campaign, Pinkerton had fully embraced McClellan's fantasy, extrapolating from the number of regiments his scouts had identified in Lee's army—most of them—into the assumption that there must be vast numbers more, unidentified. Between the detective and the general, they'd dreamed up a phantom army.[15]

McClellan's paranoia about the enemy was paired with distrust of his own side. He had actually tasked Pinkerton to spy on Lincoln and his War Department. Meanwhile, Edwin Stanton returned the favor by assigning his own agent, Lafayette Baker, to spy on McClellan and Pinkerton. The choice of Baker tells much of Stanton's own personality. Baker's only training was as a member of a band of vigilantes in the lawless city of San Francisco. The group was known for heavy-handed tactics, beating up suspects, framing evidence, and even administering the death penalty when it was convenient. Baker's inspiration was the devious and manipulative head of the French secret service police, Eugène-François Vidocq. Like Vidocq, Baker had a talent for manipulating higher-ups.[16]

It all ended in disaster. Unionists' hopes that the Peninsula Campaign would end the war were dashed. McClellan blamed intelligence failures and bad weather for his failure to press his advantage, and the war ground on. As it did, Richmond became more dirty, dangerous, and crowded. Commercial buildings and homes in the city grew unkempt. If a plank fell or a screw got loose or a gate fell from its hinges, it was likely to remain that way, as the city's carpenters were on the battlefield.[17]

The wartime city attracted an unsavory crew of prostitutes, speculators, and gamblers. Working families struggled with the pressure of rising prices. The talk around the dinner table was often about the suppertime luxuries Richmond residents enjoyed before the war, like champagne and oysters. Simple meals of Indian peas, bacon, and corn bread doused in sorghum syrup grew more common.

Injured Confederate soldiers, Federal prisoners, and the war dead came first into Richmond, thanks to its location close to enemy lines and the railroad network that had been built to service the city. Open wagons with the dead piled up in them rumbled along Richmond's streets. Rising out of one of them was "a stiff arm, shaking as it rolled down the street as if in defiance," wrote one Richmond matron.[18]

Close on their heels came the growing number of families of the injured, hoping to nurse their boys to health. Union prisoners languished in a growing number of crowded prisons. The Rebel government had commandeered a quarter of the tobacco warehouses for such use. Three thousand captured Union officers, political prisoners, deserters, and

Black convicts were imprisoned at one on Cary Street the locals called Castle Thunder. Prisoners there were routinely tortured by guards, who would hang some by their thumbs or brand them with hot irons. Another 10,000 mostly enlisted Union soldiers were held at Belle Isle, an island in the middle of the James River. There, inmates lived in the open air, without lavatories or showers, and with no blankets. In the winter, prisoners burrowed into holes in the ground to keep warm.

But it was Libby Prison that would gain the most notoriety and attention.

Elizabeth could see Libby Prison from her porch. And she no doubt heard many tales about conditions there from her paid informants. She knew the inmates were robbed of any money or valuable goods as they entered the prison. And she knew that it wasn't just inmates who were routinely flogged and tortured, but also the African American servants and slaves who worked there.

By late 1862, it was clear to Elizabeth that the situation at Libby Prison was deteriorating daily. As prisoners grew more and more restive, it became a powder keg waiting to explode. Crowding and a lack of food put increasing pressure on both the inmates and the guards. Elizabeth began conducting regular walks along the prison's perimeter. Nearly every Sunday she disguised herself as a washerwoman and, carrying a pitcher, passed in full view of the prisoners. They could see her through the upper-story windows, although she herself never looked at them, the better not to arouse suspicion. The purpose of the exercise was to allow her informants inside the prison to point her out to men that might try to escape. "There she is," they could whisper. "That's the woman, Elizabeth Van Lew. She will take you into her home and help you get through Confederate lines."

The Church Hill home had many advantages, but one that Elizabeth found particularly useful was a secret room on the third floor that ran nearly the entire length of the house. It was never an official space, more like an attic for storage. It didn't even have a real door, just a large plank of wood used to cover the opening. By shoving a chest of drawers in front of the plank, Elizabeth could hide the room. It was a perfect place to shelter Union soldiers and officers. By late 1862, Elizabeth welcomed a regular stream of escapees, many of them from Libby Prison, who always left under cover of nightfall, many assisted by Elizabeth's contacts.

One story was recounted in David B. Parker's memoir of his days as a Union soldier. [19] William H. Lounsbury was a Union lieutenant colonel held at Libby who experienced the general degradation of conditions and prayed for deliverance. The risks of injury or even death were considerable even for Union officers like Lounsbury. "To 'lose' prisoners was an expression much in vogue and all understood it meant cold blooded murder," Elizabeth wrote in her diary. [20]

Every night, the inmates at Libby were assembled for roll call. The prison clerk, Erasmus Ross, was known for swearing and abusing the inmates, who despised him. One night during roll call, Ross punched Lounsbury in the stomach and demanded he come to his office. Lounsbury knew other officers had been called to the office and never returned. His friends whispered, "Don't go, you don't have to!"

But Lounsbury went anyway, following Ross down the hallway to his office in a corner of the prison, formerly a counting room before the war. A guard stood at the door. Inside, Ross mutely pointed to a counter. To Lounsbury's surprise, there was a Confederate uniform sitting there. The young captain quickly understood what was on offer and squeezed into the uniform, which was a size too small, shrugging to get the jacket on, and then made for the door. It was just after dark, which meant it would be difficult for any of the other guards to see him. Strangely, Ross walked down a sidewalk near Lounsbury and in view of his escape route. For a second, the Union officer worried that Ross had set him up to shoot him as he tried to escape. Swallowing hard, he ran across the street to a vacant lot where he could hide in tall brush. Out of the darkness came a Black man who invited him to follow. "I know who you are, sir," he said. And the two made their way to Elizabeth's Church Hill house.

Elizabeth herself answered the door. She knew someone was coming. Ross, who was a cousin of one of the Unionists in Elizabeth's spy circle, had sent word to expect someone. When she saw Lounsbury, she quickly looked behind him to make sure he was alone and then opened the door wide. Ironically, in this house of secret shelter for Union prisoners, a large Confederate flag hung on the wall. Lounsbury may have blanched when he saw that, but Elizabeth would have quickly set him at ease, hurrying him to the hideout on the third floor and bringing him corn bread. Later, he recalled how Elizabeth instructed him to escape.

"Miss Van Lew told me the roads and where to take to the woods to escape the pickets and go down the James River, and I could, perhaps, before morning reach a place of safety," he recalled. Lounsbury not only made his way to safety but lived to start a wholesale grocery business in Jamestown, New York.[21]

But assisting one soldier at a time was becoming less and less fulfilling. In the meantime, Elizabeth had long since stopped focusing on simply bringing food and family letters to Union soldiers and officers held in the city's military prisons. She was involved in work that could only be described as that of a spy. In her first-floor study, the rectangular columns at each side of her fireplace were repositories for the secret letters and other communications Elizabeth frequently forwarded north. Some of the information hidden there concerned the Union POWs that Elizabeth aided; but increasingly more of the documents detailed Confederate military plans and troop movements, secrets that revealed her disloyalty to the Rebel cause. Atop the columns sat a pair of bronze lions. Elizabeth slipped sensitive letters and documents inside the lions' secret cavities. Those letters would later be picked up by her Black servants to deliver.

We're not exactly sure when Elizabeth found a consistently useful recipient for her information gathering, but she was clearly building her own intelligence-gathering force—what would later be lauded as the most sophisticated unofficial spying network in the Civil War.

Elizabeth described many of her efforts and her emotional journey during the war in her journal. Though she was fastidious about keeping her personal papers hidden, she kept the pages she was currently working on at her bedside so that they could be immediately destroyed were her home to be raided or searched.

Elizabeth had long since decided that some of her most loyal and committed partners were Blacks working as slaves and freemen. Most of the names of Blacks who assisted the Union cause in Richmond are lost, possibly because the exposure of their identity would have drawn a penalty of death. Robert Ford, a free Black man, worked at Libby for the Confederates but helped Union men escape. There were many others, including slaves in the Van Lew household. Oliver Lewis and the brothers James and Peter Roane were couriers Elizabeth used to take messages into Union lines. These were the people who would become the nucleus of Elizabeth's ring. They remained loyal, taking enormous risks and gambling with their lives every day.

On at least one occasion, the risk would result in catastrophe. William Roane, the man who had predicted to Elizabeth the downfall of the South, encountered a Confederate in the street and was arrested. When his captors realized the man was a member of the Van Lew household, they grew angry, Elizabeth implied in her diary, and the "life of freedom," that William envisioned would "never be realized," Elizabeth wrote. The rest of the account is missing.[22]

꘏ ꘎

THE MAKING OF AN ASSASSIN

When Rose Greenhow arrived in Richmond, she received the
welcome of a returning hero. The Union government, unwilling
to incur the bad publicity of executing a woman from high society, had
simply not known what to do with her. When confinement at her home
had failed to stop her from feeding intelligence to Richmond, Rose,
along with her eight-year-old daughter, Little Rose, were imprisoned at
the Old Capitol Prison in Washington, D.C., for several months in 1861.
But that didn't stop Rose, who continued to communicate with friends
outside the prison using ciphers and codes. Finally, under the condition
she stay within the bounds of the Confederacy, Rose was allowed to leave
Washington. Jefferson Davis, sensing an opportunity to leverage Rose's
fame, sent her to England and France to charm foreign ministers just
as she had romanced domestic ones in Washington. Richmond needed
money and support from the continent.[1]

Meanwhile, having recruited her team, Elizabeth was escalating
their plans. Even though Richmond society was full of closet Unionists,
none of them had had the courage or vision to do what it took to organize into a real resistance movement. Elizabeth, with her contrary nature
and gift for organization, was a perfect spymaster. Even as Elizabeth
lowered her profile in high society to attract as little attention as possible

from Rebel authorities, she expanded her reach and influence with the loyalists of Richmond. Loyal Unionists looked to her for leadership. The veneer of the Southern lady remained, but underneath she was plotting against the Rebels.

Her method of resistance required a low profile. For others, the war offered a chance at celebrity. While Elizabeth ducked the spotlight, John Wilkes Booth was basking in it. As the war got under way, Booth was just cementing his acting credentials. His experience in Richmond at the Marshall proved a great training ground. As his bookings increased, so did his confidence. He stopped performing under the name John Wilkes and used the family name, Booth, no longer fearful of being compared to his father.

During the theater season that began in mid-October 1861 and concluded at the end of June 1862, he gave 163 performances, nearly one a day over a period of more than half a year. He performed across the country from St. Louis to New York in leading roles. The pace was frenetic, but Booth was exploiting the opportunities that came his way and securing his reputation as an energetic and entertaining performer.[2]

The audience that had drifted away at the beginning of the war was back and desperate for diversion—and it was largely female, because America's sons and husbands were at war. Booth had done much to sharpen his appeal to that group. Aware of the importance of his physical presence in the footlights, he exercised nearly every day, and he spent a near fortune on his wardrobe. He was hounded by women. At the stage door, they pulled at his elbow and sometimes ripped his clothes. John Wilkes Booth was a star.

Some believed his performance to have elements of genius, but a friend and fellow actor Charles Wyndham said this of him: "His was not a nature to submit to discipline, adversity, or a long routine of study. When he achieved some notable triumph of his art, it was a divine flash, a combustion of elements."[3] Booth's best moments onstage, therefore, were intuitive, athletic, and high energy. Audiences ate his performances up, though some critics thought him bombastic and stagy.

In his search for recognition, Booth was particularly eager to play the Boston Museum, where he was booked for a run beginning May 12, 1862. It was a respectable high-class theater at a time that playhouses hosted everything from Shakespeare to vaudeville and animal acts. A week before the actor arrived in Boston, The *Boston Transcript* ran a story celebrating his arrival, but also noting that his father, Junius, occupied a position in city theatergoers' memory that "no other actor could ever attain." The pressure was immense.[4]

In fact, the role that Booth performed in his Boston debut, that of Richard in Shakespeare's *Richard III,* was his father's most celebrated. The younger Booth enjoyed portraying the sadistic hunchback who covets power and will do anything to achieve it. The role allowed him to spotlight his fencing prowess, something audiences across the country were eager to see. When he entered downstage right on the Boston Museum stage, the audience erupted in applause and shouts, eager to see him fight. For several minutes, he stood, his outstretched arms crossed and holding a sword, waiting for the outburst to subside. Then he began reciting Shakespeare's famous monologue—"Now is the winter of our discontent / Made glorious summer by this sun of York"—his voice even and strong. The sword fight in the last act, played right at the footlights, where the audience could see each parry and thrust, was electrifying. William H. Whalley, the actor fighting Booth, slammed his sword on Booth's, breaking it, forcing the actor to pick up the blade from the floor and continue the fight. The audience couldn't get enough, and neither could the critics. One wrote this: "That there are strong indications of genius in his acting. He is perhaps the most promising young actor on the American stage."[5] Such praise would have meant much to Booth, whose generation of actors would have included his own brother, Edwin, a successful tragedian. But there was more than just one acting dynasty in the country. Less than a year later, on March 2, 1863, Booth would find himself confronted with another, the Drews of Philadelphia.

He'd been invited to perform at the Arch Street Theatre and went there expecting a happy reunion with the staff of the theater where he had first performed. But the venue had a new manager: Louisa Lane Drew, a woman who would become the grandmother of Lionel, Ethel, and John Barrymore (and the great-grandmother of Drew Barrymore). Her family's theater credentials spanned generations, starting in London, like Booth's father Junius. At forty-three, Drew could already claim a successful stage career across multiple continents, sometimes playing multiple roles in a single play. She was a seasoned veteran and had shared the stage with Junius. She'd hired the younger Booth that season to sell seats, but something about his early success rankled her. She believed his star had risen too high, too fast. Their inability to warm to each other may have doomed the production.

The run in Philadelphia had limited success; in fact seats went empty, possibly due to Booth's discomfort with Drew, and also because the famous Edwin Forrest was playing across town at another of the Philadelphia theaters. Booth's reviews were mixed, with one critic describing the performances as a failure, and another saying he was a good actor and with some work might become a great one. He fretted over such notices, but it didn't stop the offers of work from coming in.

That year, the actor enjoyed the rewards of his popularity. He was one of the best-paid actors of his day, earning $20,000 a year at his peak, a sum equivalent to nearly $800,000 in today's dollars.[6] In the theater world, he was a success. People sought his opinions, women his attention. He dated a rotating list of theater stars, professing his devotion to actresses like the vibrant Maggie Mitchell, who played opposite Booth as Juliet to his Romeo. Booth's exploits were so well known that when an audience member asked one actor whether Shakespeare's Romeo had a sexual relationship with Juliet, he drolly replied, "Only in the Chicago production, ma'am."[7] Booth's conquests were not limited to stage actresses; he dated young fans and frequented bordellos.

Throughout the beginning of the war, Booth had struggled to contain his sentiment about the conflict. As an actor, he would have been best served not to express his political views. But he was a Southerner in spirit and a supporter of the Confederacy, a sentiment born in the

Maryland countryside, where he was raised, and reinforced by his sojourn in Richmond. As the war dragged on and his fame grew, he began to feel he lacked reach and influence where it really mattered. He could bring an audience to tears or to their feet, but when it came to the war and the North's treatment of the South, he was utterly without influence.

A turning point for Booth and the war came early in 1863. When Lincoln signed the Emancipation Proclamation on January 1 of that year, Booth could be quiet no longer. The proclamation, which freed slaves in Rebel states, was justified as a war measure to cripple the Confederacy and came on the heels of the Union's failure in the Peninsula Campaign. The aim was to stop the South from using slave labor to support the armies in the field with food and manage the home front while white men fought. But the proclamation did more than that. It officially changed the focus of the war from preserving the Union to freeing the slaves. It energized Blacks and set them on a course for full emancipation. Most important, it did not address enslavement in border states that had not joined the Confederacy. Slaves in Missouri, Kentucky, Delaware, and Maryland remained in bondage. Even within Lincoln's own cabinet, the proclamation was controversial when the president first introduced it to his inner circle in July 1862. Some considered it too radical. *Did the president actually have the power to free slaves?*

The directive drew fire in both the North and the South. Frederick Douglass called it the "greatest event in our nation's history," while in the South, it was roundly denounced.

The actor saw Lincoln's proclamation as proof of a presidential policy of coercion and punishment of the South. He believed Lincoln was a despot, and his anger at all things that injured the South was increasingly directed at the president. Booth was just finishing a rehearsal of *The Corsican Brothers* in St. Louis when he got news that Lincoln had signed the proclamation. Fuming with rage, he grabbed a prop pistol in his dressing room, shoved it into the ribs of a fellow player, and said "By—, Murphy, if you were Lincoln, what a chance I'd have."[8]

A friend of his set him up for his next round of performances, this time in Lincoln's neighborhood. Booth headed to Washington, D.C., and a seven-night run at the National Theatre on Pennsylvania Avenue, just blocks from the White House. He was playing in *The Marble Heart*, a drama well known in its day. Its story was that of a Greek sculptor reincarnated as a Frenchman whose marble sculpture eventually comes to life right before his eyes. He falls in love with the "marble-hearted" woman. Tad Lincoln came to see Booth in the play in April 1863 and found the performance thrilling. The play, which required Booth's character to laugh maniacally, as well as run about the stage and weep, was a perfect fit for Booth's physical style. The actor welcomed the boy in his dressing room, chatting easily and shaking his hand. [9]

Lincoln was a frequent theatergoer in Washington. He enjoyed all sorts of productions from comedies to straight drama, but he was a particular fan of Shakespeare and had memorized large portions of *Macbeth*. Possibly on his son's recommendation, on November 9 the president attended a performance of *The Marble Heart* starring Booth. He was part of a large party that included his two secretaries, John G. Nicolay and John Hay, and Mary B. Clay, daughter of the U.S. minister to Russia, Cassius Clay. She recalled sitting in a booth with the party very near the stage. "Twice Booth in uttering disagreeable threats in the play came very near and put his finger close to Mr. Lincoln's face." The third time Booth approached Lincoln, Clay whispered to the president, "Mr. Lincoln it looks as if he meant that for you." "Well," said Lincoln, "he does look pretty sharp at me, doesn't he?"[10]

Even so, Lincoln was a fan and asked to meet the actor. Booth turned him down more than once, describing to a friend why. His shocking answer reveals both his antipathy for the Union president and his virulent racism. The actor told an associate he would rather have the "applause of a negro."[11] The comment was meant for a private audience, not a public one. As time went on, he would become less discreet.

Washington was in fact a small town, and perhaps it should be no surprise that though Booth refused a face-to-face meeting with Lincoln, the two shared something else, a spiritualist. A belief in the supernatural, especially in ghosts of the recently departed, was common in the country's death-obsessed Victorian culture. Mary Lincoln frequently invited so-called experts in the supernatural realms to conduct seances as a way of communing with her beloved son, Willie, who had died at the age of eleven. One of the spiritualists she called on was Charles J. Colchester, a drinker and a scoundrel who came to the Lincolns' Cottage at the Soldiers' Home just north of Washington, to help Mary connect with her son. Lincoln was mesmerized by Colchester's ability to summon Willie's spirit or at least make rattling noises in different parts of the room and questioned him about his methods. As it turned out, Colchester was a drinking buddy of Booth's and, having heard Booth threaten Lincoln, actually gave the president vague warnings of threats against him. Lincoln, characteristically, did nothing about it.[12]

Increasingly, Booth's rants against Lincoln and the Union became public. Playing New Orleans, he despaired at the state of the city, the South's largest, which had been in Northern hands since early in the war. He began singing "The Bonnie Blue Flag," in full voice, a Rebel tune that was banned. He was seized by Union soldiers but managed to charm them and was released.

His next outburst had worse consequences. Booth was arrested in St. Louis after saying, "I wish the president and the whole damn government would go to hell." He was charged with treasonous remarks but was released after taking an oath of allegiance to the Union and paying a substantial fine.

In private, he was far more pointed in his comments. Friends began questioning him about his intense support for the Confederacy. If he was so adamant, why wasn't he serving in uniform? It was a question that must have both embarrassed Booth and also made him question himself. He felt bound by a promise he had made to his mother to stay out of the conflict. The two had a close relationship. Tortured by visions that he would die young, she had demanded he promise her to stay out of the war. But now he deeply regretted making that vow.

Distracted and restless by the spring of 1864, Booth began dabbling with investments in Pennsylvania oil leases. But the experiment backfired, and he lost money. He stopped acting for a time, exhausted with the demands of travel and performance. Once he was no longer forced to adhere to the exacting, disciplined routine of the theater, his mind had time to wander. He spent more time in bars talking politics and drinking too much. He became obsessed with Northern prisons and their handling of southern POWs, as well as Lincoln and the possibility of what he called "nigger citizenship." Booth's antipathy toward Blacks had crystallized into sheer hatred.

He wrote a letter to his mother describing his anguish. "For four years, I have lived a slave in the North . . . , not daring to express my thoughts or sentiments, even in my own home, constantly hearing every principle dear to my heart denounced as treasonable, and knowing the vile and savage acts committed on my countrymen, their wives, and helpless children, that I have cursed my willful idleness and begun to deem myself a coward and to despise my own existence."[13]

By August 1864, Booth decided he would be idle no more. His new role wouldn't play out on a battlefield. Even so, he would achieve fame that no other actor could.

GLORIOUS CHARGES AND YELLOW RIBBONS

On December 23, 1857, a disheveled-looking farmer walked into J. S. Freligh's St. Louis pawnshop. To Freligh, the man's air of disappointed embarrassment was typical—especially in that winter of economic distress, and thus he was unsurprised when the farmer reluctantly drew forth a gold watch and handed it over. Freligh wrote a receipt and the farmer went on his way.

Fifty-three years later, Freligh's nephew would sell the receipt for a hefty profit.

The day that thirty-five-year-old Ulysses S. Grant pawned his gold watch was a low point for a man who spent much of the 1850s battling one setback or another. It was right before Christmas, and Grant was broke, struggling to support a wife and three children—soon to be four. Farming had been so unprofitable that he was reduced to selling firewood on the streets of St. Louis. [1]

In the tumult that marked the Civil War era, the usual indicators of future success were unreliable. Wealth and power prewar could and did dissolve quickly during the conflict. Aristocratic families whose ancestors included some of the nation's founders couldn't guarantee their newest generation to be capable of heroism, much less survival. War rewarded the opportunistic and relentless. And sometimes even that was not enough.

There was little in Grant's upbringing that would have marked him for greatness. He was born in a southwestern Ohio village called Point Pleasant hard on the Ohio River and twenty-five miles southwest of Cincinnati, known then as Porkopolis because of its massive hog processing and packing factories. Point Pleasant was a world away and had more in common with the frontier than with urban living. Families carved their living from the land; most were corn and potato farmers. The little three-room clapboard cottage in which Ulysses was born was small enough to sit atop a railroad flatcar when it was toured across the country in the years after the war to educate the public on the general's humble origins.

Ulysses's father, Jesse, worked at a tannery, but his hobby was politics. Ambitious and boisterous, Jesse Grant was a large man who dominated the household with his personality and towering (to the diminutive Ulysses) height. Jesse Grant ran for multiple political offices and occasionally won. The dinner table must have been filled with talk of the local political scene. His true talent, though, was growing his businesses and wealth. As a result, by the time Ulysses was an adult, his parents lived in a fine brick home.

The future general's mother, Hannah, was Jesse's opposite—petite, a devout Methodist, emotionally controlled, quiet and humble. Her son replicated her qualities. Due to her religious beliefs, she allowed no alcohol, dancing, or cursing in the household. When Hannah became a temperance advocate, Jesse compensated by occasionally getting friends to pay for his drinks. And in that way he served his own ends, while giving lip service to Hannah's.

As a boy, Ulysses rarely demonstrated the kinds of qualities usually associated with leaders. He wasn't gregarious or a prankster. Instead, he was quiet, shy, and polite to a fault. He generally thought the best of people. The natural world was where he felt most comfortable. He loved to fish and adored horses. He became known even as a youngster for his abilities to subdue and ride the wildest of horses. He couldn't abide braggarts or bullies, and because he was physically small, it wasn't unusual for him to be the object of their hazing. Like his mother, he seldom raised his voice, but if a bully threatened a younger boy in his presence, he would readily put up his fists.

Most of his feelings he kept to himself, a habit that would endure a lifetime. And because of these personal characteristics, he wasn't particularly ambitious. He saw his future as a farmer, spending his days in the fields, tending crops and watching after the livestock, especially the horses. The young Grant was so enamored of farm animals that he couldn't stomach following his father into work at the tannery. The odiferous and brutal process of stripping hides from animals and transforming them into leather was appalling to him. Just the sight of a horse being roughly handled could send him into a fit of rage.

Thus Grant's emergence as the Union's most aggressive military leader is surprising. Not even a glimmer of the man who would earn the nickname "The Butcher" for his relentless prosecution of the war and the high casualties his troops suffered emerged in those early days.

What set Ulysses on the path to becoming the most important military figure in the Civil War was his admission to West Point. Jesse pulled the strings that allowed Ulysses to attend the premier military training facility in the United States, much to his unambitious son's dismay.

In fact, he initially refused to go. It's not just that Grant worried that he couldn't meet the entrance requirements, but he wanted to be a farmer and enjoy a quiet life away from his loud and demanding father. But in a habit familiar to all in the Grant household, Jesse would not accept no as an answer. Ulysses would surprise everyone in his small hometown by heading to West Point and breezing through his entrance exams, unusual in that many candidates flunked despite rigorous coaching.[2]

Slight, a mere five feet tall (though he would grow another six inches by the end of his time at school), Ulysses must have felt out of place among the towering young cadets. But it was at West Point where he learned the military traditions and discipline that became central to his life. At the academy, he met and got to know many of the men he would encounter on the Civil War battlefield as Confederate and Union generals.

In accord with his deep desire at the time to blend in and not call attention to himself, he finished solidly in the middle of his class, his marks neither extraordinarily high nor extremely low. By contrast, fourteen years earlier, Robert E. Lee had graduated second in his class. Young Grant—handsome, fit, with piercing blue eyes and thick auburn hair—was barely memorable except for his keen horseback-riding abilities. Grant was able to consistently jump his horses over five-foot hurdles with ease.

For Americans, the Civil War was the last great hurrah of mounted warfare. Weaponry's accuracy had already improved so greatly that the glorious assaults detailed in Tennyson's "The Charge of the Light Brigade" were a thing of the past.

Still, every horse-loving boy dreamed of being a cavalry officer. It was the glamour of the cavalry that wartime armies used to enlist men otherwise reluctant to fight. One broadside published by the 1st New York Cavalry depicted a handsome soldier astride a beautiful black horse. He sits upright, his uniform pristine. The ad promised $450, a fortune at the time, to enlistees. Many young men had read Sir Walter Scott's *Ivanhoe*, the popular romantic novel published just thirty years before, famously describing chivalrous medieval knights jousting, and like soldiers in a more contemporary war, "gaining immense superiority over the heavily laden foot soldier, slogging his dreary way through ankle-deep viscous mud."[3] Scott's books were read by Lincoln's secretary, John Hay; Henry Adams; and untold numbers of soldiers who reveled in the romantic tales.

Few of the idealistic notions of cavalry service would survive contact with reality. "The steed turned out to be an untrained, unmanageable scarecrow, requiring an inordinate amount of care; except on parade, the saber generally stayed in its rusty scabbard, since much of the fighting was on foot."[4]

One young soldier's life exemplifies the ideal template for a cavalry officer. By the end of the war, he would play a dramatic and tragic part in the lives of both Grant and Elizabeth Van Lew.

His early years couldn't have provided a sharper contrast to Grant's. Ulric Dahlgren enjoyed an idyllic childhood. He grew up in a stable family headed by a strong personality, his father, John Dahlgren. Dahlgren's upbringing, as opposed to Grant's, would seem to have been a precursor to a brilliant military career. Born twenty years after the Union general, Dahlgren came of age during the war, spending much of his time in Washington, D.C., seeing firsthand the rush to war. His father was commander of the Washington Navy Yard, where he employed his talents as an ordnance expert, inventing many of the specialized guns that would be used throughout the conflict. Smoothbore muzzle-loading boat howitzers, shell guns, and rifled guns all came from the elder Dahlgren's workshop. He was most famous for designing the soda-bottle-shaped cannons that became synonymous with Civil War battlefields. John Dahlgren's job, protecting the capital city from a Confederate assault launched from the Potomac River, was critical and put him at the center of the Union effort. As the war progressed, he became a fixture on the Washington power scene, attending state dinners and intimate White House gatherings and even mingling with European royalty. His work attracted the attention of Lincoln, who became a frequent visitor to the navy yard to see the newest inventions. Careful and methodical, Dahlgren was serious and at times taciturn, but also ambitious. He carefully nurtured his relationship with Lincoln, the natural raconteur who reveled in telling jokes and stories. The pair's disparate natures didn't keep them from becoming friends, and the elder Dahlgren brought his son into the relationship.

Raised in a setting of high expectations and ambition, the younger Dahlgren must have felt the pressure to make his mark. In fact, Ulric had been known to much of Washington even as child. Varina Howell Davis, the wife of the man who would become the Confederate president, Jefferson Davis, remembered Ulric being introduced as a toddler in a black velvet suit with a dramatic V-shaped collar made of lace and linen. His education was classical, a rarity that would have set him apart from most boys of his generation. He grew into a handsome, lithe young man with blond hair and blue eyes. His life, however, privileged as it was, was not without challenges. When he was thirteen, his mother died unexpectedly. As a result, the young boy attached himself closely to his father, accepting without question his father's advice and recommendations, a pattern he would follow throughout his life. He understood military chains of command and rarely contravened orders.

Choosing a vocation was difficult for Ulric, who considered becoming a field surveyor, which would allow him plenty of time to enjoy his favorite pursuit of riding on horseback through the countryside. But he also considered becoming a lawyer. His father continued to influence his thinking, but the emergence of the war would change everything. Concerned that Dahlgren could get caught in the conflict, John Dahlgren called for him to return to Washington from Philadelphia, where the boy had been studying law. As was true of so many young men and women, Ulric's attention was consumed by the war effort.

As the Battle of Fort Sumter loomed, Ulric's patriotism emerged. He wrote home that "the American flag should never have been insulted" by the South, adding predictably, "I would very much like to belong to a military company."[5] The hustle and bustle around Washington only reinforced his impulse to serve. Washington was a vast encampment for soldiers and weaponry. Trains arrived hourly, bringing new regiments to the capital city. Columns of infantry and artillery choked the streets, and the air was filled with band music. Crowds formed to watch soldiers drill. Fresh recruits arrived on steamboats, and the hills surrounding the scene were dotted with white soldiers' tents. It was all pretty thrilling to a young man eager to make his mark. Just nineteen at the start of the war, he began accompanying Navy seamen on their assignments.

On just such an assignment in May 1862, he went to Harpers Ferry, the mountain armory town John Brown had assaulted two years earlier. The town was under assault again, this time by rebels. Ulric assisted the small team bringing guns and ammunition by railroad to the town, control of which had switched hands multiple times. When he returned to Washington to retrieve more ammunition for Union forces, he made a late-night visit to his father, who along with President Lincoln was in the office of Edwin Stanton, the secretary of war. It wasn't Ulric's first meeting with either man, but this time they were asking for Ulric's report on the battlefield. The three listened attentively as twenty-year-old Ulric detailed his experiences and described the battle and state of the enemy. An impressed Stanton offered him an appointment to the rank of captain, and Dahlgren happily accepted. Ulric had plenty of natural talents. He was a skilled horseman and marksman, but his quick elevation to captain was largely due to his father's deep connections to Union leadership. Despite the hour, Ulric ordered an officer's uniform and was sworn in as captain the next morning before returning to Harpers Ferry.

Young Ulric was on the fast track at a time when being in the right place at the right time was critical. His future seemed preordained, a successful career attending field commanders and generals, and then who knew what might happen? His own command? An endless succession of promotions and medals and awards? If he could survive the war, he could do almost anything. It's not clear Ulric had quite thought this through, but his father was committed to the boy's success. He thought his son could achieve great things, perhaps even ascending to something John's Scandinavian immigrant parents could never have dreamed of. After all, on the basis of his own merits, intelligence, and innovation, John Dahlgren had risen to the status of a critical national asset. How far could his son go armed with the dual gifts of intelligence and connections? Ulric's future seemed bright.

Grant's career, however, was full of bumps and twists. He knew little of managing a career and didn't care to consider doing so.

At West Point, he made a pledge that would change the course of his life and the nation's. He signed enlistment papers that required him to serve in the Army for eight years in exchange for his education. For the rest of his life, Grant remained vexed by the thought that West Point grads like Robert E. Lee ignored the pledge and fought against the Federal army instead of with it.

After graduating from West Point in 1843, two critical events occurred that would have a profound effect on Grant's character. First, he met his wife, Julia Dent, a Missouri Southern belle who would provide an ideal match for the depressive, timid Grant. Julia saw the positive in most people and idolized the young Grant. Their relationship would survive a four-year engagement, enforced by Julia's father, a Missouri plantation owner who believed Grant would be unable to provide for Julia. He hoped the long engagement would fail. But while the two ardently loved each other, their families could find no common ground. Colonel Dent was a slave owner and Southern patriot, while Jesse Grant was a firm abolitionist. The gulf between the families was precisely the same as the one dividing the nation.

The second event to change Grant's life was the Mexican-American War. While Grant had daydreamed through his military classes at West Point, preferring mathematics, art, and literature, the real world was going to provide him with a crash course in soldiering. A year after meeting Julia, Grant was sent by the army to the nation's southern border, where a dispute was playing out between the U.S. government and Mexico over which of the countries was the rightful owner of Texas. The conflict quickly escalated into war, and Grant was eventually assigned a role as quartermaster, commanding supplies to feed and sustain the army. The job wasn't glamorous, but it was critical training for a man who would become a Civil War general. As the conflict ground on, Grant carefully watched the strategy and tactics of men like Winfield Scott, a star of the War of 1812 who was widely regarded as the best soldier in the world at the time (even the Duke of Wellington thought so). This was the same Winfield Scott that Lincoln in later years would come to oppose on the subject of resupplying Fort Sumter.[6] But in those early years, watching Scott was like taking a master class in military leadership. Scott's generosity to the Mexicans at the end of the war in 1848 illuminated for Grant how a lenient policy toward a conquered population could quickly bring about peace. He would follow Scott's lead at Appomattox when the Rebels surrendered seventeen years later.

During the Mexican-American War, Grant had proven himself

effective and talented as a soldier and had been promoted to lieutenant. But as was true throughout much of Grant's life, when the excitement and chaos of war was over, he was lost. As the Americans won the war with Mexico and occupation set in, a bored Grant drank to excess. To be fair, most soldiers drank and drank to excess from time to time, but alcohol rendered Grant senseless. His reaction was extreme, and his fellow soldiers were beginning to notice. Alcohol was Grant's Achilles' heel, and only the extreme demands of war or the reassuring reality of Julia's presence kept him from indulging.

He wrote to Julia not long after he "awkwardly" revealed his love to her: "You can have but little idea of the influence you have over me, Julia, even while so far away. If I feel tempted to do anything that I think is not right I am sure to think, 'Well now if Julia saw me would I do so,' and thus it is absent or present I am more or less governed by what I think is your will."[7]

The image of a Grant incapacitated by alcohol or by lovesickness couldn't be more incongruous than the reality of him in battle. During the war, he led a small group of soldiers clearing Mexican snipers from rooftops at San Cosme, where he seized a church with a view of the town's entry. He and his men broke a howitzer down into pieces and hoisted it into the belfry. That act allowed the U.S. Army to overrun the gate and end the battle. He was temporarily promoted to brevet captain. During the Battle of Monterrey, he astounded his fellow soldiers with an incredible display of horsemanship. Realizing his ammunition was nearly depleted, Grant swung one leg over his horse and, using the horse's body to protect his own from gunfire while he clung to the beast's opposite flank, rode away under intense fire, then returned the same way.[8] Under the most intense battle pressure, he would emerge calm and focused.

Unlike Dahlgren, Grant, especially at the beginning of his army career, had the misfortune of being posted far from the military's eyes. After he and Julia married, they went together to his initial assignments, one a remote post on the eastern shore of Lake Ontario in New York state, the other in Detroit. With Julia at his side, Grant was happy and productive. She became pregnant and Ulysses was ecstatic. But when Julia returned home to Missouri to have their baby, a despondent Grant began drinking again. It was a pattern that would repeat itself.

His unraveling began when the army assigned him to the West Coast, and Julia, now pregnant a second time, could not go with him, instead staying with her father and Ulysses's parents. Grant traveled to Columbia Barracks in Oregon Territory. There he would grow depressed amid the continual rain and snow, a state only made worse by his separation from Julia and his inability to see his two boys, the second of whom was named after him. Working again as a quartermaster, Grant grew bored and eventually started drinking again, going on occasional binges. His next assignment, at Fort Humboldt near Eureka, California, was similarly remote and also inappropriate to house his growing family. His drinking there drew attention. By this point, the army leadership was aware of Grant's problem with alcohol. He was a marked man. Eventually he resigned from the army rather than being fired for drinking.[9]

Returning to private life, however, provided little relief from his problems. He had no real way of earning a living outside the army. He had to borrow money to get home to Julia. The two initially lived with Julia's father on his plantation called White Haven, planning a life as farmers. But Grant, determined to make it on his own, built a log house with his own hands on land given to Julia by her father. The farm he built and named Hardscrabble was just that, a strenuous project that required all Grant's strength and effort to see through. He felled the trees for the home's construction, stripped them of their bark, and made his own shingles for the roof. This crude home was Grant's pride, and he began farming in earnest. To sustain the family until the crop proceeds rolled in, he felled trees on the property and, wearing a battered army jacket from his days in the service, he sold them on the streets of St. Louis. When an economic depression struck the country in 1857, sending commodity prices foundering, Grant hit his low, a nadir that would take years from which to recover. He pawned his gold watch and chain to sustain his family. His experiment with farming was over four frustrating years after he began. He walked the streets of St. Louis begging for day jobs, a shell of the man that could tame the wildest horses and bring order to the chaos of battle.

When the talk of secession immersed St. Louis, Grant decided enough was enough. He and his family made for Covington, Kentucky, where his father, Jesse, had built a retail colossus, several tanneries and leather goods stores. Grant would go to work in his father's Galena, Illinois, store as a clerk, reporting to his younger brother, Orvil. His fall from his years as a handsome military cadet showed on his face etched with wrinkles. He was 38.

It would take the beginning shots of the war in Charleston Harbor to revive Grant. Though he had been on the fence on the issue of slavery as a young man, his relationship with the Dents changed his mind. And the South's firing on Sumter stirred a deep patriotism. For the first time in many years, the former army officer felt a sense of purpose. He sought a commission in the army but couldn't bring himself to toot his own horn. Concerns about his drinking prevented him from being granted a commission worthy of his experience during the early days of the war, despite the Union's desperate needs for leadership. After training Galena's company of volunteers and serving on the Illinois governor's staff, he was finally appointed colonel of his own regiment, the 21st Illinois. Julia was overjoyed and foresaw her husband achieving great success in what she believed would be a short war.

And as Grant finally began to rise through the ranks in the military and to be given the responsibilities he deserved, Dahlgren looked for opportunities and stayed in touch with Lincoln's cabinet. He longed to be a hero. When the Rebels attacked Fort Sumter, he wrote his father saying that their attack was wrong and that the Union had to prevail.

A heroic reputation would come more quickly than he might have anticipated. Assigned to the staff of General Franz Sigel, Dahlgren would win the attention of not just the White House and Department of War, but the nation. In November 1862, General Sigel tasked Dahlgren with assessing Rebel strength in Fredericksburg, giving him a force of sixty men from the 1st Indiana Cavalry. The party rode fifty miles through the night, across wild and wooded country. A heavy snow was falling, making navigation difficult. At times, they followed a bridle path through the forest. By morning, they were closing in on Fredericksburg with one final impediment, a swollen river, they would have to cross. Dahlgren and four mounted soldiers went first, and then he called the rest to cross.

In a report to his *Boston Journal* editors, one war correspondent wrote this: "It was no light task to ride 40 miles, keep the movement concealed from the enemy, cross the river and dash through the town, especially as it was known the rebels occupied it in force." His account and Dahlgren's own official version were published in Northern newspapers.

The travails of the ride, while harrowing, were not the most dramatic part of the adventure, but rather what happened when they arrived in Confederate-occupied Fredericksburg. Dahlgren himself wrote: "I could plainly see the rebels gathering in large crowds in the city, and not wishing to lose time, as delay was dangerous." The young officer slowly trotted into the outskirts of the town, increasing his speed to a full gallop as the unit headed straight down the town's main street, hoping to stun an unsuspecting Fredericksburg. But he had ridden into a trap. Not only had Rebel forces learned of his approach, but they had also been recently reinforced, and now Dahlgren was undermanned. Even so, his unit shattered the morning quiet with cheering, thundering to the center of town, where they encountered two Rebel squadrons, their forces four times the size of Dahlgren's. Dahlgren found himself in just the sort of dramatic last stand epitomized in the stories of cavalry charges past. The air was filled with the sharp cracks of gunfire and the *thwip* of hacking sabers.

Despite its inferior numbers, Dahlgren's small band forced the Rebels into retreat. In the end, Dahlgren lost one man, while the Confederates lost a dozen, and the Union took thirty-one prisoners. He held the town for just three hours before leaving, but the story would catch fire, cementing his reputation as brave and resourceful. Ulric Dahlgren was a Union hero.

The next battle Dahlgren fought in marked a turning point in the war and further burnished his reputation. Over three days, July 1 to July 3, 1863, combat unfolded over eighteen square miles of sprawling Pennsylvania farmland. The Battle of Gettysburg was the single bloodiest battle of the war. Its casualties totaled more than 51,000.

But before the battle could begin, the Army of the Potomac would have to solve a big problem, which was finding the bulk of Lee's army. The difficulty of locating the enemy was something Grant acknowledged when he said, "The art of war is simple enough. Find out where your enemy is. Get at him as soon as you can. Strike him as hard as you can and as often as you can, and keep moving on."[10] It would take a mix of scouting, intelligence, and chance to track Lee's Army of Northern Virginia.

By July 2, the most serious fighting was under way. The Union had arrayed its forces in the shape of a defensive fishhook, and Lee launched a heavy assault on its left flank. Fierce fighting ensued at Little Round Top, the Wheatfield, the Devil's Den, and the Peach Orchard. Confederate assaults were waged on Culp's Hill and Cemetery Hill.

That day, Dahlgren was working for the staff of the Army of the Potomac's commander General George Meade and led a small group of cavalry harassing the enemy's rear and flank, intercepting dispatches, and slowing resupply trains. Riding with Dahlgren were ten cavalrymen, four scouts, plus Milton Cline, the shaggy redheaded star of the Union's intelligence operations, the Bureau of Military Information. Cline was known for attaching himself to a Confederate cavalry captain between February 24 and March 5, 1863, and riding the entire length of General Lee's lines, some 250 miles. It was the deepest penetration of enemy lines by either side during the war and allowed BMI analysts to develop a detailed view of the Confederate army, the order of battle.

The Bureau of Military Information was the Union's first organized intelligence agency. Edwin Fishel, who worked for the NSA for decades, discovered the BMI when looking through neglected records in government archives after World War II. In obvious admiration, Fishel described the bureau as "a sophisticated 'all-source' operation, decades ahead of its time" that "ranks alongside the war's well-known innovations, such as the control of distant armies by telegraph and the development of ironclad warships."[11]

One problem with Pinkerton's early espionage operations is that he provided information without the analysis needed to break it down into useful intelligence. Attempting to correct this, McClellan had assigned the task of summarizing the data to two young aides-de-camp who happened to be French princes in exile, one of whom was a disputed claimant to the French throne, Louis-Philippe d'Orléans.[12] Their summaries were merely adequate.

A far better "all-source" analysis would be provided by BMI, led by George Sharpe, a nondescript New Yorker recognizable by his handlebar mustache, who nonetheless had a brilliant and organized mind. Sharpe ran no more than seventy operatives, most former cavalrymen, as agents and scouts, gathering intelligence from Confederate deserters and prisoners, pilfered documents, and even newspapers. Scouts for the Bureau of Military Information were brave and daring, sometimes dressing as Confederates and working behind enemy lines. Sharpe's professionalization of their efforts and his detailed analyses of their information, complete with maps and troop strength estimates, became a critical advantage for the North. Lee didn't have a similar operation, instead relying on his own evaluation of information coming in from his Rebel network of scouts and spies and reports from the field by officers. "The belief, widely held, that in intelligence and related matters the Rebels ran rings around the Yankees is a product of popular history's romanticizing of cavalier scouts and Southern lady spies," Fishel commented in his 1996 book on the subject.[13] It was therefore to be expected that one of Sharpe's spies, the red-haired Cline, would be involved in planning this mission, and what followed.

Dahlgren's small force entering Greencastle that day was cheered by residents; even the "old and staid ministers forgot the proprieties and wept for joy." He ordered the streets cleared and climbed atop a church tower looking for Rebels. Spotting them leaving town, Dahlgren and his men swung into their saddles and rode after the squad of Confederates, taking twenty-two infantrymen prisoner. But it was the Rebel couriers riding with the squad that provided a coup for Dahlgren and his men. One nervously glanced at his saddle, where a valise was tied. Dahlgren ordered it searched, and in it his men found letters to Robert E. Lee from President Jefferson Davis. In the letters, the Confederate president denied Lee's request for more troops and detailed locations of Rebel forces. The find was an intelligence coup. Dahlgren jumped on his horse and galloped thirty miles to deliver the information to Meade on the battlefield. Some claim that the information influenced the outcome of the Gettysburg battle, by persuading Meade to cancel plans for withdrawal. Current-day historians debate that idea, but it's unquestionable that the information would have been welcome intelligence bolstering Meade in his decision to stay and fight.

Either way, Dahlgren wasn't celebrating. That night he wrote in his diary that he had captured enemy dispatches and had seen hard fighting but little more. Dahlgren's diary entries were staccato statements of facts with no embellishment. Losses for the Union over the three-day battle were estimated at 23,000 men, but Dahlgren's diary contains none of the anguish he must have felt on seeing and hearing that news. Over the next two days, Dahlgren and his men continued routing rebels and destroyed enemy communications. On the fifth, his small unit destroyed 170 wagons and captured 200 prisoners.

On July 3, the Rebels staged a massive infantry assault on Cemetery Ridge. Nearly 13,000 rebel soldiers crossed a mile through an open battlefield hoping to break the Union lines. Instead, the Federals staged a pincer movement, enveloping the Southerners in a wall of rifle fire. Only half of the men who charged the Union lines that day survived. The result was a costly but critical win for the Federals and also for the BMI. Sharpe's unit had produced reams of actionable intelligence. On July 1 alone, he wrote and processed a hundred reports from his scouts and scores of citizen scouts eager to help the Union. An amazing three-quarters of those reports were accurate.

By this time, buoyed by his own myth, Dahlgren must have felt invincible. His adventures were chronicled by embedded reporters. But his invincibility was about to take a serious hit. At Hagerstown, Maryland, anticipating a situation similar to his coup at Fredericksburg, Dahlgren led his men in a charge down Main Street. But repeated success was not to be. What differentiated Hagerstown from Fredericksburg was this: Just as Dahlgren emerged on one side of Hagerstown, a Rebel column entered from the other side. Their force was larger than Dahlgren's and was made up of infantry, cavalry, and artillery. His men were showered with bullets from streets and houses; and a deadly battle ensued. Dahlgren was wounded, shot in the foot. He called out to E. A. Paul, a *New York Times* correspondent, "Paul, I have got it at last." But Dahlgren stayed on the battlefield until a loss of blood forced him off.

Even so, the young soldier didn't consider himself seriously wounded and wrote in his diary that night, "Wounded. Did not consider it more than a ball glancing—had no idea it went through. Soon gave way from loss of blood. Laid in an ambulance all night. Foot not very painful. Slept well."

His condition worsened. After several increasingly uncomfortable days, a surgeon told Dahlgren that his foot had to be amputated. Many men lost limbs during the war because antibiotics had yet to be invented, and any open wound could lead to a mortal infection. The surgeon's solution was generally to amputate any infected limb.

With his strength failing, Dahlgren was sent home by train and carried on a stretcher into his father's home. At first he received visitors and friends, including Lincoln, but as he became weaker and as the heat of a Washington July bore down, Dahlgren lapsed into a coma. A cavalry picket was stationed near the front door to keep order. The visitor bell was silenced. Thinking that the boy wouldn't recover, the secretary of war promoted him to the rank of colonel, even though Dahlgren had seen little action.

His father, who was on duty off the South Carolina coast, wrote this on July 20: "I have been concerned beyond expression to hear of your misfortune. It was almost a foreboding with me . . . Still, I hope for the best. There is nothing good that could happen to me which by any possibility could compensate for a serious evil to any of my children. You will have the whole house at your disposal and all that I have to make you comfortable."

Dahlgren's leg below the knee was amputated and for two days he continued to linger near death. But, slowly and surprisingly, the young man began to recover. His first thoughts were a serious reflection on what he had been through. He spent time reading the Bible.

John Dahlgren attempted to shake him from his reflective, depressed state, writing: "It is not so much what we have in the world as the use we put our means to. You can do a great deal more minus a foot than most young men who have two. It's no small matter to have fought your way to colonelcy at 21, and that must lead to more."

After more convalescence and a visit with friends in Newport, Rhode Island, Ulric decided his father was right and quite literally got back on the horse, teaching himself to ride again, this time with one leg. As the weeks turned to months, he built up his strength and practiced walking on crutches. He came to realize he needed an occupation, something to do that would allow him to make his mark. He decided to see how he could help the war effort. Dahlgren, like Grant, longed to serve his country. Unlike Grant, the young colonel would have to wait for the opportunity to distinguish himself on a national stage. But his impact would be as tragic as Grant's was truly heroic.

Dahlgren's heroics, however, typified the era's Romantic conception of the premodern warrior—the noble young cavalry officer. Grant was not so lucky. At Shiloh, Grant's reputation emerged less pristine than Dahlgren's. Rumors circulated that Grant must have been drinking again, though the charges weren't likely true.[14] Newspapers didn't look kindly on the unglamorous frontier general, and many demanded his removal.

Lincoln, however, had learned the lesson of McClellan's failed Peninsula Campaign (by this time he had relieved McClellan of the chief command). Of Grant, he said, "I can't spare this man—he fights."

11

✦ ✦

BEGGING FOR BREAD

One reason Robert E. Lee invaded the North was that order
and prosperity were declining sharply on the home front. The
Confederacy's weakness forced Lee to take dramatic action. For
Elizabeth, this was a matter of both concern and interest. Already in
late 1862 her ring had begun operations to smuggle Union soldiers out
of prisons and across enemy lines. But as 1863 continued and the South's
fortunes began to turn, Elizabeth began preparation for their biggest
operation yet. As Richmond grew more desperate, Elizabeth saw that
Confederate defenses would be lower. This would be a vital opportunity.

In early 1863, the strain on the Confederate war machine placed
Richmond under tremendous pressure. Events that April would demon-
strate just how far the dream of the romantic Old South—and of delicate
Southern women—had deteriorated.

As the war progressed, Elizabeth warned the Union repeatedly about
the sufferings of people inside Richmond. She may have been an invet-
erate Unionist, but she didn't want to see her neighbors and onetime
friends starve to death. In a report to her handler, she wrote: "The price
of provisions has moderated little (not much). Flour still retails from $4
to $5 per pound. Fresh pork is $8 a pound. Dry goods and shoes have
gone beyond all reason."[1]

For most of the war, Elizabeth could avoid the privations encountered by others in Richmond because her household was supplied by her own farm. The elite in Richmond enjoyed elaborate dinners well into the war. Tables groaned with delicacies, like oyster soup, wild ducks, partridges, boned turkey, and champagne. But by 1863, shortages and high prices had touched everyone, especially the lower classes, whose wages couldn't keep up with inflation. Flour was six times its prewar price at that point, and bacon sixteen times the price it fetched five years earlier.[2]

Elizabeth understood that the food prices were creating an unstable situation. In her diary, she wrote: "Alas for the suffering of the very poor! Women are begging for bread with tears in their eyes, and a very different class from ordinary beggars . . . There is a starvation panic on the people."[3]

That panic turned to action on a chilly morning in 1863. A Richmond lady named Agnes described what she saw that day in a letter to a friend. Headed toward the capital, she set out on her usual morning stroll, her daily respite from the turmoil of the war. Her normally quiet ramble was interrupted by hundreds of people, mostly women, quietly gathering in Capitol Square. Agnes sat down on a bench to watch what was going on. A pale young woman settled down next to her, breathless. The older woman judged that she may have been a dressmaker's apprentice, based on her chafed forefinger and the elegance of her simple dress.

The girl was wasted and wan. "As she raised her hand to remove her sunbonnet and use it for a fan, her loose calico sleeve slipped up, revealing the mere skeleton of an arm," Agnes wrote. "The girl quickly pulled down her sleeve and said, with a pained laugh, "That's all that's left of me!"[4]

The young woman then told Agnes that she and the group gathered were starving and had decided to take what they needed that morning, if the government didn't yield to their demands for food. "We celebrate our right to live!" she told Agnes. The plan that morning was first to meet with Governor John Letcher and ask for food. If that produced no benefit, they planned to break into the stores only a few blocks away and rob them of whatever they could get their hands on—bread, eggs, bacon. Agnes could see some of the women clutching weapons, such as axes and hatchets. At least one had a pistol.

The Bread Riot that followed on April 1, 1863, is famous in Richmond history as a rebellion led by poor Southern women for food. Before the war, the middle and lower classes in Richmond had been supplied by the farms surrounding the city in Henrico County. Vegetables, fruit, milk, butter, and eggs arrived by one of the five railroads serving the city, or by the James River via canal boat. Goods were also brought in via an elaborate network of roads—some dirt, others modern turnpikes.

But during the war these roads degraded because local governments didn't have the money to maintain them. Railroads were burdened with transporting soldiers. And often the railroads were out of commission due to a lack of labor and equipment to repair them. The canal systems suffered for the same reasons.

Bad weather that winter had made it difficult for food to travel from local farms into the city. Storms dropped as much as twenty inches of snow. The roads were quagmires of snow, ice, and mud, virtually impassable.[5] Even the wealthy had trouble stocking their warders, and Elizabeth praised the family hen, whose eggs kept them from starving.

Others blamed speculators for the exorbitant prices. The *Richmond Examiner* described speculation as the "most mortifying feature of the war." *The* [Lynchburg] *Virginian* declared that prosperous farmers were "grinding the faces of the poor and destroying the cause of their country."[6] Fingers were pointed at Yankees, Jews, and native Southern merchants who were said to be exploiting the problem of a lack of goods.

The situation turned some into hoarders. The *Richmond Examiner* reported on one man who bought and stored 700 barrels of flour and criticized a planter who bought so much food that his yard looked like a wharf where ships had unloaded their cargo. But while some in Virginia did engage in speculation, that alone wasn't the cause of spiraling prices.

The real culprits were various and difficult to ameliorate. First, the city's population had grown dramatically during the war. Prewar census estimates put the total population at just 27,570. Richmond at that point was barely a city. By 1860, the numbers had swelled to 37,910, and by the middle of the war, Richmond was home to 100,000 native- and foreign-born whites and Blacks. Fewer and fewer goods were being spread among more and more people. Inflation was the natural result of more mouths to feed.

The Confederate military's need for goods to feed, clothe, and move its soldiers also put pressure on prices. The Virginia countryside that had housed military encampments for three years had been scoured clean of food that could sustain soldiers. Farms, especially in the northern part of the state, were bereft of animals or food stores. As a result, Lee's army was subsisting on half rations.

Increasingly, the military simply seized the food, fuel, slaves, and other commodities it needed to run the war effort. The output of grain mills and bakeries was largely consigned to the war effort in just this way. It didn't help that because the male members of families were serving in the army, area farms were producing less. For a period, the government even outlawed shipping of wheat not intended for the army. [7]

The Virginia legislature passed an impressment law that set up a convoluted bureaucracy to allow the government to set prices. Across the South, state boards of impressment were organized, charged with purchasing goods and sending commissioners into the field to negotiate prices with farmers. But when Confederate losses mounted a few months after the Rebels lost at Gettysburg and Vicksburg, and government buyers demanded price schedules that were 50 percent below market rates, farmers and Richmonders alike were enraged.

Tax officials seized what was needed, leaving a trail of IOUs in their wake. Horses were especially vulnerable to seizure. Avoiding the impressment tax agent became a way of life. Elizabeth hid her horse in the smokehouse and then moved it into the house. She needed the animal for her spying activities. "We spread straw on the study floor, and he accepted his position and behaved as if he thoroughly understood matters, never stamping loud enough to be heard," Elizabeth wrote in her diary.[8] Some people impersonated impressment agents to feed their families.

Meanwhile, government initiatives proved useless. The legislature's efforts to write a law preventing speculation failed to pass. Elizabeth's Rebel minder, General Winder, attempted to set prices, essentially freezing them for goods sold at the public markets operated by the government, two-story brick buildings nearly a block long. That didn't work, either, because grocers refused to sell at prices that would force them to take losses.

The largest wartime food riot in the Confederacy had started the night before the morning when Agnes met the starving girl on Capitol Square. That night a group of desperate women gathered at a church on Oregon Hill, in the city's southwest quadrant, alongside the James River. They discussed their options, deciding to choose a committee to call on the governor to ask for relief. The women wanted to buy food at government storehouses at the same prices the government had bought them. When Agnes caught up with the group the next morning, Governor Letcher had put them off, telling the women to come back later in the day.

The women flooded back into the square, their anger fueled by pangs of hunger. A cry of "Bread or blood!" went up, and the women half walked and half ran to provision stores along Main Street, pulling out their axes and hatchets. The sounds of glass shattering pierced the air as the women smashed store windows and made their way inside, bypassing locked doors. The crowd swelled in size to a thousand as others, including Richmond men, joined in. They carried out flour, bacon, and other foodstuffs. A sort of mania swept through their ranks as rioters expanded their target to include not just food but shoes, bonnets, silks, and jewelry. Some merchants tried to stop the crowd; others stared helplessly.

To quell what had become a full-scale riot, the city's alarm bell shrieked and a public guard, a company of armory workers, flooded the square. Letcher confronted the crowd, describing their behavior as "disgraceful." He asked Mayor Joseph Mayo to read them the riot act. The governor gave the protesters five minutes to disperse, or the guard, he said, would open fire on them. The threat made the women pause, but their anger held them in place. They refused to leave.

Next, Jefferson Davis appeared, riding in the back of a wooden wagon. He stood atop it to address the crowd. A detachment of Confederate troops stood behind him. He told the crowd that their continued rioting would only dissuade farmers from bringing more food into the city. They were at first unmoved by his logic.

He tried to evoke their patriotism, telling them that they needed to stand united against the enemy. Still the women would not leave. Finally he flung the money from his pockets in front of them and told them to take it. And, pulling out his watch, he said he would authorize the guard to fire on them unless they dispersed in five minutes. Only as the clock ticked down a second time did the crowd finally begin to break up. Guardsmen swept in, arresting forty-seven individuals. At least a dozen were convicted.[9]

Few among wealthy Richmonders, the media, or city leaders would have sympathy for the rioters. In fact, most denounced them. The protestors were seen as possible Union sympathizers or simply as criminals. The *Richmond Examiner* described them as "prostitutes, professional thieves, Irish and Yankee hags and gallow birds from all lands."[10]

Elizabeth stepped in with her usual empathy, paying legal fees for many of those rounded up that day in downtown Richmond.[11] But the riot there sparked uprisings across the South that spring. Similar uprisings occurred in Atlanta, Augusta, Columbus, and Macon, Georgia; in Salisbury and High Point, North Carolina; and in Mobile, Alabama.

In Richmond, the city council debated what to do over the course of four meetings, finally deciding to offer goods at significantly reduced prices from market value. Only what the council defined as the "meritorious poor," those who didn't participate in the riot, were allowed to buy food.

Whether you watched the riot or participated in it that spring, it was hard not to conclude that the Confederate government was unable to protect the public. The breakdown in public order had a profound effect on Richmond's population, contributing to the further dissipation of confidence in the Confederate cause. For Unionists, like Elizabeth, it had the opposite effect. The South was reeling and losing control; Unionists' position was more solid than ever. It was time to begin planning how they could help bring an end to the war.

The fall of Richmond was the long-term goal, but the first serious step in that chain reaction would be accomplishing the most important Union objective inside the city—liberating the Union officers in Libby Prison.

TOO CLOSE FOR COMFORT

The knock at the front door of the Church Hill mansion was un-expected. One of Elizabeth's servants—possibly Mary—alerted her that the visitors that late September afternoon in 1863 were two Confederate detectives, sending a panic through Elizabeth's household. Only a year ago, Confederate Captain Alexander, the malevolent warden at the prison known as Castle Godwin, had chided Elizabeth, telling her she had been reported several times for giving too much attention to Union soldiers. And now there were two detectives standing at the entry to her home. They planned to search the premises. This was no request for entry. It was a demand. She had much in the house that could implicate her.

For one thing, there were the letters hidden in the stone lions that the detectives passed on their way into the house. Caught by surprise, Elizabeth must also have been thinking of her diary, lying exposed on her bedside table.[1]

But Elizabeth knew the biggest threat was on her third floor. Hidden in a secret room were Union POWs newly escaped from Confederate prisons. Elizabeth had transformed her home into a way station for fleeing Union prisoners. She fed them, clothed them, and gave them directions for the quickest route to Union lines and freedom. They were waiting in the darkness, sitting in the unfurnished attic of her home, marking time until they could start their escape under the cover of darkness. Discovery by the detectives would be a disaster for them and Elizabeth. Would they keep quiet?

Both mother, Eliza, and daughter, Elizabeth, had been living in fear of reprisals since March of 1862, when their family friend John Minor Botts had been ripped from his bed and imprisoned at the direction of General Winder, a man Elizabeth knew all too well, and most important, who knew her. Elizabeth must have wondered whether it was her turn to be dragged away from her home. But while Botts sympathized with the Unionists, he was no operative and certainly no spy. Increasingly, that was the role Elizabeth was taking on.

Spying during the Civil War was a democratic endeavor. Men of course participated, but so did women. Blacks, free and slave, spied. Because the conflict played out in the cities, towns, and countryside where people lived, anyone might come across information that would be valuable. Upper-class women, like Elizabeth, were particularly suited for the role because their class gave them some protection.

Elizabeth must have remembered how Rose Greenhow built a fifty-member spy ring that spanned several states, but her undoing was her careless handling of incriminating documents. Elizabeth had vowed not to make the same mistake.

Rose was the first of what historians later came to call the Big Five, a quintet of female spies that included Belle Boyd, Antonia Ford, Pauline Cushman, and Elizabeth. By 1863, all of them except Elizabeth had been jailed.

But that year it became clear that prison wasn't the worst sentence Elizabeth might get if she was caught.

Even events that Elizabeth welcomed, like Lincoln's Emancipation Proclamation, ended up rebounding in ways that made the spy ring's work more dangerous. Lincoln's proclamation that slaves in states still in rebellion as of January 1, 1863, be forever free came after the Union's victory at Antietam. But the proclamation was not enthusiastically embraced even in the North. Privately, Lincoln's chief military officer, McClellan, expressed reservations to his wife. Perhaps his concern had to do with the fact that a late addition to the proclamation was a sanctioning of the enlistment of Black soldiers. Though Blacks would serve with distinction, whether they should participate in the war was hotly debated in the North and in the South and was vociferously denounced. Davis wanted the South to retaliate by putting to death captured Black soldiers as runaway slaves. He believed their white officers should be charged with fomenting slave rebellion and executed.[2] The Richmond newspapers spat vitriol. *The Enquirer* called Lincoln "a savage" and described the Emancipation Proclamation as "servile insurrection."

In response to Lincoln's controversial proclamation, the Virginia legislature passed a resolution granting immunity to anyone killing any person attempting to enforce freedom for slaves. In other words, Elizabeth and members of her spy ring faced the possibility that their antislavery Unionist views could result in their execution by anyone.

All of this may well have raced through Elizabeth's mind as she watched the detectives crossing her threshold, one of the last sanctuaries of Union sentiment in Richmond. For them, to step into the Church Street mansion was to enter a rarefied setting. They may have been unnerved as well. The home's entry hallway was eighteen feet wide. A chandelier hung above their heads. Plush Persian rugs covered the floors and carved mahogany benches provided seating.

Perhaps she calculated that her elegant home and her gracious manners might disarm these two. And so she assumed her most natural disguise: loyal Southern lady. She smiled at the men, putting on her best face of Rebel hostess loyal to the cause, and warmly welcomed them into her home. She treated them as old family friends, promising refreshment at the end of their tour of the house, and tasked her servant with preparing tea and cakes, which they could consume when finished. The goal was to charm and awe the men, making their intention to carefully search the house seem like an *impossible* breach of convention and respect.

Elizabeth had worked hard to train her servants for just such a situation. Now she had to hope and pray that they knew what to do as she took the guests on a personal tour. Heart hammering, she led the detectives to the basement kitchens, where the duo peered into cupboards and even the fireplace. They couldn't have failed to notice the long sweeping views to the James River below. Slowly and surely, they made their way to the rest of the house. A detailed tour might reduce the length of the inquiry, Elizabeth must have reasoned. After all, even detectives get hungry. She led them through the first-floor rooms, passing through the sitting room and the drawing room past expensive chairs, soft sofas, antique tables, and priceless vases. Her study was thankfully clear of any incriminating papers.

Bedrooms occupying the second floor similarly failed to yield anything of interest to the detectives. And then, Elizabeth was obliged to take them to the third floor, the most dangerous, exactly where her Union friends were hiding behind a hole in the wall covered by an old chest of draws. Had Mary had time to tell the men to hide and keep silent? Elizabeth's elegant antebellum black silk dress clung to her back as a cold sweat broke out. She must have worried her heart was beating so loudly they might hear it.

The secret room was at the end of the hallway. A simple bump against the wall by one of the Union men or a cough could mean disaster. But that did not happen. Instead, the two detectives stood and chatted for a moment with their charming hostess and then turned to go back downstairs, where applesauce cookies and tea awaited.

She was safe—this time. Her team's cool under pressure had held up. But they were about to face the ultimate test of their organization and nerve.

THERE WAS NO MISSING GENERAL BENJAMIN FRANKLIN BUTLER WHEN he walked into a room. He was distinctive in his look. What was left of his hair curled along his neck, but his head was balding. He sported a full dark beard and a mustache speckled with gray. His eyes were so hooded, he appeared cross-eyed. His stomach stretched the tunic of his uniforms to bursting.

And by the time Butler came to Virginia in late 1863 to oversee Union operations in Virginia and North Carolina, his reputation was already legendary. "The Beast" is what a lot of people called him, or "Damnedest Yankee," or in reference to allegations he had looted wealthy Southern families, simply "Spoons," for the silver he was said to have stolen. Those were the nice names.

When it came to Butler, Rebel vitriol was eloquent. One Confederate woman in New Orleans said, "Ever since you came among us, we have felt for you hatred so violent that no words can express it. We have always regarded you as a monster in whose composition the lowest of traits were concentrated; and 'Butler the brute' will be handed down to posterity as a by-word, by which all true Southerners will 'remember thee monster, thou vilest of scum.'"[3]

One reviewer described the man as much "cussed and discussed." He was possibly best known for his controversial seven-and-a-half-month administration of New Orleans, when it was occupied by the Union forces in 1862. He could be harsh, executing a Rebel and professional gambler who, in a fit of patriotic pique, tore down a U.S. flag. Local gambler and Confederate sympathizer William Mumford had then dragged the flag through the streets and made a show of pulling it apart. He was hung on a scaffold after a military commission that Butler had appointed found Mumford guilty of showing contempt for Federal laws.

But to Southerners, that wasn't the worst of it. Far more offensive was his issuance of the "Woman Order," General Order No. 28, which sought to contain Rebel women who were spitting on Union soldiers, insulting them, and trying to provoke the men into insulting them back. The fact that Confederate ladies would leave the church pew they were occupying if a Federal sat next to them was unbearable for Butler. To end their insolence, he ordered his soldiers to treat such offenders as prostitutes, which is to say that their behavior would make them subject to arrest. He dealt with the mob-like behavior of New Orleanians by banning the display of the Stars and Bars and demanding loyalty oaths and the surrender of firearms. He even shut down newspapers and lectured the populace on their insolence.

His heavy-handed actions were meant to bring stability to New Orleans, which was in disarray. Many of its population were starving and living in acute poverty and filth. He attempted to reset the balance of power in that city, taxing aristocratic wealthy families and using that money to pay thousands of poor whites and Blacks to do the much-needed labor of reconstruction. He ordered the streets and sewers cleaned. He sent paid Black laborers to plantations where crops were in danger of rotting in the field, turning the tide in the city's fight against hunger. A month before Lincoln's Emancipation Proclamation was issued, Butler enlisted Black men into the U.S. Army. Butler concluded, "Better soldiers never soldiered a musket." In fact, The Beast may have been the most enlightened of Union military administrators. He recognized that women were more than victims to be protected, and that Black men were more than field hands.

Butler was assigned to lead the Departments of Virginia and North Carolina on November 2, 1862. He oversaw the Army of the James against Richmond and set up shop at Fort Monroe in Hampton, Virginia, the southern tip of the Virginia Peninsula. To do that job, he needed one thing: intelligence.[4] He began searching for a spy to provide reliable information on the Rebel government and its military.

It took a daring prison outbreak to connect Elizabeth to Butler, one that used all the Richmond ring's resources and cunning. And it wouldn't be the last breakout to change Elizabeth's fortunes. Attempts to leave Libby Prison were common, but not many were successful. That's why the escape of John A. McCullough, a Wisconsin soldier and assistant surgeon, and his friend Harry Catlin, a scout for Butler who went by the name Captain Harry S. Howard, was notable. The operation, planned by Elizabeth's Union ring, was led by an unlikely field agent, a fifteen-year-old girl, Josephine Holmes, the daughter of Unionist Arnold B. Holmes, one of Elizabeth's ring.

She had appeared unbidden at the prison hospital and handed McCullough a bag of tobacco to smoke. At the bottom of the bag was a note, bidding him to meet her if he wanted to escape. He did, and at a second meeting, she whispered her plan. McCullough would be laid out as a corpse, his body covered with a blanket and moved to Libby's morgue. He was to lay there all day, as still as possible among the dead bodies. At dusk, inmates in on the plan were to stage a fight, allowing McCullough and his friend Howard to escape. Howard would cart McCullough out of the prison yard still pretending he was dead.

On the night of December 8, 1863, the men did just that, following directions to trail Josephine on foot. They walked behind the girl keeping their distance as they followed her white handkerchief just visible in the gathering gloom. She led them to her home. The men were then transferred to the home of William Rowley, Elizabeth's trusted partner, where they stayed for a week, while Josephine and another friend of the ring sewed them Confederate uniforms out of blankets. Another ally and railroad superintendent, Samuel Ruth, secured passes for the two men to leave the city.

After safely crossing Union lines, Howard and McCullough shared their rescue story with Butler, who told the pair he had been looking for someone who could supply his office with reliable information on the Rebel capital. The author of Howard and McCullough's dramatic escape plan, Elizabeth, seemed just the right person. But first he would check her out. He reached out to Commander Charles Boutelle of the Coast Guard survey office in Washington, a friend of Elizabeth's and well-regarded engineer, whom Butler knew from his service in New Orleans. Butler asked whether Elizabeth was a "true Union woman, as true as steel," and could serve the role as a correspondent writing him via the post office's flag of truce, a system which civilians used to correspond through enemy lines. Boutelle confirmed Elizabeth's loyalty and capability. Butler set in motion the steps to sign her up for service.[5]

In January 1864, Howard headed back to Richmond and Rowley's home to meet with both Rowley and Elizabeth to formally recruit them as Federal espionage agents. Next, he introduced them to the tools they would need. First, he showed the two a letter from Butler that, at first glance, looked like a family missive from James Ap. Jones to his "dear Aunt." When one applied heat and acid, Butler's words, written in invisible ink, came into view on the paper. "I cannot refrain from saying to you, although personally unknown, how much I am rejoiced to hear of the strong feelings for the Union which exists in your own breast and among some of the ladies of Richmond."

Howard gave Elizabeth one more thing, which would become a critical tool: a cipher, a square piece of paper that contained a chart for converting letters into a numerical code. This tool allowed her to encode her messages. She would carry the cipher in her watch case for the rest of her life.

In short order, Elizabeth's efforts gathering intel from her network of informants redoubled. She reviewed information, pulled it together into reports, sharing her intel in weekly and sometimes daily missives that were sent to Butler via the James Jones address in Norfolk. No matter was too small for her to share. She wrote of Richmond's privations, spiraling food costs, and hunger. Troop movements, prisoner health, and even rumor were all part of her repertoire. Six months after starting work with Butler, she was running more than a dozen agents in addition to Mary Bowser and her other Black servants. Butler asked for reports on Rebel rams, boats built to slam Union ships, the Rebels' North Carolina strategy. She sent intel on developments at the Richmond Navy Yard.

She didn't stop there. When Butler asked her to go to the Henrico County Courthouse on Richmond's Main Street and recruit a source in Winder's offices in March 1864, she immediately complied. Philip Cashmeyer was one of Winder's "pug uglies," a group of notorious gang members from Baltimore that the general had brought to Richmond to restore order. The special detective was already suspected of having

Union sympathies and had been arrested by the Confederacy after he was caught handing information to a Union prisoner aboard a flag-of-truce boat bound for City Point. The papers included detailed orders from Winder himself. Cashmeyer was thrown in Castle Thunder on March 9, 1864. The detective managed to get himself reinstated to his job in Winder's office, claiming he was only trying to impress his wife with his importance in the Confederate bureaucracy. So, when Elizabeth called on Cashmeyer, the special detective was already being watched. Wasting no time, she pulled a letter from her blouse and handed it to Cashmeyer. As he read it, his face turned deadly pale. The note stated that Butler wanted to meet with Cashmeyer as soon as possible in a safe location. The special detective begged Elizabeth to never come to the office again. He did, however, visit Elizabeth at her home and became a member of the underground.[6]

Butler had struck gold, and he was so enthused by the performance of Elizabeth and her ring that he sent them $50,000[7] to recruit even more agents.

Elizabeth's very first report to Butler, written on January 30, 1864, would change the course of the war and topple a series of dominoes that would impact the White House itself. The report was written in code using invisible ink, just as Butler had instructed. The January 30, 1864, dispatch was addressed to her "Uncle" and signed by "Eliza A. Jones." In it, Elizabeth revealed how Confederate leadership was planning to move prisoners of war south. Davis and his cabinet, she said, had begun to believe the prisoners were a magnet, and feared Federal forces would come to set them free. The Union prisoners were a problem not just for Lincoln but for the Confederacy as well.

"It is intended," she wrote, "to remove to Georgia very soon all the Federal prisoners; butchers and bakers go at once." Then Elizabeth did something unusual, especially for a novice Union spy: she gave advice on the size of force it would take to attempt a raid of Richmond and a rescue of Union soldiers held prisoner there:

Because of new and rash council! Beware! This I send you by direction of all your friends. No attempt should be made with less than 30,000 cavalry, from 10,000 to 15,000 infantry to support them, amounting in all to 40,000 to 50,000 troops. Do not underrate their [the Confederates'] strength and desperation.[8]

Elizabeth had written her first missive in code and invisible ink as instructed. The January 30, 1864, dispatch was addressed to her "Uncle" and signed by "Eliza A. Jones." That news fired as a rifle shot through Butler's offices and those of the War Department.

Another missive based on Elizabeth's reporting has been held in the National Archives and received little attention. The report is stored with the materials from Grant's Secret Service and is a synthesis of material from Elizabeth and Samuel Ruth, a man who worked for the railroads but reported information on troop movements to the Union. The material from Elizabeth bears her distinctive tone and style and is virtually copied from her letters. It appears to have been delivered shortly after or even as part of the January report.

Describing how Richmond could be quickly taken, she is quoted as saying: "It can be done either by forcing Lee to retreat there to winter, or by the *capture of Davis,* [emphasis added] which would not be a feat hard to accomplish. Davis is the head and front of the rebellion; with his capture, it would go to pieces. He has many enemies (all Union men) who, with his fall, would be glad to welcome again the Stars and Stripes." She goes on to describe the route that Union cavalry and soldiers could take, "land on the Pamunkey at dark and ride unmolested to Richmond." Once there, they should

burn the government buildings, release the federal prisoners, and carry off Jeff Davis. This could be effected with less risk than would appear at first glance. There are no troops on the road except a small picket at Mechanicsville, (which could be avoided) until you get within the defenses of Richmond proper. There are two companies of cavalry to meet. There are but two pieces of artillery in position but no men to man them. A well digested plan would succeed.

She goes on to describe how this move by the Union would topple a series of dominoes that would result in "the people returning to their allegiances; county after county would yield and the backbone of the rebellion is broken."[9]

She went on to detail the sorry state of Lee's army taken from a recent letter to the Confederate secretary of war: "Five thousand men are barefooted, and many are without blankets." She goes on to detail the numbers in Lee's army, their location, and the fact that only 2,500 men are "scattered about and around Richmond."

The explicit and ruthless nature of Elizabeth's suggested plans reveals just how much she had changed from the bluestocking Southern lady she'd been at the war's start. In the beginning, she was very much a Victorian character, interested in great events and wanting to participate but at a safe remove. Some might have described her as a dilettante. By this time, though, she had seen her friends thrown into prison. She had completely lost any acceptance by her neighbors. The social network she was protected by during her youth had turned its back on her.

These missives reveal just how thoroughly she had returned the favor.

Federal officials got more than they bargained for with Elizabeth. Not only was she incredibly well informed, with contacts willing to share information in some of the most critical Rebel offices, but she also was opinionated and eager to give the government advice based on her extensive knowledge. If Union officials had been expecting small kernels of intel from a genteel Southern lady, what they got instead were detailed reports with actionable information from a woman weary from three years of surreptitiously fighting Rebels. She was rewarded with a response directly from General George Meade, who by this time had been replaced as chief of the Union army by Ulysses S. Grant. Mysteriously, she kept the note, even though its discovery would have been disastrous.

She wanted to instigate reprisals against the government that had stolen her beloved Virginia and turned it into a killing field. The naiveté and hopefulness with which she had begun her campaign of resisting the Confederacy had hardened into a fury. The time was now, she believed, for the Union to take Richmond, the capital, and end the war. She was finally in touch with the Union command, and the relationship would give her support for her most ambitious gambit yet.

But the Union military had far to go. Grant set Richmond as his first objective after Lincoln appointed him the head of all Union armies in February of 1864. His very first encounter with Lee, the Battle of the Wilderness, on May 5 was a bloody draw. Elizabeth was dismayed by early reports that Grant had been defeated. "It seems we have suffered past all excitement. Nothing elates me," she wrote. "I have calm hope. But there is much heart sadness in it." The next morning, May 14, Elizabeth was awakened to the sounds of guns firing and the white smoke of battle drifting from the north. Already, the second battle in the Overland Campaign, the Battle of Spotsylvania Court House, was under way. She sent Mary Jane to hunt for news while she ran to the mansion's roof, staring north of the city to try to understand what was going on. Already, she had sent news to the Union that most of Richmond's troops had been sent to help Lee. Richmond was unguarded and the streets and shops closed. Grant's Overland Campaign wouldn't settle the war, but it would demonstrate the general's tenacity. He cabled Lincoln with this determined message to "fight it out on this line if it takes all summer." Elizabeth was ready for a fight, and she was as tenacious as Grant.

⤜ ⤛

THE JOURNEY THROUGH RAT HELL

In the 150 or so military prisons that sprang up throughout the country during the Civil War, men held there dreamed above all of one thing: escape. Some captives achieved a measure of independence by asking for special paroles to work as gravediggers or kitchen help. In Richmond, some prisoners worked at the Tredegar Iron Works, making cannons that would blast their brother soldiers fighting for the Union to smithereens.

Creativity was sometimes rewarded with freedom. Some prisoners walked through the front door disguised as slaves, covering their faces with charcoal. Others threw themselves down among the dead and were carted out for burial.

But as the war ground on and conditions became increasingly dangerous inside the prisons, inmates took more and more risks. Some hardy souls rushed prison walls, threw themselves over, and ran like hell. Others employed handmade ladders to do the same. Even more daring escapes were made by attacking guards, though this strategy was seldom successful, since most guards were armed.

Escapees became famous, their exploits covered in newspapers. Absalom C. Grimes of Hannibal, Missouri, was captured five times during the war and escaped each time. One of his arrests occurred after the Springfield, Missouri, prison commandant challenged Grimes to join him for dinner at his home—and Grimes did just that. In an even more strange ending to his story, the Confederate achieved his goal of returning home when Lincoln gave him a stay of execution. [1]

The establishment of prisons was generally haphazard in both the North and the South and in no way developed with an eye to the thousands who would ultimately march through their doors. Existing prisons used to incarcerate criminals were immediately overrun. In Richmond, tobacco warehouses were confiscated by the Confederate government and turned into prisons. Their large rooms and sturdy construction seemed ideal for the purpose. But ultimately, almost any structure might be converted for the purpose of holding POWs. The Union converted forts along the coastline to prisons. Basic training camps were ringed with fences to house the ever-increasing stream of prisoners. And sometimes, as at Belle Isle outside Richmond, men lived in tents on the open ground. In later years, as supplies grew thin, there were no tents to give the prisoners and the men faced the elements unprotected. In the winter, they dug holes in the ground to sleep in.

It wasn't just Union prisoners of war held in Richmond jails. At Castle Godwin, referred to as the "Negro jail" in Lumpkin's Alley (as Wall Street had begun to be called, named for Lumpkin's jail), Richmond residents suspected of disloyalty were imprisoned. The roundups of suspected Unionists under martial law began with the imprisonment of 30 prisoners initially, but within five months the facility held 250.[2] It was here that the Van Lew family friend John Minor Botts was taken.[3]

The practice on the battlefield was to march newly captured prisoners to the back of the lines and strip them of all personal items. "They took possession of overcoats, blankets, and the contents of our pockets. They also took what under the circumstances was the most serious loss for men who had a long march before them, our shoes," wrote George Putnam of the 176th New York State Volunteers. Putnam was held at Libby.

By the time they reached the prison gates, most prisoners said they had been robbed four or five times. It was impossible to hold on to cash, though they tried. Men hid their money where they could, in socks and hats. One man rolled it between tobacco leaves and chewed it, dropping it into his hand as he was searched.

Arrivals of new prisoners were often scheduled for daylight hours so that city residents would come out to meet them. Richmond's train lines dispersed Union soldiers into the most heavily trafficked area of the city. As they began their walk to prison, they passed through streets lined with women, children, and the elderly, who would taunt and throw things at them. As the war ground on, prisoners reported seeing displays in store windows of effects taken from prisoners. The idea was to intimidate and subdue new arrivals.

Arrival at the prison was no less trying. As new entrants arrived, existing prisoners would cry, "Fresh fish!" Depending on the state of the prison at the time, the new inmates would either be greeted by POWs looking for people they knew and news of the field, or they would be robbed yet again.

Once inside, the prisoners had little to do but spend the day standing in line. Queuing up for roll call, rations, and water consumed much of the day. Monotony, depression, and anxiety consumed those who were held. Raised in a culture that prized family relationships, some succumbed to what was called "nostalgia," or homesickness. But some prisoners were able to find ways of overcoming the brutalizing conditions. Soldiers from the same towns or states would band together, forming a replacement family to sustain each other.

In those early days, Libby prisoners set up debate circles and language clubs and exchanged books distributed by Chaplain Charles McCabe, who sang to the prisoners in a deep baritone. Copies of *David Copperfield*, *Bleak House*, and *Arthur O'Leary: His Wanderings and Ponderings in Many Lands* circulated the prison. Officers with special knowledge held lectures on topics as diverse as military tactics and hypnotism. Inmates even organized a complaint committee to air grievances and discipline their own officers.[4]

Elizabeth's ring worked to aid Union prisoners throughout the city, but as the war dragged on, she focused on Libby Prison. It was the toughest nut to crack, and the one full of the most strategically important prisoners. Libby was a prison for officers, and inmates there got better treatment than foot soldiers held elsewhere. Instead of one meal a day, Libby prisoners got three, at least at the beginning of the war. Stays were short at that time, the result of a robust prisoner exchange program. Union prisoners would be swapped for Rebel ones. Inmates cycled in and out in weeks or months.

But when the prison exchange program slowed and larger conflicts yielded growing numbers of prisoners, crowding increased and food became scarce. The 6-by-2-foot space originally assigned to each prisoner shrank. Inmates were forced to sleep on the floor spoon fashion, their bodies squeezed together like sardines in a can. Men ate their meals immediately, so their food wasn't stolen from their lips. Over the war, some 125,000 prisoners would cross Libby's threshold.

Seen from the Rebels' point of view, Libby's isolated location was ideal. Situated in a warehouse district next to the canal away from the hustle and bustle of the main shopping district, Libby prisoners could be closely watched.

Along Cary Street, the building was three stories high, but facing the canal, it was four stories. Thick plaster walls divided the interior floors into three large rooms. Low ceilings with exposed beams made the place feel claustrophobic. Four small windows on the outer wall of each room were barred and provided little light. Inmates were told to stay away from the windows, and a three-foot empty zone was strictly enforced by guards who were authorized to shoot those who broke the rules. Prisoners occupied the two top floors. A kitchen, hospital, and offices were located on the first floor. The basement was a hellhole for holding prisoners who were badly behaved; it was later a repository for the dead. When the building flooded, as it sometimes did, bodies floated into the street.

The prison was run by a motley crew. Though Elizabeth's protector, Winder, oversaw the entire Richmond prison complex, individual jails had their own overseers. While Libby was run by Thomas Turner, the most hated of the Libby overseers was his cousin, Richard R. Turner, known as Dick Turner. Young—just twenty-three—he was a large man and a former plantation overseer. He lost his West Point appointment when he was convicted of forgery. Prisoners cringed at his brutality. He didn't hesitate to use physical punishment to keep inmates in line.

Despite the bleak situation, inmates could take courage in the fact that if they could manage to escape, there was an active and powerful ring of Unionists led by Elizabeth that could help them flee to Union lines. Her ring and their work were well known and served as a beacon to inmates, firing their courage and willingness to take risks.

In July 1863, two days before the Union army would crush the rebels in the bloodiest battle ever fought on American soil then or now, Gettysburg, inmates at Libby made an unusual decision. They would celebrate the Fourth of July, a Union holiday marking the adoption of the Declaration of Independence and the separation of the colonies from Great Britain.

Leading the celebration was Union colonel Abel Streight. A mammoth man for the time, over six feet tall and 200 pounds, Streight had been a successful businessman before the war, the owner of a publishing company and a lumberyard in what was then the frontier city of Indianapolis. He led an unusual and ill-fated raid on Southern cities, his cavalrymen riding mules. After he was taken prisoner near Gaylesville, Alabama, he became known for sending a series of highly critical letters to Union and Confederate leadership about the plight of prisoners, especially himself.

Standing below a homemade Stars and Stripes, Streight delivered a long speech, delighting prisoners and angering their captors. A Confederate sergeant ordered the flag removed, and when the prisoners refused, the officer clambered into the prison rafters and took it down himself. Undeterred, prisoners sang "The Star-Spangled Banner" and "Yankee Doodle." Rebel guards fumed.

Two days later, as the news of the Union victory at Gettysburg spread through Libby, the prisoners spontaneously gathered and sang a new song whose lyrics had just been composed by Julia Ward Howe, "Battle Hymn of the Republic." The song's slow cadence matched the gravitas of the moment. "Mine eyes have seen the glory of the coming of the Lord," the men sang, their voices echoing from the rafters. Gettysburg marked a true turning point in the war, as it meant that the Confederate invasion of the North was ended, and its soldiers would return to defend Richmond and Virginia. The tune became Libby's theme song and a signature song for Union forces. Chaplain McCabe taught the inmates the words. When he was released later that year in a prisoner exchange, he sang it in front of the House of Representatives. President Lincoln was on hand. Listeners were stirred by McCabe's performance and sang the chorus with him.

The desire for liberty seemed to infect all the inmates at Libby Prison. But in late 1863 no man was more dedicated to that cause than Colonel Thomas Ellwood Rose, a leader of the 77th Pennsylvania Infantry. Before the war, the stout red-haired Pennsylvanian was a teacher and a school administrator. Poor preparation, one would think, for battle. But as a soldier and a leader, Rose was well regarded. He survived the unprecedented carnage of the Battle of Shiloh and took over leadership of two companies of Pennsylvania men at Stones River, Tennessee, when its commander was mortally wounded. Rose led his men again at the Battle of Chickamauga. This battle, fought September 18 to 20 along a northern Georgia creek, was one of the war's bloodiest. *Chickamauga*, a Cherokee word, means "river of death" in English. The battle proved the name apt. There were 35,000 casualties, including 16,170 Union soldiers and 18,454 Rebels. Even so, the Confederates won, turning a tide against the Union momentum gained from their massive victories at Gettysburg and Vicksburg. Rose was among the Union soldiers taken prisoner there.[5]

The move from battlefield to prison must have been shocking to the system. Rose immediately attempted to escape, leaping from a train that was transporting the POWs to Richmond. In the fall, Rose broke his foot. He gained a single day of freedom but was recaptured. In Richmond, Rose endured the usual gauntlet of taunts from Richmond citizens.

Taken to Libby, Rose quickly began surveying the prison for a way out. He spotted workmen climbing into a sewer on Canal Street behind the prison. Surmising that the sewer emptied into the Kanawha Canal along the James River, he began to formulate a plan of escape. On a nocturnal exploration of the prison, he made his way to the cellar, a nasty place overrun with rats and filth. The room had been set up as a kitchen and the place stank of rancid grease and rotten food. The darkness there was impenetrable. Suddenly Rose bumped into someone.

Major A. G. Hamilton, a member of the 12th Kentucky Cavalry, was also searching for a way out of the prison. He was small, underweight, with a dark shock of hair. He'd been at Libby since his capture at Jonesboro, Tennessee, in September. Before the war he had been a homebuilder. In later years, he told his story at length, and much of what we know today about the escape is from the pen of Hamilton or from the reporters who interviewed him.

Throughout the next four and a half months, Rose and Hamilton plotted the perfect escape. Rose believed the safest and best option, the one least likely to be detected, was tunneling from Libby's foul basement to the sewer and then following the sewer out to Canal Street. Again and again, they tried.

A first attempt was shut down when Confederates closed off the basement kitchen and sealed a stairway. Rose and Hamilton decided to try again, still believing the cellar was the best route. With the east cellar closed off, they settled on using the cellar room adjacent. Tying a rope to a supporting post and dropping the line through a hole in the kitchen floor, the two could shimmy to the ground floor and potentially out to freedom. Several fellow prisoners were brought into the scheme to fight off any guards that got wind of the attempted escape. Their optimism was fueled by the discovery of an unobstructed doorway onto Canal Street. Perhaps they could just walk out under cover of darkness!

After a week of watching guards' patrol routines covering the facade on the canal side, Rose and Hamilton decided they were ready. But their flight was quickly ended by guards swarming into the prison who had gotten word of the escape attempt. Hamilton and the men shimmied up the rope and into the first-floor kitchen, sneaking to their rooms. Rose was the last up. The guards were too close for him to run farther. So he quickly settled himself at the kitchen table, shoving a pipe in his mouth as the guards ran by, oblivious to his actions. As it turned out, Rose was a fair actor in addition to being the prison's best escape artist.

Far from defeated, the two decided to try again, returning to the original plan, a tunnel dug by hand. The question was where to start it? They needed a new way into the east cellar and decided to create their own opening, a passage behind the kitchen fireplace on the first floor. It took eleven days to make the excavation through brick and masonry. Using his expertise as a builder, Hamilton carved an S-shaped tunnel running down through the kitchen's fire wall to the east cellar, breaking through a brick wall to gain access. His tools were nothing but a pocket-knife and a chisel.

The passage was dangerous, and Rose nearly suffocated to death the first time he tried to move through it. They expanded the portal and set about trying to decide how best to tunnel out of Libby, returning to the plan to access Canal Street via the sewer, twenty feet away. Deciding that the work would require more manpower, they recruited their closest friends to join them. But their first serious tunneling operation failed when Rose hit water, a great torrent of it, and nearly drowned. Apparently, they had tunneled too close to the canal. Failure, again. The tunnel had to be abandoned.

In short order, they restarted their efforts. The addition of fellow prisoners meant they had additional new tools: a hatchet and an auger. The work proceeded quickly, and then, again, tragedy. The second tunnel caved in. Worse yet, it was visible to guards from the yard. Several of them gathered around the hole, scratching their heads. But the tunnelers were safe because the guards believed it was burrowing rodents, not burrowing prisoners, that had created the hole. At last, the nasty critters proved useful.

In January of 1864, Rose and Hamilton started a third tunnel, convincing the men they had been working with to return to the project. They worked in shifts to speed up the progress of the tunnel. When they reached the sewer, they realized it was lined with dense oak that would be difficult, if not impossible, for their poor tools to penetrate. Penknives broke and candles snuffed themselves due to a lack of oxygen. When the wall was finally breached, a stinky sewage began pouring in. The odor was so bad some men fainted. Discouraged, several of the men quit. Tunnel three was officially abandoned.

In the meantime, Northern newspapers were calling insistently for the rescue of Union soldiers held in Southern prisons. "They must not be permitted to perish," said the *New York Herald.* Escapees from prisons throughout the South had described the brutal conditions in detail, and newspapers and magazines carried detailed descriptions of Belle Isle's filth and the brutality at Andersonville in southern Georgia. The Senate weighed in with an ambitious yet fanciful plan calling for a force of a million citizen volunteers from all over the North to descend on the prisons and free their inmates. The pressure on Lincoln and his wartime administration ratcheted higher each day.

Colonel Streight, meanwhile, was languishing next to the east cellar, where the Confederates put him in special confinement. His legs were in irons and his rations were limited to bread and water. But the colonel was eager to prove he wasn't beaten. In November 1863, he organized the men to execute a "Great Escape Plot," a wildly ambitious idea for liberating Union POWs and seizing Richmond itself. Rose was one of four "brigade commanders" chosen to start the massive uprising. The plan was that 13,000 prisoners, all the Union men held in prisons across Richmond, would overwhelm their captors at the same time and overtake all of Richmond. Its industrial power base, Tredegar, was to be seized and Jefferson Davis and his cabinet captured. The Libby inmates were enthralled by the idea—so excited, in fact, that prison guards overheard them talking about it. Prison administrators doubled the guard. Confederate artillery aimed cannon muzzles at the prison walls. The Great Escape Plot was abandoned.

But the idea of such a raid by prisoners kept Confederate leaders up late at night. It wasn't just that a unified showing of effort by prisoners could wreak havoc on the city, but that their sheer numbers were taxing Richmond's resources. Prisoner rations were cut to subsistence levels, and even the prison's guards were hungry. In truth, all of Richmond was starving. Children came to the prison's windows begging for food from the inmates.

Despite the problems and stumbling blocks, Rose and Hamilton kept going, at least in part because of what was waiting for them on the outside. Elizabeth's ring was furiously organizing to assist their flight and keep them safe if they could just clear the prison walls. With the help of ring member Abby Green, Elizabeth located a captured Black Union army teamster named Robert Ford, who was willing to work with them. Ford was working as stableman for the notorious Dick Turner. The two women fed him all manner of intelligence valuable for a breakout. They told him the number of Libby guards they might encounter, the arms stockpiles outside the prison they could raid, and the strength of Richmond fortifications they would encounter on their escape north. Ford gave the information to the plotters. In return, Ford fed Elizabeth information he gleaned from inside the prison's walls. In addition to providing information, Elizabeth also alerted ring members willing to share their homes that an escape was imminent and told them to prepare to house escapees on the run.[6]

After the collapse of the Great Escape Plot, Rose and Hamilton went back to work with a new idea for a fourth version of the tunnel. Avoiding increasingly suspicious prison guards, who were poking their noses in the prison's many dark corners, including the east cellar, Rose and Hamilton started again in their usual configuration. Rose dug and Hamilton fanned as much breathable oxygen in Rose's direction as possible. This time they decided to avoid the sewer and aim for a longer tunnel that would end at a tall fence and tobacco shed. The downside was that they had to traverse the entire prison yard, a distance of fifty yards just below the feet of the prison guards. The good news was that they would be burrowing their way above the water table. With any luck, their tunnel would not flood or cave in or fill with sewage.

Other men who had joined in earlier efforts were convinced to help dig. At its narrowest, the tunnel itself was just sixteen inches wide. Men moved in and out, gulping air on the outside and dumping fresh dirt into pans and cups. Their efforts seemed to be working: they were advancing about five feet each night. One night, one of the diggers became convinced he made it across the entire yard and started digging for the surface, gulping in the cool nighttime air. Unfortunately, he was still on the wrong side of the fence and nearly gave away the plot to Confederate guards.

Hours later, Rose returned, assuming that the guards would not inspect the area on the Sabbath. Sunday, even for guards, was a day of rest. He was correct, and sensing that his time to finish the tunnel was limited, he worked nonstop for hours, worried the whole effort could be discovered at any time. By the time he withdrew, it was night again and he was exhausted. During these difficult moments, Rose could sustain himself with the knowledge that Richmond Unionists would come to his aid once he cleared the prison walls. Green had sent the men directions to safe houses they could hide in until arrangements could be made to help them get out of the city. Elizabeth's money, perhaps some of the cash Butler had given her circle, was used to pay for the communications lines between Rose and his circle and the spy ring. If he could just clear the short distance between his cell and the prison wall, he could find safety.

The next day, Rose decided, would be the end of it, one way or another. He dug like a demon, his body trembling and covered with sweat. And just as his willpower was about to give out, he encountered a fence post. He knew he was close. Energized, he began to dig higher, closer to the surface. The ground above him gave way. Dirt spilled into his nose and eyes.

With effort, he gained his feet and looked around. His tunnel had ended inside the tobacco shed as planned. He had made it. Tunnel four was a success. It was still dark, barely one a.m. Making sure he was clear of the sentry, he tried the gate, unlatching it with his dirt-encrusted fingers and stepping into Canal Street. Freedom. Rose could have run right then and secured his own freedom, but he did not.

Rose was disciplined. He had a plan for freeing a number of Libby prisoners, not just himself. And he returned the way he had come, sharing the news of his success with his gang of fellow diggers. They were ecstatic.

The following day, Tuesday, February 9, 1864, was the designated date for the escape. But the men had decided to wait for the cover of darkness. The party of fifteen tunnelers would go first, including Rose and Hamilton. The chosen dropped through the kitchen portal one by one and shimmied through the narrow portal. The entire process took fifteen minutes for each escapee.

Rose and Hamilton had planned for an orderly exit for the men who had been involved in excavating the tunnel. A password was given out to the lucky few who would escape. The idea was that the portal would be closed and the fireplace sealed off so that the next night more prisoners could escape.

The one thing Rose had not anticipated was that other prisoners who had not been part of the planning would see prisoners running down Canal Street to freedom. Soon the prison was full of the shouts of wild excitement. Men began pouring out of the upstairs rooms and to the kitchen, jumping down the chute. One of them was Colonel Streight, still robustly built despite his time in Libby. When he became stuck at the tunnel's narrowest point, just sixteen inches in diameter, he reversed course, came out the other side, and took off his clothes to reduce his bulk. Tying his clothes to his feet, he wriggled through the tunnel nearly naked. All the while, Rebel sentries outside passed by oblivious to the drama playing out below their feet.

In all, 109 men would escape Libby that night. Most walked down

Cary Street, a major commercial street running right through one of the busiest commercial districts in the city, Shockoe Bottom. Stores were still open and people congregated on the sidewalks. Rebel soldiers were a part of the crowd. The escapees wandered, dazed, silently praying they could make it to a more rural area before being spotted.

Elizabeth and her ring, though they didn't plan the breakout, could be fairly credited with creating the conditions that allowed it to happen. They developed safe houses for escapees and helped escaped prisoners make their way to the safety of Union lines. The promise of that assistance, well known to inmates, emboldened men like Rose. For that reason, some stopped at Elizabeth's house the night of the breakout looking for shelter. Ironically, Elizabeth's Church Hill home was not among those who took some of the prisoners in. Though there was a knock at the Van Lew door that night, Elizabeth was not home. Her favorite servant, Mary, likely turned away the visitors, anxious that they might be Rebels in disguise. The master spy was away, helping her brother to escape from Richmond. He was dodging the Rebel draft and Elizabeth was trying to help him. The Libby breakout would make it impossible for John to run. Rebel soldiers would be questioning everyone they found. Later, Elizabeth said that while she knew of the efforts by inmates to dig their way out of Libby, they didn't know exactly what night the men might break out. In this case, her family was her priority.

Back at Libby the next morning, Erasmus Ross went through roll call twice to confirm the mass of men missing. Confederate command sprang into action trying to understand how so many men were able to disappear in such a short period of time. Roads and bridges surrounding Richmond were searched for the missing officers. Guards who had failed to spot the escape were arrested, assuming that they were in on the plot. The news hit the afternoon papers and the story became a sensation, the escape described as "extraordinary." That week people began congregating around the prison, straining to see evidence of the tunnel. "The Great Yankee Wonder" became an exhibition and people came to take tours of the facility.

Streight sought shelter in one of the underground's safe houses for a week, waiting for the Rebel forces to assume he was long gone. While there, he asked to meet the legendary spy that made his escape possible. Elizabeth went to the safe house to meet him. In her diary, she described the meeting with Streight and three other men who'd escaped with him. She described herself as "so overcome for terror for them that I quite lost my voice." She relished meeting them, though, particularly when one placed in her hand a chisel used to dig the tunnel through which they escaped. But she regretted her conversation with Streight. When he asked her what she believed had caused the war, she responded with the answer her hero John Minor Botts always gave, "Democracy," meaning the Democratic party's rashness. She fretted over the answer and later sent Streight a letter describing what she truly believed to be the cause: slavery.

Meanwhile, her ring secured Streight's safety by getting word to the press that he had already made it to Washington. The search for the colonel was ended. But other men were rounded up. Of the 109 who escaped through the tunnel, fifty-nine reached safety, two drowned and forty-eight were captured. One of those was Rose. He had hidden for days, traveling at night and sleeping hidden during the day. His flight was arduous. He fell in the Chickahominy River and the cold temperatures froze his clothing. Setting a fire to warm himself, he immediately fell asleep and awoke to find the fire had burnt his boots. He crossed paths with Confederate soldiers multiple times, managing to talk himself out of trouble twice, but he was finally caught by Rebels wearing Yankee uniforms. He was marched back to Libby and thrown into the basement dungeon.

For Elizabeth, there was good news from the Libby breakout. She appealed to Winder to be allowed to see Belle Isle prison. The tightly controlled visit took place on February 27, 1864. A traumatized Elizabeth wrote this in her diary: "It surpassed in wretchedness and squalid filth my most vivid imagination. The long lines of forsaken, despairing, hopeless-looking beings, who, within this hollow square, looked upon us, gaunt hunger staring from their sunken eyes." Her words were no exaggeration. To a twentieth-century eye, the images of some of the survivors of Belle Isle—photographs taken at an Annapolis, Virginia, hospital after the war—are similar to photos taken in Nazi concentration camps after World War II.

The miserable condition of Belle Isle and the success of Libby's breakout may well have encouraged Elizabeth to set in motion a more ambitious plan to free Richmond's Union prisoners. A grander scheme implemented with the assistance of Union forces could end the Confederacy's mistreatment of Federal troops and officers. But a failure would put all her efforts at risk.

❧ ❦

THE UNDERTAKING IS A DESPERATE ONE

As a Southern belle, Elizabeth had attended her share of balls. But she had never seen anything like the scene in front of her on that cold February afternoon in 1864. The soldiers of the Army of the Potomac had built a makeshift ballroom smack in the middle of a muddy battlefield in Virginia's Piedmont region. Soldiers had scoured the area for wood, ripping apart abandoned buildings and felling trees, to build their "palace of pleasure," as they called it. The whole place smelled of pine. All this work, and it was substantial, intended for a single night of merriment, a ball to celebrate Washington's Birthday.

Had she poked about, taking care to avoid the worst of the mud because of her handmade boots, Elizabeth would have found an expansive and charming interior. The ballroom was 90 feet by 60 feet. Its white tents were spotless, its kettles gleamed. Regimental flags and evergreen boughs draped its walls and ceiling. Rifles and bayonets served as decoration. At one end of the hall, a display of soldier life was mounted on an elevated platform.[1]

The whole scene may well have brought tears to the eyes of Elizabeth, who normally saw Union soldiers under the duress of incarceration, hungry and depressed. Here they were merrily running about, sawing and hammering, the anxiety and boredom of daily camp life temporarily forgotten.

The gala was the event of the social season. All of Washington's best-known and well-connected were invited for four days of festivities. Most made the sixty-mile trip by train wearing coats and gloves to protect from the February chill. Vice President Hannibal Hamlin, a Supreme Court justice, and a number of senators and representatives attended. General George Meade, baggy-eyed and taciturn, was on hand to officiate. The blond-haired Ulric Dahlgren dashed about on a black stallion, his crutch lashed to his saddle. But most exciting, at least to the soldiers, was the arrival of three hundred young female socialites, their laughter and rustling dresses infusing the scene with excitement. Their wary-eyed mothers followed.

Neither Elizabeth, her mother, Eliza, nor F.W.E. Lohmann or two other members of Elizabeth's spy ring were on the official invitation list. They had traveled by train. All, with the exception of Elizabeth and her mother, sat far away from each other. Secrecy was important. Were the Rebels to learn of their attendance at this celebration of the Union, they would never have been able to go home again. Elizabeth and her band of Union spies and sympathizers were here for one thing and one thing only, to help plan a raid on Richmond.[2]

OVER MEALS OF HARDTACK AND SALT PORK AROUND THE CAMPFIRE, news of the Libby Prison escape had spread rapidly among Union soldiers. Little more than half the escapees managed to make their way back to Union lines to tell the tale firsthand. But mostly, the story traveled by word of mouth among soldiers who had *not* been there. The men reveled in the thrilling tale of escape but were haunted by details of the inhumane and brutal conditions at Libby, where hunger, pneumonia, diarrhea, and dysentery were common. The idea of being held in such a place sapped soldiers' resolve like pine straw.

Northern newspapers pumped up the outrage among their readers.

The *New York Times* headlines described "disease, starvation and death . . . shocking pictures of destitution and abject wretchedness." [3]

And in the White House itself, where strangers roamed the halls at all hours eager to gain Lincoln's ear, some approached the harried president with pleas for help. Please, they said, look after my son, my husband. Free these men. Other Union leaders, not to mention Elizabeth, realized that the Libby Prison escape couldn't be allowed to halt the momentum toward the fall of Richmond. The rest of the prison had to be liberated.

Already, one plan to free the prisoners had failed. Encouraged by Elizabeth's insistent advocating for the captives and set in motion by General Benjamin Butler, in early February a force of 6,000 Union cavalry had been launched toward Richmond but had been forced to turn back a tantalizing twelve miles from the Confederate capital. Their raid was abandoned after word of it leaked to Confederate forces, giving the rebels time to muster an overwhelming reception.

So in the days after the Libby breakout a second plan was hatched to free Union prisoners in Richmond. The author of that plan was not Lincoln's high command but a young, self-assured, and brash cavalry officer, Hugh Judson Kilpatrick. Slight and short, like most cavalrymen, the New Jerseyite sported sandy-colored wispy sideburns stretching from the top of his ear to his jaw.

His primary trait, however, was his ambition. As a cadet at West Point when war broke out, Kilpatrick petitioned Lincoln to move up their graduation so he could enter the fight immediately. The president did just that. The young captain quickly established himself by becoming the first Union officer wounded in the Civil War, in the war's first engagement, the 1861 Battle of Big Bethel. When soldiers around him flagged, he spurred them on. Kilpatrick's superiors were impressed by his leadership. His star rising fast, he was upped from lieutenant colonel to colonel to brigadier general in two short years. He was just twenty-eight years old.

Although Kilpatrick had convinced his superiors of his prowess, he had a reputation for recklessness among his men, who came to call him "Kill-cavalry" behind his back. Colonel James Kidd of the 6th Michigan Cavalry wrote this about Kilpatrick: "He was brave to the point of rashness, capricious, ambitious, reckless in rushing into scrapes, and generally full of expedients in getting out, though, at times, he seemed to lose his head entirely."[4]

That rashness on the battlefield led him to embellish reports to his bosses, placing them in the best light possible. Colonel Charles S. Wainwright questioned the officer's veracity. Recalling Kilpatrick's account of the Battle of Falling Waters, part of the Gettysburg Campaign, he wrote this: "A good deal of talk is made about a fight on Tuesday last at Falling Waters, in which General Kilpatrick claims to have charged a large body of rebel infantry in breastwork and to have captured two cannon, three battle flags and some 1,500 prisoners. It sounds like a big thing for the cavalry, but the fact that Kilpatrick makes the report leads to some doubt of its accuracy."[5]

Despite Kilpatrick's shortcomings, he had one quality that the Union desperately needed: boldness. Despite the Union victory at Gettysburg, Lincoln viewed his top military leadership as somewhat timid, the latest unsuccessful raid on Richmond just one example. The president was ready for a strong hand, and Kilpatrick had been training for that role for a lifetime.

Traveling to Washington just three days after the Libby Prison breakout, Kilpatrick's appointment was not with his bosses, the cavalry commander Alfred Pleasanton or even General George Meade, the commander of the Army of the Potomac. Instead, Kilpatrick had been called by the president himself to discuss a plan to free the prisoners, a face-to-face that the young officer had helped set up by tapping his extensive Washington contacts.[6] He must have been thrilled.

In Washington, Kilpatrick encountered a city that had none of the grandeur of European capitals. The nation was still just eighty-four years from its founding, and the capital city was still not much more than a swampy town. The Capitol was unfinished, as were many other government buildings. Henry Adams, the great-grandson of U.S. President John Adams, described it as "an idea set in the wilderness."[7]

So it was, on February 12, 1864, Kilpatrick, a brigadier general with no experience setting wartime strategy, sat down with the Union president for a frank conversation about the plight of Union POWs. Though no record exists of the exchange, the two quickly found common ground. Kilpatrick wanted to lead an offensive cavalry raid on the capital of the Confederacy to free Union soldiers held in the city's prisons, Libby and Belle Isle. Lincoln was facing enormous pressure to do just that.

But Lincoln also had another agenda. It was critical to the president to communicate to Confederate soldiers his design for light treatment were they to surrender. The Union had gained momentum at Gettysburg seven months prior, though at considerable cost, and the president didn't want to lose it. He knew Rebel soldiers were hungry for an end to the war and wanted to circulate an amnesty proclamation among them, hoping they would drop their arms once they saw his generous terms. Only the highest officials would be barred from complete amnesty, and those taking advantage of the offer would only have to swear loyalty to the North.

For the president, there was little time to take advantage of his momentum, for another election was looming. A war weariness had settled in on both sides. Fresh voices were calling for a negotiated settlement of the conflict. Were Lincoln not to finish the war in short order, those voices could gain ascendancy in the next election, oust Lincoln, and change the course of American history by either opening the West to slavery or allowing the Confederacy to be separately governed. The clock was ticking. Action was required.

At the meeting, Lincoln and Kilpatrick discussed both the immediate goal of freeing the prisoners from Libby and Belle Isle prisons and Lincoln's message for Rebel soldiers. He urged Kilpatrick to coordinate with the War Department directly, bypassing his immediate bosses. The young general happily agreed and, on the next day, briefed Secretary of War Stanton, Lincoln's chief war strategist, on the broad outlines of his plan of attack. Stanton sent him back to camp to draft a detailed plan.

There was just one very large problem: The raid was scheduled to take place immediately, and that meant moving before the temperatures warmed. Fighting between the two armies usually took place in the spring, summer, and fall to avoid the worst of winter storms. Kilpatrick and his forces would have to pray for decent weather.

The shape of Kilpatrick's plan was classic military strategy—a pincer movement in which the Union force would split, arriving at the Confederate capital's doorstep from two different directions. One was a feint, the other a surprise blow from an unexpected direction. It would start twenty-one miles northwest of Richmond at the Rapidan River, the site of severe fighting throughout the war. A force of 4,000 cavalry would sneak past General Lee's army and then split up. A smaller force of just 500 would swing west and south, where the city was largely unguarded, to open prison doors and set free Union soldiers and officers held prisoner. Kilpatrick would strike a more direct route south to Richmond. Both would be charged with tearing up critical railroad and communications lines along the way.

The plan was clever. But it was about to change. That's because Ulric Dahlgren, perhaps the youngest colonel in the Union army, had gotten wind of the raid and was eager to join in. For Kilpatrick, this was good news. Dahlgren was the ultimate connected Washington player: his father John A. Dahlgren, was a close friend of President Lincoln's. In fact, young Dahlgren had met with Lincoln a week before Kilpatrick, on February 1, easily chatting with the president as he was shaved. Including Dahlgren would enhance Kilpatrick's daring raid, raising its stature and the stakes for success.

Dahlgren's heroic reputation would also counterbalance Kilpatrick's poor one, though he had never commanded a force as large as the one he would lead in the Richmond raid. Soldiers who fought with him regarded him as a fair fighter, kind to the soldiers who labored under him. His manners, as one soldier later described him, were "soft as a cat's." But this raid would be his first foray onto the battlefield since his injury at Gettysburg; and he would be fighting with a wooden right leg. No matter,

Dahlgren no doubt reasoned, he had been training for weeks, regaining strength, even relearning how to ride a horse.

Given the two men's experience and reputation, it would be logical to expect that the brash Kilpatrick, a veteran of the battlefield, would do everything he could to achieve his objectives. The charming but inexperienced Dahlgren might falter. But in the strange way history has of upending expectations, it would be Kilpatrick who would lose his nerve.

Days before joining up with Kilpatrick's forces, Dahlgren penned a letter for his father—to be opened only if the raid failed and he never returned. He was eager both to please his father and to make a name for himself. He wrote:

> there is to be a grand raid to be made, and I am to have a very important command. If successful, it will be the grandest thing on record; and if it fails, many of us will *"go up."* I may be captured, or I may be *"tumbled over,"* but it is an undertaking that if I were not in, I should be ashamed to show my face again. With such an important command, I am afraid to mention it, for fear the letter might fall into the wrong hands before reaching you. I find that I can stand the service perfectly well without my leg. I think we will be successful, although a desperate undertaking . . . If we do not return, there is no better place to *"give up the ghost."*[8]

The raid relied on the speed and flexibility of horses. Astride horses, cavalrymen not only engaged directly with the enemy slashing at them with sabers and leveling them with carbines, but also protected long and straggling lines of their own infantry marching long distances. They were well disposed to spy on enemy lines and transport information.

On the battlefield, cavalry could leverage the weakness of conventional battle-line formations, flanking enemy lines and striking where they were most vulnerable. Cavalry could also cut the lines critical to running a war efficiently, telegraph lines and railroad lines, which transported critical information, food, ammunition, and soldiers. Only horses could cross the bramble-filled terrain and climb the steep hills of the rural Virginia countryside at speed. No mechanized vehicle yet existed; wagons were hopeless for most of these tasks. And while the Civil War's toll on human life is much cited, as many as three million horses are estimated to have died in the conflict.

General William Tecumseh Sherman wrote in 1863 that the Confederate cavalry was the best in the world, saying they were "splendid riders, first rate shots, and utterly reckless," adding ominously they were also "the most dangerous men this world has ever turned loose on the world" because their fortunes were destroyed by war. In other words, they had nothing left to lose.[9]

Over time, however, experience turned out to be an effective teacher for Union cavalry, and by 1864, Northern cavalrymen were not only competing but winning. The nation's most celebrated cavalry officer, George Armstrong Custer, made his name in the Civil War as a young officer, best known for his leadership in the Shenandoah campaign. The Battle of Little Big Horn, where Custer made his famous last stand in the Great Sioux War, losing to the combined forces of three native American tribes, the Lakota Sioux, the Northern Cheyenne, and the Arapaho, was still eleven years in his future. But at this point in American history, the blond mustachioed Custer was about to play a critical role in Kilpatrick's raid, distracting the enemy and shutting communications lines. He was a tender twenty-six at the time.

On the eve of what would become the war's most daring and largest cavalry raid, it's shocking to understand its details were better known in fashionable Washington circles and among journalists than by the soldiers that would fight it. At the Willard Hotel, which author Nathaniel Hawthorne described during the war as "more justly called the nerve center of Washington and the Union than either the Capitol, the White House, or the State Department," the raid was the talk of the well-heeled guests. Maps of the assault's planned routes circulated in newsrooms.

And in Richmond and at the Army of Northern Virginia's headquarters, where Confederate leaders had been bracing for an attack on the capital city for months, suspicions flew.

And thanks to the gathering for the wilderness ball, Elizabeth actually joined the intrigues of Washington society. According to Lohmann family lore, Elizabeth and her band met multiple times directly with Kilpatrick, who would lead the raid. They likely met in Stevensburg, at the general's headquarters set in a tree-bordered mansion. There they reviewed maps and planned out just where members of the spy ring would meet the raiders and guide them to Libby Prison and the White House of the Confederacy.[10]

The mansion was crowded with visitors. The most powerful of guests came to see Kilpatrick, hoping to get the latest information on the raid, which had long since ceased being a secret. In fact, it was the talk of the weekend. The young general was so excited at the prospect of leading the raid and possibly ending the war that he shared nearly all the details in a speech to the weekend's visitors. Animated by high spirits or perhaps whiskey, Kilpatrick rode his horse through the main hall of the house, leaving a trail of hoofmarks for future generations.

That Saturday night, the party began in earnest. Chinese lanterns and hundreds of candles transformed the ballroom, filling it with a warm glow. An elaborate feast was served. Elizabeth would likely have been stunned by the display, given that only a few miles south many in Richmond were starving. Officers, soldiers, and ladies crowded the crudely finished wooden dance floor, whirling, laughing, and flirting. A military band provided music. Entanglements were made and forgotten. A slight young woman with long blond curly hair, Miss Sally Marsten caught the eye of many young men eager for a dance. She was engaging and merry and asked many naive questions, the soldiers' tongues loosed by liquor.

But the young woman was really a man, Confederate spy Frank Stringfellow. A member of the Hampton Scouts, a Rebel cavalry unit known for their reconnaissance abilities, Stringfellow had managed to steal a pass intended for a woman to attend the party. He asked a circle of young women he knew to loan him a ball gown. They drilled him in etiquette and feminine behavior. He dressed carefully, with a pair of derringer pistols in the pockets of his pants, carefully rolled up under his dress. At the party, a major told him that Grant would soon take over the Army of the Potomac. The official announcement wouldn't go out for two weeks. Stringfellow was eventually pulled aside and taken for questioning that evening, but when he was, he pulled out his derringers and made his escape.[11]

The next day, a happy but tired General Meade presided over an elaborate review of his troops. The climax of the ceremony was a cavalry charge led by Kilpatrick and played right in front of the grandstand, where Meade and the ladies were seated. A bugler sounded the charge and the men rushed in, holding sabers high over their heads. The men stood in their stirrups, galloping past the audience, which erupted in shouts and applause.

Only a few days later, some in the audience would be left to wish that Kilpatrick's showing on the battlefield was as good as what they saw that day at the review.

Kilpatrick's idea for the raid was not new; after all, General Butler's expedition had failed only weeks before. But everyone expected another attempt on Richmond would surely allow Kilpatrick and his men to correct the mistakes made on the earlier attempt. General Meade's words to his wife via letter were hopeful, but practical. "The undertaking is a desperate one, but the anxiety and distress of the public and of the authorities at Washington is so great that it seems to demand great risks for the chances of success."[12]

With high expectations and well wishes all around, Kilpatrick and his team of 4,000 men from units across the Union, including Dahlgren, who was assigned to command 500 of them, began to assemble on February 28 at Stevensburg, Virginia, then a tiny town on a road leading to Richmond, only eighty miles away. The rural Virginia landscape that met these cavalrymen as they crossed into enemy territory was war-weary. They encountered few adult men. Fields were fallow or destroyed, churches ruined, buildings deserted.

Into this scene rode Custer and his 2nd Michigan Cavalry Brigade, known as the Wolverines, southwest toward Charlottesville. Their mission: destruction, and more important, confusion. They were to divert General Lee's attention from Kilpatrick and Dahlgren's forces, and along the way they were charged with destroying a railroad supply depot before returning to camp. To that end, Custer directed the soldiers to make as much noise as they could; the 1,500-member force began singing an Elizabethan folk song of love and loss, "The Girl I Left Behind," at the top of their lungs.

As Custer deflected, Dahlgren's forces moved south during the late afternoon to cross the Rapidan River at Ely's Ford, where shallow river water allowed easy passage for horses. His forces watched him closely, as many had never seen the young officer before. He tried to inspire confidence by looking men in the eye, appearing calm and confident, but it was likely he was anything but tranquil. The stakes were high for him, his men, and the entire Union effort. By the time the sun set, the temperature had turned cold, but the sky was clear. Starlight illuminated the backs of Dahlgren and his men as they crossed the Rapidan. With them was a band of Rebel soldiers who had been surprised and taken hostage along the way. It was the first of many rivers they would attempt to cross in the next forty-eight hours, some unsuccessfully. Already, the element of surprise, a critical advantage for raiders in enemy territory, was evaporating.

Crossing seventeen miles as quickly as their horses could go, some of the route from the river to Spotsylvania Court House made at a full gallop, the men crouched low into the backs of their horses. According to some accounts, Dahlgren and his band had already been spotted by the so-called Iron Scouts, an intelligence network of Rebel soldiers stationed behind enemy lines on a permanent basis to provide military intelligence to their generals.

Meanwhile, Kilpatrick's force of 3,500 men departed Stevensburg at eleven p.m., crossing the same river, the Rapidan, as Dahlgren had hours earlier. Both forces rode throughout the night. Kilpatrick's destination was also Spotsylvania Court House, and he arrived there well after Dahlgren had swept through, on his way to Frederick Hall's Station, crossing ever deeper into Confederate territory. The forces sped ahead, with Dahlgren in the lead as he prepared to sweep south to the James River and cross it to enter the capital city from the south. But even as the two made their way, hitting each mark as planned, storm clouds were gathering, reducing the light by which they traveled and threatening bad weather.

The next day, at Frederick's Hall Station, Dahlgren's men checked another item off their list of objectives, cutting the telegraph wire and tearing up the track of the Virginia Central Railroad. In one of those strange ironies of war, only moments before they arrived, none other than the commander of the Army of Northern Virginia, General Robert E. Lee, passed through aboard a train.

Meanwhile, Kilpatrick's troops moved on to another train depot on the Virginia Central line at Beaver Dam, setting the town afire and shutting down the telegraph operator, the men dancing afterward in the firelight, celebrating their own unchallenged success. But harder times were coming. Snow, sleet, and wind fell on the soldiers as they crossed south. At times, the men could barely see ahead of themselves, relying on the horses to follow the one in front of them. Icy snow stung their eyes. Beards caked with snow and cold hands could barely handle weapons, much less fire accurately. Rebel soldiers on leave, home guardsmen, and others began to harass their lines with sniper fire.

Farther south, Dahlgren's troops fared no better. He stopped his weary men for a brief rest, displaying an attitude that inspired them, saying, "We'll have some supper and two hours' sleep. Then you'll see how bright I am." One soldier wrote: "Who could complain of weariness when he looked at the colonel, still weak from his wound, riding along quietly, uncomplainingly, ever vigilantly watching every incidence of the march?"

Two days after the raiders had embarked, Richmond residents began to hear faraway cannon fire and rifle shot. They grew fearful and anxious, watching preparations in the streets for defense against a possible Union assault. Rumors flew. Were Union forces led by Kilpatrick 5,000 strong or 50,000? No one knew, but everyone worried. Families armed women with every remaining gun available. Men and boys ran to join the defense of their hometown. It seemed that the nightmare Richmond had long braced itself for, a Union strike, was about to become a reality.[13]

"Every reliable man was called out," recalled Elizabeth in the pages of her diary. She had returned to the city after the exciting trip to the battlefield ball. "There was an awful quiet in the streets, the heavy silence was impressive . . . At night we could hear the firing of the cannon from ten till eleven o'clock."[14] Crowds gathered outside the capitol building waiting for definitive word of Union advances; while churches threw open their door to welcome those who would pray for deliverance.

At dawn on March 1, after sleeping on the ground in icy rain, Dahlgren's men moved out. Stopping just twenty-one miles from Richmond, he sent about a quarter of his men, 100 of the 500 he started with, along the north side of the James. Their job was to render useless canal locks, boats, and mills, eliminating as much support for Rebel troops as possible. The detachment, led by Captain John Mitchell, was scheduled to rejoin Dahlgren's main troops in Richmond.

Reaching the James River in the late morning, his last obstacle to the Rebel capital, Dahlgren prepared to cross. His guide was a free Black man, Martin Robinson, a bricklayer who had lived nearby. Finding a safe place to cross was critical to the raiding party, and finding the right point required local knowledge. Well-regarded by Union forces in Washington, Robinson had distinguished himself by assisting Libby Prison escapees on their journey north. But for some reason—either Robinson got lost or perhaps he changed his mind about helping Dahlgren's forces—the guide couldn't find a place to cross. The river ran deep. There were no shallows permitting horses to traverse.

Dahlgren must have been furious at the turn of events. Everything depended on crossing the James. Failing to get across this major barrier would slow, if not stop altogether, the execution of Kilpatrick's plan. Failure would mean there would be no release of Union soldiers in Richmond. The turn of events was too much for Dahlgren. He ordered Robinson hanged on the spot.

Deciding what to do next was critical. Captain John Mitchell and his small force managed to find Dahlgren, and the two conferred over a campfire. Unable to admit defeat, Dahlgren intended to continue and find a way into Richmond. There was no dissuading him from attempting to complete his orders. Later that afternoon he ordered the men to mount and resume their march to the capital city.

Meanwhile, Kilpatrick was closing in on the city from the opposite direction, the north, his men just five miles outside its limits. But he had no idea where Dahlgren was and was loath to attack without knowing his partner was close enough to play his assigned role. The whole idea, after all, was for Kilpatrick to draw the few Richmond forces defending the capital to the city's northern perimeter, while Dahlgren attacked from the south. But the flares that were to be used for communication between the two parties were worthless under the weather conditions. They simply couldn't be seen. The plan had been to attack at sunset. But with no real source of information, Kilpatrick hesitated. And hesitated. The self-assured brashness he was so well known for deserted him, and his 3,500 men sat and waited while Kilpatrick stewed.

Had Kilpatrick instead led his contingent straight into the city, he could have easily taken it. But instead of attacking, the general ordered soldiers to investigate and probe the earthworks and trenches that stretched ahead of his forces; occasional shots rang out. His cannon fire was barely answered. By early afternoon, Kilpatrick's forces had barely advanced two miles.

Later that day, a new fear seized the Richmond residents as news of the imminent approach of Dahlgren and his 500 men reached their ears. The bell on Capitol Square sounded an alarm, calling for the home defense brigade to muster. Richmond residents turned to action. Dropping their pens, tools, and schoolbooks, clerks and factory workers, elderly men and schoolboys making up the home defense brigade made their way to the battlefront. A shocked Elizabeth could even spot her own Union friends drilling alongside them. "I drove out in the afternoon, and I saw all the militia drilling, among them Northerners, and some I know to be Unionists," she wrote in her diary. "So potent is fear to blind conscience!"[15]

Along the streets of the city, the faces of women and children could be seen, peering out upstairs windows, some holding ancient firearms. They waited and prayed.

According to some accounts, prison officials panicked, imagining the prisoners would be freed by the intruders and attack their captors and the rest of the city. General Winder knew prisoners at Libby had crude weapons and rumors of a raid might set them to mount yet another effort to escape. Only a handful of guards manned the prisons against thousands of inmates. With approval from Secretary of War James Seddon, Thomas Turner, the Libby Prison commander, found a dangerous solution. Explosives were buried in the basement of the prison, to be detonated in the event of a successful Union advance into the city.

Richmond residents weren't the only ones panicked. As rain turned to snow, Kilpatrick worried about what appeared to be an amassing of guns by the rebels. He sent troops again to probe the city's defenses. As he awaited their reports, trained Confederate soldiers fired on his forces. The longer he waited, the more his window for striking the capital closed. By afternoon, he called an end to the attack. There would be no raid on Richmond that day by Kilpatrick's troops.

Meanwhile, Dahlgren had finally found another crossing of the James. As he closed in on Richmond, the colonel heard that Kilpatrick had been stopped, not by loss of nerve but by Confederate forces. He was told by scouts that Confederate cavalry units roamed the area. Dahlgren had a choice. Continue or turn back? He could see his one last chance at glory—at ending the war or dramatically shortening it—slipping away right here. He couldn't let that happen. Even with the hope that the planned raid could free Union prisoners fading, Dahlgren elected to proceed anyway, deciding they could get invaluable information about the defense of the capital.

And so Dahlgren and his forces, diminished by the difficulties of the ride and the weather and the lack of food and comfort, proceeded ahead, dumping equipment that would slow them down, like the signal rockets. They also abandoned hundreds of Black slaves who had followed them, seeking safety and freedom. They were left to fend for themselves.

Several miles from Richmond, the force hastily routed Rebel scouts. They found more resistance from the Richmond city battalion closer to the city, but that infantry was no match for the mounted, trained Union forces, exhausted though they were. Lieutenant Merritt, a soldier with Dahlgren, wrote about their chase of Rebel forces: "It was a scrub race, across fields, fences and stone walls, we pressed after them, rallying, and scattering them repeatedly as they attempted to dispute our advance whenever a wall or house afforded shelter. Between formidable works, over rifle pits, ditches and every obstruction, with a cheer, a run and a volley from our Spencers, we crowded them back to the edge of the city."[16] The sky darkened and gas lights provided the only illumination. Dahlgren was inside the city limits, but barely. Having fought his way to Richmond's door, he and his troops were overwhelmed by determined Rebels defending their homes, surging forward like a wildfire through a dry forest to protect everything they held dear. Dahlgren, bitter with disappointment, was forced to reverse course.

Returning the way he had come was difficult. The soldiers were deep inside hostile territory. Any Rebel boy, furloughed soldier, or old man could pick up a gun to chase Dahlgren and his forces down. Dahlgren's men made their way across the fields they had just crossed, picking up their injured and placing them under the supervision of a medical officer who volunteered to stay.

They must have thought things couldn't get any worse, but at just this moment, a storm rolled in, a fierce wind driving rain, snow, and sleet into the very faces of Dahlgren's meager forces. Visibility was nearly impossible. Forward movement was agonizingly slow. Heavy pines overgrew the road; fallen trees blocking their passage had to be cleared from the little-used path they crossed. Exhausted, the men fell asleep in their saddles, astride their horses, relying on the animals' instincts to follow each other in a single line to proceed forward. When they finally reached Hungary Station, they realized that Captain Mitchell and his party, charged with protecting their rear quarters, had become separated from them.

In fact, Mitchell had managed to find Kilpatrick and his larger force; Dahlgren was left to ride northeast to try to reunite with General Butler's forces located at Gloucester Point, near Williamsburg. It was painfully slow going. They crossed two more rivers without incident, the Pamunkey southeast of Richmond and the Mattaponi. For the next several hours, they encountered repeated skirmishers, which slowed their movement through the countryside. On that long ride, Dahlgren had plenty of time to contemplate the raid and its failure. Did he blame himself and his own foolish optimism? Or Kilpatrick's raging ambition?

By evening Dahlgren and his men were able to make camp just north of King and Queen Court House. There, the men cooked their first meal in thirty-six hours. By now, Dahlgren's forces were reduced to just 70 men from 500 originally. Their ammunition was mostly exhausted and many of the men had none. All were bone-tired and weary, many injured.

But they had to keep moving. After just three hours sleep, Dahlgren had the soldiers roused and mounted an hour before midnight. The march resumed through drizzling rain and a thick pine wood. As before, visibility was low. And then, more bad news. A picket of three men, sent ahead of the main group's halting pace to warn them of an enemy advance, disappeared. Dahlgren and his men proceeded quietly, the young officer riding near the head of the advance, pausing as they heard noises ahead.

In front of them, hidden by the dark of night, was a small detachment of Rebels, some home guards who had never seen action, as anxious as Dahlgren's men were exhausted; others were sharpshooters, battle-hardened and home on furlough, assigned picket duty. All were arrayed along the sides of the road, ready to ambush Dahlgren and his men.

A noise startled a young Union private, who nervously called out, "Who are you?" And, Dahlgren immediately followed on, yelling, "Surrender or we will shoot you!" He raised his pistol and fired, but only the cap exploded. The next instant a heavy volley of gunfire poured in upon the Union soldiers, the flash of that gunfire illuminating the Rebels' position fifteen paces ahead. Parallel with the road, men fired from every tree; bushes poured a sheet of fire. The trap sprung, it now closed as fire opened on the small unit's rear. Chaos followed as the horses reared and stampeded. Fences lining the road trapped the men for a time, until some of the rails were torn down.

Panicked, those who could escaped into the night. Not all did. Face down in the muddy road, lay Dahlgren, dead, the back of his uniform torn open by bullets, his blood mixing with the rain. [17]

In the coming hours, the failed raid would have a shocking coda, a fire that would spread from man to man across the entire country. And the match to light it was in Dahlgren's own pockets.

✦ ✦

ULRIC THE HUN

The fighting had ended, and the sleet and snow had stopped. In the quiet, snow-blanketed night, soldiers on both sides prepared to rest for a few short hours. The Federals crept to a nearby pine grove and bedded down with only their uniforms for warmth, believing they were surrounded by Rebels. Although the ground was cold and hard, they dared not light fires for fear of exposing their position. The men debated their tenuous situation. Some planned to steal away in the early morning, while others saw no hope for escape. They were twenty-five miles from Union lines, surrounded by swamps, the Mattaponi River, and the enemy.

Only a few hundred yards away, the Confederates also prepared for bed, chatting easily and warming themselves at fires. Most of them anyway. A desperate few surveyed the site of the ambush, looking for treasure. It was a grisly yet common practice during the war to rifle the pockets and persons of the dead after an engagement. Money, rings, watches, and knives were the objects of such searches, but so were the soldiers' most common items of dress and equipment—boots, jackets, pants, and shirts.

That night, a thirteen-year-old boy among the scavengers found an unusual prize. William Littlepage was a member of a company of schoolboys that served the Virginia home guard. He was eager to find a gold watch, but what he discovered that night was something far more valuable. It didn't look like much at first: a cigar case, a memorandum book, and some papers. Disappointed, Littlepage turned the lot over to his schoolteacher, Edward Halbach, who was part of the Confederate ambush party. Halbach stowed the papers for reading in the light of day and returned the cigar box to the boy. At least, he thought, the child had something for his efforts.

Littlepage wasn't the only one to search Dahlgren. Other soldiers stripped him, taking his clothing, and, with some difficulty, removing his wooden leg. Another severed the little finger of Dahlgren's right hand to take a ring. They buried his nearly naked body at a crossroads in a muddy hole, a shallow grave. But his body wouldn't stay there for long.

Back in Richmond, residents remained wary as a gray sky announced the dawn. A sprinkle of snow fell on the city early that morning. The home guard, stationed around the perimeter of the city along its fortifications, stared into the muddy field in front of them, worried about what might come next. They knew of the previous day's cavalry raids and had been watching for hours for a strike against the capital city.

On Church Hill, Elizabeth would have been on her guard as well. The spymaster had probably already received the crushing news of the raid's failure from the agents she had sent into the field to greet the Union cavalry. When the Union failed to show, her spies would have made their way to Church Hill, hidden by the night, to give her the news. Despite Elizabeth's planning and hard work, there was no liberation of Libby or Belle Isle, no abduction of the Confederate president. It was all for naught, and now she had to immediately start considering whether she and her ring had been exposed. She likely was possessed by equal parts fear and anger, knowing that at any moment Confederate soldiers might knock on her door to take her and her family to prison.

As the day dawned back at Mantapike Hill, the site roiled with the activity of the soldiers and horses breaking their primitive camp. The scene was still littered with debris from battle, exploded shells, manure left by panicked horses. An odor of sulfur still permeated the air.

The rebels rounded up Union soldiers under Dahlgren's command who failed to make their escape. Officers who had opted to run were corralled at the home of a plantation overseer who had deceived the Union officers into thinking they were being sheltered by friends. They, too, were held prisoner.

Amid the hubbub, Halbach pulled out the papers confiscated from Dahlgren to figure out what Littlepage had discovered. The first thing he noticed was the official stationery of the Army of the Potomac's Cavalry of the Third Division. Unsure how to proceed, he turned the papers over to Lt. James Pollard, who had commanded the rebels in the skirmish. The next day, Pollard handed the materials over to Fitzhugh Lee, the nephew of General Robert E. Lee, and a man known for his high spirits and high emotions. The papers would contribute to both.

The documents contained Dahlgren's notes from a planning meeting with his superior, Kilpatrick. Including a timeline for a campaign of destruction in the capital city, the inexperienced colonel detailed the exact weapons of destruction to be used in the Richmond raid. He couldn't afford to forget a single item.

It would have been apparent to even a casual reader of the orders that the mission's objective was more than just setting the prisoners of war free. The text of a speech Dahlgren had planned to deliver to his soldiers was part of Littlefield's treasure trove:

> We hope to release the prisoners from Belle Isle first, and having seen them fairly started, we will cross the James River into Richmond destroying the bridges after us and exhorting the released prisoners to destroy and burn the hateful city; and do not allow the Rebel leader Davis and his traitorous crew to escape. The prisoners must render great assistance as you cannot leave your ranks too far or become too much scattered or you will be lost.

But in a separate set of instructions for Captain John F. B. Mitchell of the 2nd New York Cavalry, who led the separate detachment down the north bank of the James, there was this: "The bridges once secured, and the prisoners loose and over the river, the bridges will be burned, and the city destroyed and *Jeff. Davis and his cabinet killed.*"[1]

Fitzhugh Lee must have read the following line from Dahlgren's detailed itinerary more than once: "Jeff. Davis and his cabinet must be killed on the spot." For Lee, the Union objectives were as outrageous as they were surprising. Dahlgren's men, with the help of a vengeful group of prisoners, were to decapitate Confederate leadership, murdering the president and his cabinet. The questions came fast and furious. Had Union leadership approved these orders? If not, who had written them? Dahlgren's notes continued to fly up the Confederate ladder of command. Lee took the papers to President Davis, who, familiar with threats, didn't take this one too seriously at first. Davis is reported to have laughed out loud when he read the papers to his secretary of state, Judah P. Benjamin. "This means you, Mr. Benjamin," he joked.[2]

But at the War Department, Davis's chief military advisor, Braxton Bragg, was outraged. He sent the papers to Secretary of War James A. Seddon, demanding they be made public to call the attention of "our people and the civilized world to the fiendish and atrocious conduct of our enemies."[3] The very next day Dahlgren's orders appeared in every newspaper in Richmond. The documents lit a fire in Confederate hearts. The *Richmond Sentinel* reported that Dahlgren "was the willing instrument for executing an atrocity, which his superiors had approved and sanctioned."[4] The *Whig*, describing Dahlgren's forces, wrote: "Are these men warriors? Are they soldiers, taken in performance of duties recognized as legitimate. Or are they assassins, barbarians, and thugs?"[5]

Elizabeth must have been shocked. She hadn't called for an assassination of the Confederate president, and to her knowledge, neither had the Union. She had been part of the discussions at the Washington Ball. Murder wasn't part of the plan. She came to the only conclusion left to her. Elizabeth steadfastly, and somewhat naively, believed that the Rebels planted the orders on Dahlgren. The young colonel, she believed, was innocent of anything other than a fierce commitment to his assigned job.

She believed the real tragedy was the treatment of Dahlgren's corpse at the hands of the Rebels. On March 6, a day after Dahlgren's orders were made public, his body was, under Rebel orders, disinterred from the muddy grave barely two feet deep where he had first been buried after the deadly assault. His body was taken to the York River Railroad Depot and put on display. There, scores of Richmonders filed past to get a glimpse of the man headline writers had dubbed "Ulric the Hun." His body had been dressed simply in a linen shirt and trousers. Elizabeth was among the crowds, describing the parade as an "insult to decency" in her diary. Both Elizabeth and her circle regarded putting his body on display as barbaric, but for most of Richmond, it represented just deserts. "It would seem something of the curse he came to bestow on others lighted upon his own carcass," sneered the *Richmond Examiner*.[6]

Elizabeth knew as well as did many Americans that assassinating a sitting head of government or his cabinet was considered uncivilized. The physical threat of war was supposed to occur on the battlefield, not in the homes and offices of state leaders.

But the rules of war were under revision on both sides. Early in the conflict, Lincoln had advocated a soft-war policy, which would protect not only persons and property of Confederate civilians but also establish an obligation to return slaves to their masters. Lincoln had written this: "Let us show to our fellow-citizens of these States that we come merely to crush the rebellion and to restore them to peace. They have been told that we come to oppress and plunder. By our acts, we will undeceive them."[7] But Lincoln's forgiving attitude couldn't survive an increasingly bitter war fought not on a remote battlefield but on the farmland and in the backyards of citizens, most of them Southern. A new code of war acknowledged these challenges and recognized both women and Blacks as potential combatants.

No code sanctioned the murder of a head of state. But the rules protecting state leaders weren't inviolate. Kidnapping public officials of high rank was permissible. In fact, the first raid on Richmond to set free prisoners, which had been approved by Lincoln and his secretary of war Edwin Stanton, included specific instructions to abduct "some leaders of the rebellion."[8] Major General Benjamin Butler instructed the commander of the raid, Isaac J. Wistar, to first liberate Richmond prisoners and destroy the city's buildings and a store of ammunition and firearms. After that, the men were to capture Confederate leaders. When Wistar wrote out his own detailed version of the plan for Major James Wheelan, who was to lead 300 troopers of the 1st New York Mounted Rifles, it directed him to "turn to the right and capture Jeff Davis" at the Confederate White House on Clay Street.[9] Butler's plan never became a reality as it was turned back by Rebel forces a dozen miles short of Richmond.

Kidnapping the leadership of one's foes had a definite air of desperation. But by this point in the war, both sides were eager for a way to end the fighting quickly and declare victory. The South was reeling after major Union successes on the battlefield at Gettysburg and Vicksburg. And Lincoln faced reelection at a time that Northern appeasers, the Copperheads, were gaining political traction. The question for either government was: How would you capitalize on abduction? Would you conduct a trial? Press charges of treason? Hold the leader for ransom? What if the leader was to die as he was transported to enemy encampments? The questions were academic at this point, given the raid's abject failure.

The news caught Union generals and politicians off guard. Dahlgren's father, among many others in the North, insisted the orders were fabrications, a view taken up by many in the North. But in the South, the *Richmond Examiner*'s indignant views were common: "The depredations of the last Yankee raiders, and the wantonness of their devastation equal anything heretofore committed during the war."[10]

The exposed orders carried by Dahlgren had become a flashpoint for the entire country. The issue divided Americans along regional lines.

If the reaction in the South was anger, in the North it was disbelief. The first headlines in *The New York Times* on the story were these: "The Manner of Col. Dahlgren's Death and the Capture of His Men: They Are Shot Down from a Midnight Ambush: Confinement of Prisoners in Dungeons and in Irons; Their Prompt Execution Demanded. Barbarous Indignities; Cruelties and Passions." And in the story, Dahlgren is described as "brave almost to rashness," maintaining "he expressed a willingness to sacrifice his own life in an effort to rescue his brave countrymen from the Bastille in which they had been for months confined."[11] *Harper's Weekly* labeled Dahlgren "sturdy and courageous."

Their incredulity isn't too surprising given how out of character such a mission appeared to be for Dahlgren, who was a celebrity in his own right—handsome, well-mannered, and clearly destined for great things. His prominence in antebellum high society and lionization by the newspapers for his bravery at Fredericksburg and Gettysburg made these allegations of dishonorable intentions seem implausible. For him to execute such a devious plan simply didn't square with what newspaper readers felt they knew about the man.

His father, Admiral Dahlgren, was inconsolable and demanded the return of his son's body to Union soil. Once the admiral saw the orders firsthand, he made a discovery that he believed proved his son's innocence. The young colonel's signature was misspelled on the lithographed copies of the orders. The discovery whipped the North into a frenzy. According to the *New York Herald,* "Dahlgren Papers Are a Bare-Faced, Atrocious Forgery."

Elizabeth believed the misspelling proved her conviction that Dahlgren had no malevolent intentions on the Confederate president or his cabinet. "The pretended order of Dahlgren as given by the Rebel Press spelled his name wrongly, which is, of course, proof present that he never signed it," she wrote confidently in her diary, adding "said paper was prepared in Richmond . . . to irritate and inflame the Southern people."[12]

It was time for answers. General Lee wrote to the Union's top military officer, General Meade, with the most important question: Did the instructions in Dahlgren's letters originate with the federal government or his superior officers? In other words, who ordered the decapitation of Confederate leadership?

Meade ordered Kilpatrick to headquarters to find out, but the brash colonel preempted his request, writing a letter of denial, stating that Dahlgren received no orders from him to pillage, burn, or kill. Plus, he wrote, there were no such instructions from his superiors. In other words, it was the fault of Dahlgren, now dead and incapable of defending himself. In his letter back to Lee, Meade said he didn't approve the orders and Kilpatrick did not authorize or sanction such actions.

But Elizabeth and the Northern newspapers were wrong. The orders were genuine. It would take fourteen years for a compelling explanation of the misspelling to come to light. It was Confederate general Jubal Early who solved the puzzle. The orders had been copied by the process of lithography, which required that the original be blemish free. The originals were written on a thin paper, and where Dahlgren's signature appeared, lettering on the opposite side showed through. When the orders were prepared for wider dissemination, the lithographer touching up the document exacerbated the problem by deciphering the signature as best he could. The signature in his amended version did read as "U. Dalhgren," rather than "U. Dahlgren," but not because the name was forged; it was quite simply an error introduced by copying the document.[13]

Meanwhile, in the days after the failed raid, General Meade found additional confirmation that the orders were genuine. Worried that he would be blamed for the attack's failure, he ordered Dahlgren's personal effects brought to his office. He demanded his subordinates Alfred Pleasanton, commander of the Army of the Potomac's Cavalry Corps, and Marsena Patrick, the army's provost marshal, search their files for anything that might bring clarity to the situation.

Patrick returned with an entry from his own diary, in which he logged his conversation with Captain John McEntee, a Union spy and member of the Bureau of Military Information. McEntee had ridden with Dahlgren on the fateful attack, and when he returned from the raid, he sat down with Patrick in the brigadier general's tent. The two swapped stories of their contempt for Kilpatrick. And when Patrick probed McEntee about the orders, the spy shared that he believed the orders were authentic. Why? Because when the two were together on the raid, Dahlgren described them to him. In other words, the orders weren't planted on Dahlgren and forged by Rebel leaders, as Elizabeth and so many others had surmised. Dahlgren himself had confirmed them. But Meade's hands were tied. Officially, he had to stick to the story that neither his office nor the government had any role in the scheme.[14]

That led to an obvious question: If the documents were authentic and not forged, who could have written the orders?

The revisions of the rules of war were reflected in the choices of Union leadership. Lincoln, failed by McClellan, had turned to brash western frontier generals like Grant and Sherman. But was he ready to translate that approach to war strategy to the dirty war of assassination? Was the man who scoffed at the Baltimore Plot, unwilling to believe people would stoop so low, ready to make such a decision himself?

Maybe the decision originated at a lower level. But while Kilpatrick was given to dramatic display, he didn't possess the kind of cold-blooded courage that such a plot would require. And Meade rejected the idea that Dahlgren would take it on himself to design such a radical plan. The captain had been raised to respect military authority, and his record of service revealed a young man eager to execute the orders of his superiors to the letter, not invent his own.

It was the general's suspicion, though he didn't say so publicly, that there was a plot orchestrated not by Kilpatrick or Dahlgren but by someone in the military or political hierarchy in Washington. Meade retraced Kilpatrick's footsteps in seeking approval for the Richmond raid. In fact, Kilpatrick had consulted with precious few people while devising his plans. The cavalry officer had met directly with Lincoln, who in turn sent him to Secretary of War Stanton to firm up the details. Lincoln's authorship of the dark purpose of the raid, however, seemed highly unlikely. There were no documents linking the president to the plot, and his interest in the scheme was to deliver his amnesty proclamation to Confederate soldiers. Though Lincoln had approved an earlier raid on Richmond to free prisoners, it set as a secondary goal abducting senior Confederate leadership, not killing them.

Only one other person had left fingerprints on the raid's planning, and that was Edwin Stanton, the secretary of war. Lincoln had sent Kilpatrick directly to Stanton to detail his plan. Throughout the war, Stanton was credited with providing strong leadership to organize the North's resources and with guiding the Union to victory. But his methods were controversial. He pressed for war without limits, a concept called total war, which expanded military targets to include civilians and the infrastructure that supported an enemy. At Stanton's direction, Francis Lieber's more liberal code of the proper conduct of war was distributed to all Union officers. Under that code, for example, women were no longer automatically assumed innocent, but had to pass a loyalty test, a change demanded by the participation of women like Elizabeth as spies and soldiers. Lincoln's call to enlist Blacks was seen as a part of that strategy because it acknowledged that Black men could fight with the same competence as white—in other words, that they were men and not chattel. Confederates were outraged by what they perceived as an attack on their property, robbing Southern farms and plantations of manpower and therefore sapping the Confederacy of support for its armies.

Noted historian Stephen W. Sears wrote that "circumstance and logic" point to Stanton as the author of the Dahlgren orders to burn, pillage, and kill. "The idea of liberating maddened prisoners and exhorting them to carry out death sentences and the pillaging was a masterstroke of rationalization and perfectly in character for the secretary of war." [15]

That November, Stanton asked Francis Lieber, who was by then in charge of the Confederate archives, to bring him all the papers and documents dealing with the failed raid. The papers were delivered on December 1 and have never been seen since.

As a military stratagem, the Dahlgren raid failed miserably. Its losses were substantial: 9 officers, 331 men, 583 horses, 90 Spencer rifles, 59 Spencer carbines, 338 Sharps carbines, and 516 Colt army pistols, with no gain for the Union in territory or prisoners.

But the raid's significance was not on the battlefield. Its import was the indelible imprint it left on the minds of Americans generally. The entire affair had the effect of hardening views and inflaming people on both sides of the conflict. Among military planners, it gave cover to ideas that would have sounded outrageous just a few months earlier and would have been dismissed as immoral or unethical. Sherman found a use for Kilpatrick on his march to the sea. Defending his choice to select the hotheaded brigadier, Sherman said, "I know Kilpatrick is a hell of a damned fool, but I want just that sort of man to command my cavalry on this expedition."[16] In both the Union and especially the Confederacy, appetites were whetted for vengeance, retribution, and retaliation.

Despite setbacks, Grant achieved victory after victory in the western theater of the war. His success at Vicksburg split the confederacy in two, representing a major Union victory. He did continue to battle his demons. He appeared drunk in public a few times in 1863, though allegations that this led to his failures at Shiloh are generally considered false by historians. Legend has it that when critics brought Grant's drinking problem to Lincoln, the latter responded by saying that "if he could find out what brand of whiskey Grant drank, he would send a barrel of it to all the other commanders."[17]

Bolstered by his victories in the western theater, Lincoln promoted Grant to make him general in chief of all the Union armies.

Wrote the *Richmond Sentinel*: "If the Confederate capital has been in the closest danger of massacre and conflagration; if the President and Cabinet have run a serious risk of being hanged at their own door, do we not owe it chiefly to the milk-and-water spirit in which the war has hitherto been conducted?"[18]

Ironically the failure of the very raid Elizabeth had called for increased her value to the Union, rather than the opposite. She was very much in demand. This was partially because as Grant was elevated over Meade to take command of all Union armies, he put a special emphasis on intelligence. The general knew firsthand the value of trustworthy information, having nearly lost the Battle of Shiloh because of a lack of it. As army chief, he immediately elevated the senior officer of the Union's Bureau of Military Information, George Sharpe, whose role had been diminished by General Meade after Gettysburg. Grant promoted Sharpe to brigadier general, and he worked as a senior advisor to Grant. When Grant moved operations to City Point, Virginia, to oversee the siege of Petersburg, Sharpe went along. Taking Petersburg was essential to Union efforts because the town just south of Richmond was a critical Confederate supply hub. Railroad lines converged at Petersburg, bringing essential supplies for the Rebel army. The town's proximity and importance to the Rebel capital made Richmond a critical center for intelligence during the nine-and-a-half-month siege.

Although Van Lew had been Butler's asset, Sharpe began personally supervising the network and Van Lew in those critical months. That change alone propelled Elizabeth and her team from keen amateurs to critical assets. That Sharpe would in later years be deemed the father of modern military intelligence is due in no small part to the contributions of Elizabeth and her ring. During World War II, Sharpe's techniques and structures were copied in the formation of the Office of Strategic Services, which eventually became the Central Intelligence Agency. His groundbreaking "all-source" intelligence analysis allowed information to be cross-checked against different sources, verified, and analyzed.

Under Sharpe's direction, Elizabeth instructed her ring to focus less on the prisoners and more on the Confederate war machine, or what was left of it. Sharpe posed the questions for Van Lew's team to answer, while she deployed the agents and compiled their intelligence into readable reports salted with her vivid insights. Her role as spymaster and ringleader was then parallel with what Sharpe was doing on a wider basis, but with her own personal twist. When describing how a road had been mined to block Union forces, she mentions that the information came from the very men who put the explosives in place.

She began churning out a report a week, then two reports a week, and then three. Her notes were sometimes scrawled on scraps of paper delivered by farmers, store clerks, and factory workers, members of her expanding ring. Sometimes they were carefully placed in a hollowed-out egg in a basket of real eggs or in the specially made heels of servant's shoes. Longer missives covering the city's defenses, troop movements, the morale of the city's populace, rumors, and economic conditions in the city were encoded. By this point, she was managing information from several dozen operatives, including agents in the Rebel government, and because of this, her reports grew increasingly critical to the Union war effort. One of her informants was a clerk in the Confederate adjutant general's office who stole details on the strength of Rebel regiments, brigades, and divisions and their movements. Another was an agent in the Confederate engineering department who sent her plans of Rebel defenses around Richmond and Petersburg.

For months, Elizabeth's reports had been picked up by couriers at her family farm located near the Richmond-Henrico County line; it was one of the first of five stops along the James River where Butler's agents could pick up or drop off messages and reports. But as Elizabeth's reports increased in frequency, Sharpe set up a special steam launch to pick up her coded reports. Under cover of darkness, a Union scout would meet with one of Elizabeth's many couriers and safely transfer the information into Sharpe's hands. Other times, Elizabeth had Samuel Ruth, a railroad employee who ran his own espionage operation and fed her own, carry communications on trains. But these encounters were dangerous. Rebel scouts nearly captured one of Sharpe's men meeting a Van Lew courier near the Chickahominy River. As the Confederates rode up to him, he jammed the slips of paper in his mouth and swallowed hard.

Elizabeth's speed and efficiency was such that an eager Ulysses S. Grant could sit down over breakfast every day with a comprehensive survey of Richmond's defenses and the status of the Confederate army, next to a fresh bouquet plucked from Elizabeth's garden that morning. He often sent the reports on to Lincoln, describing them as penned by "our friend in Richmond."

In Van Lew, Sharpe found the intelligence source he had been looking for. He could rightfully brag that Elizabeth and her spy ring could answer virtually any question Grant could conceive about Richmond. And inside Confederate war offices, officers lamented the fact that it was nearly impossible to keep information secret. Their plans and frustrations seemed to fairly routinely find a way into Union hands. Elizabeth wasn't just an important Union spy; she was now its most important one.

TOTAL WAR

The Dahlgren Affair, as it came to be known, infuriated just about everyone—whether they were angry at Union leadership over the targets of the raid as described in the young colonel's orders or at the Confederacy for planting the orders on Dahlgren's dead body. From that deep well of anger sprang rash acts that had unintended consequences from Richmond to Washington.

On Church Hill, Elizabeth stewed. Her aim had been a surprise attack by an overwhelming Federal force that could free prisoners in all of Richmond's prisons and on Belle Isle; a secondary goal was the abduction of Jefferson Davis. To be sure, she wanted the Union to win the war, but not by murdering Confederate leaders in their beds and offices. But no, she couldn't believe the orders were real. John Dahlgren was right; the signature was not his son's. Ulric Dahlgren remained a hero in her mind, and the Confederacy's treatment of his body was criminal. She promised herself she would find the grave Dahlgren had been taken to after being put on display at the train station and she would see his remains recovered and sent to his grieving father. Elizabeth vowed to run her own raid with her own people. Her most trusted agents would take on this most dangerous assignment locating Dahlgren's body to "remove his honored dust to friendly care," as she wrote in her diary. The Union might not have been able to run a successful raid on Richmond, but Elizabeth was certain she could.

LESS THAN A MONTH LATER, ELIZABETH'S FAVORITE OPERATIVE, F.W.E. Lohmann, assisted by his brother John and Martin Meredith Lipscomb, who had the grisly day job of burying Yankees, made their way into Oakwood Cemetery on Richmond's east end as quietly as they could under the cover of darkness. The night was moonless and cold. Rain pelted on the backs of the three hunched men as they followed a fourth man, the groundskeeper. They stumbled across the muddy ground, slick with water, their tense faces intermittently etched by lightning.

It was a night fit for grave robbers, and that is exactly what they were. Thunder rolled as if God himself was commenting on their work. The groundskeeper, a free Black man risking his life to be there, pointed to the spot the three had come to see. Breaking out crude shovels of iron and wood, they began to dig. Their objective was Dahlgren's flimsy pine coffin. The boy had been dead more than a month.

The three risked detection at any moment by Confederate soldiers. The penalty for moving the body, if discovered, would be extreme. Death by hanging or perhaps by a firing squad. Neither option was appealing, so they kept at their work, moving quickly and quietly, their hearts in their throats.

In short order, they located the casket. Next came the worst of their assignment, prying it open to make sure it was the right one. They couldn't risk alerting the enemy by lighting a torch against the dark, so once they got the casket open, Lohmann shoved his hand inside, his fingers feeling for the body. No right leg below the knee. The man was also missing the little finger of his left hand. They had gotten it right. The decaying body of Lieutenant Colonel Ulric Dahlgren was back in the hands of Union operatives, though not yet back on Union soil.

The men lifted the coffin containing the remains of Dahlgren, an easy burden, as the slight man was made lighter by the rot of decay spreading through his body. The coffin and its occupant were hoisted high and then carefully lowered into the back of the mule-drawn wagon the men had arrived in. The men jumped aboard and settled in. The wagon creaked ahead.

Next, the three drove the wagon a short distance to the home of another of Elizabeth's prized agents, William Rowley. There, they placed the coffin in an outbuilding at his farm, a wooden workshop. They left for home. Loyal Rowley stayed up all night with the body in the dark, keeping vigil over their prize and listening for Confederate soldiers. The job wasn't over yet.

The next morning, Elizabeth met her ring at Rowley's farm, eager to reclaim Dahlgren. She likely wore the skirt and jacket of a farm woman to conceal her identity. She moved quickly to the workshop, steeling herself for what she was about to see. Crossing the threshold, Elizabeth immediately noticed a smell like rotten eggs. But the stench didn't stop her. She was familiar with the odor of death. Dahlgren's body was laid out on a table, and encircling him were her Unionist agents, her friends and confidants.

American culture, following the example of Victorians, was obsessed with death. Cultural practices and habits were important because they helped prepare a dying person's soul for the afterlife. A calm look on a dead person's face signaled they were at peace and ready for death. It was important for Elizabeth to comfort his family with a story of a serene demeanor. The only problem for Elizabeth was that Dahlgren had been cut down on the battlefield. The last thing on his mind was meeting his maker. As a result, his face bore a look of agony. Elizabeth would have to improvise. She leaned down and got a closer look at his face. Her fingertips skimmed his chest and what was left of his limbs. The skin was dirty and scratched. His face was yellow green, with the most exposed parts of it, like his nose, dried out and brown. His eyes were opaque. The blue irises were glazed over. His jaw was bloated because of the gases expanding in his body. He was wearing a coarse shirt the Confederates had no doubt dressed him in and his uniform pants, likely worse for the wear. *Poor Dahlgren,* Elizabeth thought.

The kill shot to his back had left a large wound. Elizabeth must have wondered whether Dahlgren had been caught by the fatal blow as he was fleeing the scene. *Was he running in fear?*

But there was no time for such second thoughts. She knew her very presence here on this remote farm was dangerous. She was alert for the sound of hooves, men on horseback, the slap of a rifle butt against a thigh. Any of it would portend exposure of her work and her companions. She must finish her task.

Following the requisite tradition, she moved to cut off a lock of his reddish-brown hair to preserve and send to his father. But the dried-out locks broke and fell into her hand. She scooped them up anyway.

At Elizabeth's instruction, the group held a mock funeral cere-mony, complete with prayer and the singing of hymns. She ordered the body moved to a safer location farther out of the city and buried where Confederates weren't likely to see it. The men transferred Dahlgren's body into a metal coffin and placed both on Rowley's wagon to be transferred to the new burial site some twelve miles away. They hid the coffin from view by setting young peach trees around it in the bed of the wagon. The cover for the entire operation was nearly blown when the wagon carrying Dahlgren was stopped by a Rebel picket post. Thinking quickly, Rowley was able to convince the guard on duty that the load on his wagon was nothing more than peach trees bound for a neighbor's farm. Had Rowley been less convincing, Elizabeth's entire operation and her spy ring would have been discovered. It wasn't the first time she had been lucky.

They all took a massive risk for an insignificant payoff. In the interim, the Confederacy had agreed to return the body to John Dahlgren. When they went to dig it up at Oakwood, it was gone. John Dahlgren got word from Butler that the body had been moved and was in safe hands, but in the meantime, Confederate officials knew they had Unionists to blame for Dahlgren's disappearance. Elizabeth and her ring were in more danger than ever.

ON CAPITOL SQUARE IN RICHMOND, JEFFERSON DAVIS WAS PONDERING his own response to the Dahlgren raid. He needed to answer the insult contained in the military orders Dahlgren carried. He couldn't allow a threat to Confederate leaders' lives, his own included, to go unanswered. The newspapers were turning against him. His reviews on their editorial pages were not good. The South's editorial writers were baying for blood, describing his administration as imbecilic.

"Let every Yankee marauder die the 'ignominious death' which their late leader expected for the stragglers of his pack of hellhounds," said the *Richmond Examiner* on March 19. "And let us begin at once with the picked gang of marauders, whose fate should be decided not by the amount of mischief which they actually accomplished but by the outrages which they came to perpetrate."

Davis wanted to retaliate, but not in the way the newspapers were suggesting. He was considering a new kind of warfare altogether. He wanted to take the fight behind enemy lines. With his resources flagging and the ranks of his soldiers diminished, Davis needed a way to strike at his enemy where they least expected it. Newspaper editors may have wanted better performance on the battlefield, but Davis was intent on developing a campaign of subterfuge and surprise elsewhere.[1]

The Confederacy had operated spies since the beginning of the war. They leveraged every possible source in the public domain, including newspapers and maps relayed by couriers or mailed in boxes. Richmond's mercantile class reported important news and gossip they heard from relatives and business contacts living in the North. In the field, Confederate engineers and members of the Signal Corps kept watch on roads and weather, information critical to moving armies and cavalry. Captured soldiers provided critical information.

Possibly the richest source of information was Washington itself.

Even in the Union's most elite circles, there was support for Confederate aims. And because so many Southern sympathizers lived in Washington, D.C., and were members of the government even after the war began, information flowed from every federal department, including the Union's own secret service agency. [2]

The job of developing intel was so important that Davis, a man who loved detail, assigned the task to himself. His intelligence system had no Richmond address or offices—it ran out of Davis's home and the offices of his cabinet. The system was so decentralized and unofficial that friends, relatives, and even neighbors of Confederate leaders might be pressed into helping in an intelligence operation.[3]

But as the Dahlgren raid made clear, Davis needed more than just timely information. He needed to convert his intelligence operation into a military one, strike fear into the Northern populace, and convince average people that the time for peace had come. Northerners had seen little of the war up close; most of it had been fought in the South. It was time for that to change. Davis's goal was to convince Lincoln to seek peace on Rebel terms, by which Davis meant disunion: The Confederacy would continue as a separate nation, as would slavery. He needed operations that would make the Northerners feel the war was at their doorstep.

The Confederate Congress had provided the means to do just that in mid-February of 1864, when they had set up a special fund to finance Secret Service operations. Information on the fund is scant, but what is clear is that on April 25, 1864, only weeks after the Dahlgren raid had failed and the orders had been made public, Davis signed off on a request for $1 million from the fund by the Confederate secretary of war Judah P. Benjamin. On it was written the name Thompson.[4]

ON OCTOBER 18, 1864, BOOTH ARRIVED BY TRAIN IN MONTREAL, A CITY some called "Little Richmond," because of its many visitors from the Rebel South. The actor traveled with his entire theatrical wardrobe. Two large wooden boxes were packed with capes, velvet suits, crowns, swords, and hats, as well as scores of annotated scripts. He had told his brother, Edwin, that he intended to hire a blockade runner to ship his belongings south to Richmond, where, he said, he was looking to move.

But Booth had bigger plans on his mind. By late 1864, he had turned his attention away from theater and toward what he would later call a "noble duty."[5] He was ashamed of the fact he had never put on a real uniform—only an imitation for the stage—and fought on behalf of what he called "my countrymen." His promise to his mother not to enlist weighed heavily on his mind. Relieved of the duties associated with acting—the endless rehearsals, the memorization of lines, and travel—he had more time to ruminate. And plan. Never one to do a task in half measures, Booth was desperate to reset the war's footing on his own terms. He was preparing a plan to abduct President Lincoln in Washington, convey him to Richmond, and turn him over to the Confederate government, to be held as a hostage for the exchange of prisoners.

Once off the train, he headed straight for St. Lawrence Hall, well known as the city's unofficial Confederate headquarters. The huge neoclassical pile with its columned porticos and classical motifs attracted the wealthiest of Rebel schemers and plotters. Southern families had been rushing there since the beginning of the war. Former Florida senator James Wescott had taken up residency there and claimed he might never leave.

It wasn't Booth's first visit to the city. Henry Hogan, the proprietor of the St. Lawrence, remembered Booth as "most genial and gifted" and a "great favorite with theatergoers" when he performed at the old Theatre Royal in Court Street before the war. The admiration was mutual. Booth felt comfortable among St. Lawrence Hall's mostly Southern clientele, swapping stories with Wescott and playing billiards in his ample spare time. And he wasn't afraid to show his true colors that October. It was here that an inebriated Booth shared his antipathy for the U.S. president, saying "It makes little difference head or tail. Abe's contract is near up, and whether he gets re-elected or not, he will get his goose cooked." He earned the staff's gratitude by showering the bellboys with silver pieces whenever there was an announcement of a Rebel victory.[6]

In truth, there were few victories to celebrate. The fall had brought Rebels multiple failures as the war had turned against the South. On September 1, 1864, Union general William T. Sherman's campaign to take Atlanta, begun four months before, finally bore fruit when he took the city. One of the largest cities in the South was back under Federal control. Two months later the general would begin his march to the sea, unprecedented in its destruction. Meanwhile, Phil Sheridan pulled off major successes against Jubal Early in the Shenandoah Valley that September. Residents remember his campaign as "The Burning," because the cavalry commander destroyed every barn, mill, railroad, and factory over an area of 400 square miles. Voter enthusiasm followed battlefield successes in the North. Talk of Lincoln's reelection was widespread. Though many of the nation's founding fathers had served two terms, no president in living memory had done so, and Booth judged the ambition to serve a second term as evidence of Lincoln's despotism.

John Wilkes Booth loved playing at the edge of history. And just as he had been on hand at the hanging of John Brown four years earlier in Charles Town, Virginia, he now moved to the center of the Union resistance. Although his initial intention may have been only to hire a blockade runner to move his wardrobe south, the Montreal he arrived in was a hotbed of Confederate plotting, one that would encourage the development of his ideas into an actual plan.

Canada's status as a Rebel refuge had been encouraged by none other than Richmond itself. Davis saw Canada as a natural ally. Britain's official policy toward the Confederacy was neutrality, but in reality, it was in small ways supportive. After Lincoln allowed Rose Greenhow to return to the South, Davis sent her to Britain and France to represent Confederate interests in 1863. She settled in London to write her memoir. British fans snapped up copies of the slim volume. As Rose was returning from that tour, her ship ran aground off the coast of Wilmington, N.C., trying to escape a Union gunboat. Rose fled by rowboat, but it capsized, weighed down by the $2,000 worth of gold sewed into her underclothes.

Davis nurtured a network of Rebel operatives along Canada's eastern border with the United States, out of the reach of Union generals but just within striking distance of Northern population centers. And, it was there, in Toronto and Montreal, that a growing group of former soldiers, Confederate agents, ne'er-do-wells, and refugees gathered, eyeing their opportunities and living off the gold provided by Davis's government.

Jacob Thompson, a former Mississippi congressman, and Clement C. Clay were chosen by Davis to run the covert military operations that the Confederate president hoped would bring the North to its knees. The Confederate money directed their way by Davis was to be used for bribes, waging retaliatory warfare on the North's own territory, and even sparking counterrevolution. At all costs, Lincoln's reelection should be stopped. [7]

Joining the two were several men, many of whom Booth would come to meet during his trip to Montreal. Dr. Luke Blackburn, an expert in yellow fever; Nathaniel Beverley Tucker, an American diplomat who became a Confederate purchasing agent; and Dr. Montrose Pallen, who spied on the American consulate office. The blockade runner, Patrick C. Martin, was one of the Confederacy's principal agents in Montreal, and became a close confidant of Booth's. Another Booth contact was George N. Sanders, a radical agent and Confederate principal who had been associated with European nationalists plotting to assassinate Napoleon III of France. It's no leap of imagination to assume Booth was seeking the backing of these men. And more than that, because Booth was such a social animal, he no doubt also wanted support and companionship. He got that and more. When he left the city after a ten-day stay, he had in hand $1,500 and a list of Rebel agent contacts based in Northern Virginia, men who could assist Booth in spiriting an abducted Lincoln to Richmond. [8]

Did Booth's plan have the approval of Richmond? Had Jefferson Davis gotten wind of his plot? Because of Davis's decentralized approach to running these "black ops," there are no letters or memos with Booth's name. But the actor was famous. Even people who didn't attend theater knew of Booth, since his name had been emblazoned on theater circulars and in newspapers for five years, sometimes in the Rebel capital. The gossip mills in Confederate circles in Montreal would have been full of his name and activities. Because of that, it's very possible Davis had heard of Booth's plans, or at least of his interest in conducting his own raid. The larger question of whether Richmond had assigned Booth the job of kidnapping the Union president in the first place is similarly unanswered. No paper trail links Booth and Davis in such a plot. But in the frenzy of rapidly developing Rebel plots to strike the Union at home, it hardly even matters. The red-hot anger and desire for revenge lit by the Dahlgren Affair mobilized men to take actions they might never have otherwise considered.

The operations run from Montreal were haphazard, though one, conducted the day after the actor arrived in the city, had moderate success. Sixty-seven miles south from Montreal, a band of roughly twenty men backed by Rebel money conducted what would be the northernmost land action of the entire war. The site was St. Albans, Vermont, a small but prosperous town near the border.

The raid was led by Lieutenant Bennett Young, a twenty-one-year-old Kentuckian who had abandoned his career as a Methodist divinity student and joined the Confederate army as a private. Tall, with a head full of brown hair, hazel eyes, and evenly shaped facial features, Young was eager to establish his own reputation with a novel assignment: He would help replenish the Confederacy's rapidly diminishing coffers by robbing banks in the North.

On October 15, 1864, Young and Lieutenant William Hutchison led a small group of Confederate soldiers across the Canadian border into the small town of St. Albans. Three days later, Young walked out of his hotel and, brandishing his Navy Colt revolver in his hand, yelled out that the town was under the control of the Confederacy. Passersby stared. Some laughed. But when four Confederate raiders on horseback charged down Main Street howling the Rebel yell and firing guns, townspeople vanished from the street. Young shot and killed one of the few men who managed to fire a gun at him from an upper-story window.

Members of the raiding party burst into the city's banks. One of them grabbed a bank teller by the throat, telling employees huddled there, "You have been in the Shenandoah Valley, burned our houses, and wasted our property, and now we propose to pay you back in the same coin." The intruders required the people in the bank to swear an oath of loyalty to the Confederacy.

Young and the other raiders rode out late that afternoon with more than $200,000, nearly $8 million in today's currency. The money never made its way to Confederate coffers, as the robbers were caught, but the incident had at least some of its anticipated effect, sowing fear and distrust throughout the area.

More elaborate Confederate plans were being hatched daily. In Richmond, Davis gave approvals to a particularly convoluted one. The Confederate president believed members of a radical wing of the Democratic Party, peace Democrats, also called Copperheads, would be an important ally in his mission. Across Ohio, Iowa, Indiana, Illinois, and Michigan, thousands of antiwar dissidents joined societies with secret handshakes and symbols and pushed for peace. They called themselves the Knights of the Golden Circle, the Sons of Liberty, and the Order of the American Knights. Some served as congressmen while others operated underground. The more violent Copperheads burned government buildings and military warehouses and ransacked homes of Union soldiers. All wanted the war ended.

Davis planned to use the Copperheads to start an uprising that might help him crush Union will. To that end, he engaged a twenty-three-year-old captain from Kentucky with a boy's face and a straggly black mustache who looked eerily like John Wilkes Booth. Thomas H. Hines had already spent time operating behind the lines in the North with great success. And he was ambitious to make his mark.[9]

Months earlier, Hines had come to Davis presenting a dramatic plan of sabotage and raid in the Northwest, what came to be known as the Northwest conspiracy. It was a bold plan calling for the freeing of POWs, the looting of banks, and the setting of fires in heavily populated Northern cities. When Hines had first presented the plan, Davis had rejected it as too vengeful. Now the Rebel president thought it the perfect response to the Dahlgren raid. But Hines, despite Davis's backing, was never able to get much traction on his goals. The pacifist Copperheads refused to engage in violence or even organize in the numbers Hines believed possible.

That didn't mean that Rebel plans to take the fight to Northern states were over—far from it. In fact, the plans grew grislier. The Confederates tried their hand at biological warfare, using a plan developed by the aforementioned Luke Blackburn, a Kentucky physician expert in treating patients with yellow fever. Secretly, he collected the clothing of men who died of the disease, assuming that their shirts, pants, coats, and blankets were contaminated with the cause of yellow fever. Taking trunks of this clothing to Washington, D.C., Blackburn delivered them to an auctioneer who he hoped would sell the clothing, thus distributing contagion throughout the capital. He even hoped to get a box of infected shirts into the hands of Lincoln himself. In the end, Blackburn was unsuccessful, mainly because his science was wrong. Yellow fever is a virus transmitted by mosquitoes, not by physical contact by people who are infected.

Ironically, one plan set in motion by the Montreal operatives threatened the lives of both Booth and his brothers. A month after Booth's visit to Montreal, he and his brothers planned to perform together for the first time in Shakespeare's *Julius Caesar* at the Winter Garden in New York City. Ticket sales benefited a fund to erect a statue of the Bard in Central Park.[10]

But in the second act, strange noises emanated from the back of the theater. The audience turned, and soon the smell of smoke permeated the theater. One of the Canadian Confederate agents had set fire to his third-story room in the Lafarge House, a hotel next door to the Winter Garden. His room was located over the entrance of the theater.

A panic ensued as firefighters burst into the Lafarge. The crowd didn't calm down until an enterprising scenic artist painted the words "There is no fire. It has already been extinguished" on a large piece of canvas and placed it before the footlights. Only then did the audience return to their seats. Fortunately, no one was seriously injured.

The performance continued, picking up just thirty minutes after the disruption. The event proceeded as planned, with only a few in the audience noting John's amendment to the script. Though he played Mark Antony, he stole a line from Brutus, uttering, "Sic semper tyrannis," the motto of Virginia, which translates as "thus always to tyrants." Shakespeare had put the words into Brutus's mouth, to be said after his murder of Julius Caesar. But John added it to Mark Antony's funeral oration.

His performance in *Julius Caesar* was one of John Wilkes Booth's last. From then on, he abandoned his acting career and dedicated himself to his "noble duty." To accomplish his plot, he needed help. He turned first to two men he had known since childhood. Samuel B. Arnold was a classmate from his days at St. Timothy's Hall, now a farmworker. Michael O'Laughlen was a friend from his boyhood in Baltimore. Both men had served the Rebel army, but their exploits in the intervening years had been unimpressive.

Booth summoned the two to the Barnum Hotel in Baltimore, where he ordered cigars and wine for the table. The three hadn't seen each other since they were children, and the actor appeared larger than life. Arnold was bowled over, describing him as "a deep-thinking man of the world . . . With highly distinguishing marks of beauty, intelligence, and gentlemanly refinement." Over the next several hours the three became reacquainted. The talking grew louder as the drinking continued. Just as Arnold and O'Laughlen were evaluating Booth, so Booth was evaluating the two men, their Confederate sympathies, and their willingness to be led. When he became comfortable with the two as partners, Booth revealed his true reason for bringing them together. He wanted them to work with him on his plan to abduct Lincoln. He even had figured out locations where the president might be lightly guarded and easily spirited away to Richmond—where he could be held hostage for the exchange of prisoners—a hospital for wounded soldiers outside Washington. The two agreed to sign on. The actor had charmed and, to some measure, bullied the men into becoming the original members of his ring. He plied them with cigars, alcohol, and the offer of friendship. [11]

During his trip to Canada, Booth had established other contacts, Drs. Samuel Mudd and William McQueen, who would be critical to his plot. The two were Confederate sympathizers, locals to Charles County, a rural area Booth and his band would have to pass through on the way to Richmond from Washington. Just thirty years old, Mudd was a married farmer with four young children and a thriving medical practice. He was well regarded in the community for his kind and peaceful nature. But he led a secret life hiding Southern soldiers and delivering contraband mail. McQueen was similarly prone to Southern sympathies but older. The war had destroyed his wealth; his dozen or so slaves had escaped or been emancipated. The two were ripe for Booth's advances. But the actor needed more than just conspirators. He also needed horses, guns, and local knowledge of the roads and byways through which he would transport an abducted Lincoln.

In turn, Mudd introduced Booth to men who were more than just loyal Rebels. Confederate agents Thomas Harbin and John H. Surratt were men who had confidentially run errands for Jefferson Davis and were well apprised of sympathizers in the area. Harbin was the Confederacy's principal spy in lower Maryland and had made a name for himself when he shot his way out of an ambush by a dozen Union cavalrymen. Meeting Booth, he was at first bemused by Booth's melodramatic approach, but he became convinced of the actor's seriousness and pledged to help him abduct the president.

To gain Surratt's allegiance, Booth followed the same script he had used to secure O'Laughlen's and Arnold's loyalties, plying him first with cigars and wine as he carefully probed his true loyalties. Surratt was educated, having studied to become a priest. But when Booth met him, he had abandoned that vocation. Surratt ran his family's tavern, which sat along a smuggler's network and carried Rebel mail and contraband along with produce from his family farm to Washington. For cover, he carried a glowing biography of John Brown.[12] Surratt claimed to know every crossroad, bypass, and hiding place in northern Virginia and southern Maryland.

Between the two of them, Mudd and Surratt introduced Booth to the people who would complete his league of conspirators: George A. Atzerodt; Thomas A. Jones; Harbin's brother-in-law, David E. Herold; and likely Lewis Powell.

Booth employed all his acting skills to bring the network together and keep them on board. This was no small feat. What he was proposing, which Surratt would later describe as "unparalleled in its audacity," was a dangerous mission that could go wrong any number of ways. Though abducting a sitting president and spiriting him away to what was at the moment a separate country was risky, the conspirators believed it was better than waiting for the Union to win the war, which increasingly seemed inevitable. Most regarded their actions as honorable.

Booth pursued the idea with an intensity and near recklessness that at times shook his co-conspirators' resolve. It didn't help that Booth was drinking heavily, dogged by the habit that had burdened his father. He was also prone to mood swings. The crisp physique that thrilled audience members during his theater years was disappearing, his body growing bulkier. But his new circle of conspirators hadn't known him long enough in his adult years to compare his puffy and pale countenance to that of his prewar visage. Ultimately, Booth's persistence and their own desire for a quick end to the war brought them on board and kept them loyal.

During the fall of 1864, the actor was energized by his new criminal project, traveling between New York, Washington, and rural Maryland securing the tools, weapons, and horses his team would need. He wrote to his mother, explaining why he had decided to engage in such a dangerous mission. The letter wouldn't be delivered in time for her to stop him, but the words make it clear he was committed to a duty for the "sake of liberty and humanity due my country."[13]

For the most part, the circle's efforts were an abject failure. Over the first three months of 1865, Booth and his band attempted to kidnap Lincoln three times and failed three times. First, Booth planned to seize the president at a performance by Edwin Forrest, the preeminent actor of his day and a draw for Lincoln, well known for his love of theater. Booth had access to a steady stream of information about the performance, including famous members of the audience, because he roomed with the stage manager and John McCullough, an actor in the company whom Booth had known for a long time. It seemed like a perfect setup for Booth to achieve his goals but it failed. The reasons were unclear, but Lincoln never showed up at the theater that night, disappointing the actors and Booth. [14]

The next attempt to abduct Lincoln occurred at the Campbell Hospital, a military facility on the city's northern edge, where Booth expected Lincoln to attend a performance by the hospital's amateur acting troupe on March 17, St. Patrick's Day. Booth's conspirators assembled at a nearby restaurant, carbines at the ready to spirit the president out of the city. But Booth had gotten it wrong. The president wasn't coming to the hospital, but was speaking at the actor's own hotel, the National. Booth, agitated and angry, rode back into town quickly enough to catch the speech. As Lincoln spoke, the actor stared at him, anger pouring from his eyes. His performance was so intense people there took note.

Resentful and frustrated, the gang scattered until Booth summoned them again on March 25, telling them that the *Washington Evening Star* was reporting First Lady Mary Lincoln had secured tickets for an opera at Ford's Theatre on March 29. But again, Booth's information was wrong. The president was at the front and didn't return to the city until April 9. Failure again.

The team was disintegrating. Surratt was nowhere to be found. Herold talked of traveling to the Idaho Territory. Arnold wanted to pull out altogether. At a meeting with Arnold and O'Laughlen at the National Hotel, Booth seemed defeated. He was done with the business of abduction and planned to return to acting. He told the men to keep their weapons.

The plan to abduct Lincoln was officially over. Booth walked away.

SWELTERING SEA OF FIRE

The war had grown more savage than ever during the spring of 1864. Casualties were appalling. Sixty-five thousand Union soldiers and 35,000 Confederates were injured or died in little more than a four-week period. Grant had attempted to leverage an opportunity to take Richmond by sending his army to move on the capitol from a small perch at Cold Harbor, ten miles northeast of Richmond. His goal was to move quickly and decisively but he was slowed by bickering commanders. Troop movements took longer than he expected. On June 3, he launched a massive assault with 50,000 soldiers, but it ground to a halt in only a couple of hours. A lack of accurate intelligence led Grant to believe that Confederate defenses at Cold Harbor were light, and he had no knowledge of the elaborate fortified defensive works his army would encounter. Rebel soldiers had buried themselves deep in the Virginia swamp and built a labyrinth of trenches. They shot Union soldiers by the tens of thousands, littering the ground with the dead and wounded. A Copperhead newspaper called out Grant as a butcher, a name that stuck. Cold Harbor became a byword for senseless slaughter.

The experience stung Grant, and for a time, he appeared depressed and saddened. Lines began to etch his face. But then, as he often did, the general took lessons from the experience and executed a 180-degree change in strategy. Instead of a direct attack of the Army of Northern Virginia, he would focus on a siege of the city of Petersburg, the second largest Virginia city and a critical supplier to both Richmond and the Confederate army. The Petersburg Campaign played out over eleven months as Grant closed down five railroad routes into the city one by one. Grant believed that taking the critical city would ultimately result in the fall of Richmond and Lee's army.

Grant's first step in that campaign was a miraculous feat of engineering that would allow his army to quickly cross the massive 2,000-foot-wide James River, a barrier that had confounded many during the war. His men constructed a bridge by stringing a series of flat-bottomed pontoon boats across the river and anchoring them in place. Grant's cavalry and army, their cannons and guns, crossed the river along a wooden walkway installed by the engineers.

The rest of the campaign would not be so easy.

The Union army had set up its supply headquarters twenty-two miles east of Richmond at City Point. The scene there stood in sharp contrast to that of the starving Confederate forces at Petersburg. Located at the confluence of the James and Appomattox Rivers, the site was a hub of activity. Warehouses were stocked with supplies, ammunition and equipment. Two hundred Union ships crowded eight wharves. Hospitals cared for the Union wounded and sick. It was here that Grant had set his headquarters, and here that Elizabeth's reports arrived like clockwork, giving BMI agents critical information about the enemy's strength and planning. In the evenings, when Grant was not in the field, he and his officers on duty would gather, sitting around a fire, smoking and discussing the latest information from deserters and interesting stories from Rebel newspapers. Elizabeth's reports were always of particular interest.

The Petersburg siege would require a talent that Grant had seldom displayed, patience. His plan was to starve Lee and his forces, who were embedded in zigzagging trenches four to six feet below the ground's surface. As the siege progressed, the trenches became muddy ditches filled with lice and rats. Union forces easily outnumbered Rebel ones,

115,000 men compared to just 60,000. The battle lines stretched seventy miles as Grant forced Lee to string out his army over a wider and wider front. When winter set in, many of Lee's men holed up in town. Tens of thousands abandoned the army. Grant began shutting down rail lines one by one. It took nine long months for the siege to bear fruit.

It was during this time that Elizabeth's ring forwarded information that illuminated the sad state of Rebel forces. Lee had ordered the men of Richmond's fire brigade to round up able-bodied men in the city to reinforce Rebel forces. There were so few, in fact, that a blind man was said to have been one of those corralled. Likewise, the ring reported that the city's major iron manufacturer was out of iron and therefore unable to produce nails or spikes. The reports encouraged the Union officers sitting around the City Point campfire, but it was the ring's reports on the location of Jubal Early's Rebel Army of the Valley that allowed them to take action. Early's job was to threaten Washington and harass Union forces in the Shenandoah Valley to prevent Grant from focusing all his efforts on Lee in Petersburg and taking Richmond. Elizabeth and her ring kept Grant informed of the flow of reinforcements back and forth between Early's army and Lee's. By August, the ring learned and reported that Early was being denied supplies and being told to "subsist himself or starve." Grant ordered Phil Sheridan to attack Early's army and destroy the crops in fields sustaining them. Another critical coup by the ring was intelligence gathered at a meeting of prominent Rebel generals at the Confederate white house. It's unknown whether Elizabeth's servant Mary was responsible for gathering information from that meeting, but it was clear from the report that Lee's options were narrowing and the Rebel lines protecting Petersburg were growing thinner and thinner. The ring followed up with reports on rumors that Richmond itself would be evacuated.[1]

As the siege went on, Elizabeth's position became more and more precarious, though her pace of reporting only increased. In the fall of 1864, Confederate forces investigated Elizabeth and her mother. This time, the government finally had a source who could give them a glimpse directly into the Van Lew household. Elizabeth's sister-in-law, Mary C. Van Lew, gave a deposition to Confederate authorities describing Elizabeth as disloyal and citing as evidence the fact she had sent a Black woman north to be educated.

Over a few tense days, Elizabeth must have worried that their entire operation would be exposed. However, the charges were dropped. Lack of evidence was one reason, but a deeper one was revealed in one tribunal member's dismissal of the case: "Miss Elizabeth Van Lew of this city is very unfriendly in her sentiments toward the Gov't . . . [but] it does not appear that she has ever done anything to infirm the cause—Like most of her sex she seems to have talked freely—and in the presence of female friends, who have informed on her. The question is whether she shall be sent beyond the lines because of her opinion?"[2]

Elizabeth had once again benefited from being underestimated. Mary's charges were deemed insufficient to merit action. But the rupture between Elizabeth and Mary would never be mended. Mary's daughter, Eliza, was taken from her mother by John and brought to Church Hill to live, where Elizabeth raised her. Months later, Confederates would conduct another roundup of Unionists, throwing them in prison cells where they would languish until the evacuation of Richmond. Elizabeth was not among them, but Lohmann was. Meanwhile the stranglehold that Grant was putting on Confederate resources was starving the Van Lew household. Elizabeth noted as much in a missive to City Point. "May God bless you and bring you soon to deliver us," she wrote. "We are all in an awful situation here. There is great want of food." Even so, the ring was resolved to continue until the bitter end. It was soon in coming.

By March 1865, Grant, emboldened by Elizabeth's reports about the weakening Rebel army, prepared for a final assault. On March 24, the general launched a massive final bombardment. Hundreds of artillery pieces, heavy siege guns and mortars, unleashed a devastating and continuous barrage on Confederate lines. The sound created by the assault was so loud that Elizabeth could hear it twenty-four miles away in Richmond. Lee's final supply line was taken April 1 at the Battle of Five Forks, a resounding win for the Union as lines of Rebel soldiers weakened by hunger disintegrated under Union attack. Petersburg was stormed by a flying wedge of Union soldiers. As his generals captured thousands of Confederate soldiers, Grant rode his horse into the elaborate defenses of the Confederate army. Union soldiers seeing him erupted in a thunderous cheer. Lee retreated with a small group of Union soldiers.

COMMUNION WAS CELEBRATED THAT WARM SUNDAY MORNING APRIL 2, 1865, at St. Paul's Episcopal in Richmond, well known as the church home of Jefferson Davis and Robert E. Lee. Davis himself was on hand for the service, his lanky frame perched on a wooden pew. The Greek Revival style church, located just across the street from the State Capitol, was where Davis had been sworn in as president three years before. But this Sunday he wasn't likely thinking of those early ebullient and exciting days.

He knew the siege of Petersburg was floundering and may even have been praying for a miracle when a telegram was thrust into his hands by a courier from the nearby Confederate war offices. Lee had written the telegram as he waited for the darkness of night to cover his army's withdrawal. "I see no prospect of doing more than holding our position here til night. I am not certain I can do that. I advise that all preparations be made for leaving Richmond tonight."[3]

The meaning was simple. Lee was telling Davis that in a few short hours the protective screen of Confederate soldiers separating Richmond from the Union army would be gone. The very people Davis had sworn to protect would be vulnerable and the fate of the Confederacy very nearly sealed. The government had to flee.

Davis rose, put on his coat, and walked calmly out of the church, watched by the entire congregation. One of them, a Confederate lady, described the scene in her diary, "He rose instantly, and walked down the aisle—his face set, so we could read nothing."[4] The meaning of his exit wasn't clear to the congregation, but it was unnerving even so. One by one, the members of the church stood and followed him out the door.

For days, Davis and his cabinet had been some of the few in Richmond who understood the full details of the Army of Northern Virginia's perilous situation. Over the course of that Sunday, though, everyone in Richmond would face that reality. Summoning up the feelings of many Southerners, especially those in the capitol, Josiah Gorgas, a Confederate general, wrote this: "The crisis of our fate is rapidly approaching." [5]

Already, some of Richmond's well-heeled had left. Diarist Mary Chesnut, whose husband had served as an aide to Davis, had left the year before to nurse soldiers in a Columbia, South Carolina, hospital. Varina Davis, wife of the Confederate president, was gone as well. She could have no illusions about the future after her husband wrote her these words: "If I live you can come to me when the struggle is ended, but I do not expect to survive the end of Constitutional liberty."

Elizabeth had not run. She remained at the mansion at Church Hill even though she no doubt understood the extent of the threat to Richmond. She may have known as much of the battles and their outcomes as Davis, since she had sources on both sides. She, too, had to prepare for assault. If the government was leaving, her Unionist network must be protected during the Rebels' departure. Any kind of change, even a welcome one, could be dangerous.

After leaving church, Davis began his preparations to evacuate, assembling his cabinet in his office in the capitol building to discuss evacuation. There he updated them on Lee's position and informed them that they must pack, load, and leave the city within twelve hours. The plan was for the government to abandon Richmond. Davis and most of his cabinet would take a train to Danville along Virginia's southern border. Lee's army would move west, where he planned to regroup and consolidate.

But first the government's money, or what was left of it, anyway, must be moved from the imperiled capital. Government gold and silver and Confederate coins were stashed aboard trains for evacuation. Official documents were burned outside government offices. There was no official announcement of the government's departure until four p.m. April 2, barely four hours since Davis had received his telegram to evacuate from Lee. Until that time, crowds gathered at popular hotels and near government offices to hear news of Richmond's prospects. Some wept openly. As it became clear the government was fleeing, residents prepared to go as well. Residents fled on horseback, in carts or carriages, aboard trains, on canal barges, skiffs, and boats. The streets filled with people feverishly preparing and, at the same time, fearing their plans might be interrupted at any moment by flanks of blue-suited soldiers bearing long guns or cavalry hoisting sabers.

Still, some refused to believe the news. One of those was Virginia governor William Smith. At a late-afternoon meeting of the city council, he told all assembled that Lee had not in fact lost Petersburg and that victory was at hand—a Confederate one. His words did not persuade the council, and Mayor Michael Mayo informed the group they must prepare for the evacuation of the Confederate government and find ways to keep the remaining populace safe. To that end, he asked that two companies of militia remain behind to keep order in the city. And the council decided—fatefully, as it turned out—to destroy all alcoholic liquors to prevent soldiers and residents from getting drunk and rampaging in the streets.

As night fell, hysteria and panic rose. The trouble started at midnight, when the militia struggled to find an expedient way to follow Mayo's orders to destroy alcohol in the city's saloons and warehouses. It was a large task and there was little time. An anxious and exhausted Richmond lady named Agnes, the same one who had written about the city's food riot, described the scene from her room at Spotswood Hotel in a letter:

> I expected to sit by my window all night as you always do in a troubled time, but sleep overtook me. I had slept, but not undressed, when a loud explosion shook the house—then another. There were crashing sounds of falling glass from the concussion . . . All was

commotion in the streets, and agitation at the hotel. The city government had dragged hogsheads of liquor from shops, knocked in the heads, and poured spirits in the gutters. They ran with brandy, whiskey, and rum, and men, women, and boys rushed out with buckets, pails, pitchers, and in the lower streets, hats and boots, to be filled. [6]

When Confederate soldiers moved to destroy the city's tobacco, cotton, and food stores to keep them from falling into the hands of Federal soldiers hours later, these now-drunk city residents who had endured privation and hunger for months saw for themselves the great stores of goods accumulated by the government in warehouses throughout the city. Smoked meat, flour, sugar, and coffee—basic goods that had been unavailable or simply too expensive for many Richmonders—were there for the taking.

Using every wheelbarrow and cart they could find, the mob rushed from one storehouse to another, loading their conveyances with supplies and then dumping what they'd collected altogether when something more valuable was spotted. The scale of looting surged as some in the crowd commanded furniture wagons and drays.

Ladies who earlier in the war had once sent wounded Confederate soldiers elaborate meals on silver trays loaded with the finest china and damask napkins from their own kitchens now loaded their arms with boxes of stolen loot and scurried through the streets on foot. Confederate soldiers joined the melee. Some who had recently been released from holding the city's lines ran frantically through the streets, their faces illuminated by the firelight.

BACK ON CHURCH HILL, ELIZABETH OPENED HER DOORS TO UNIONISTS seeking shelter. Three of them were members of her ring who had been imprisoned at Castle Thunder for helping refugees cross into Union lines and giving secrets of Rebel troop movements to the Federals. As a last act before fleeing, the Confederate government had ordered prison inmates to be moved south to avoid being claimed by the advancing Federal army.

F.W.E. Lohmann and two other Unionist agents, John Hancock and William White, were hustled that night through the chaotic streets by Confederate guards. But when those wardens paused to drink whiskey from the gutters, the trio slipped away, running to Church Hill. It's not clear whether all three made their way to Elizabeth's house. But once inside the mansion, they would have joined Unionists of all sorts who had gathered there, seeking shelter and community against the storm that raged on Richmond's streets. That night, beds were hastily set up in the parlor to accommodate the refugees.

Elizabeth had not abandoned her neighbors. She allowed them to stash their gold, jewelry, and china in her closets. They feared Federal troops or looters might steal their heirlooms from their houses and judged that Elizabeth's Northern roots might protect their valuables. But while she was still willing to assist her neighbors, she didn't necessarily trust them. That night, Elizabeth shut off the lights in the room where her guests were sequestered, worried that it might attract unwanted attention from neighbors.[7]

WHILE ELIZABETH TENDED HER REBEL NEIGHBORS AND UNIONISTS, IN the city, the destruction of anything that might be valuable to the Federal army was under way. By one o'clock in the morning, Mayor Mayo was ordered to set the city's four principal tobacco warehouses on fire. The mayor resisted but was overruled. Already several boats, including the gunboat *Patrick Henry,* were set ablaze, shooting fireworks above as the fire hit ammunition stores.

The arsonists didn't stop at the warehouses but also set ablaze houses in the area, turning the entire downtown core of Richmond into one large conflagration. The liquor in the streets and alleys and along the curbs served as incendiary agents. Laboratories, arsenals, artillery shops—a two-mile stretch of the city—blazed. The pride of

Richmond, the Tredegar Iron Works, survived, but the navy yard at Rocketts did not. At 4:30 a.m., the earth shook as Confederate ships were set on fire in the James River, their artillery exploding, the blast so strong it knocked down nearby buildings.

Three of the city's bridges were in flames, the entire skyline illuminated by fire, and beneath them all, the James River sparkled. "Every now and then, as a magazine exploded, a column of white smoke rose up as high as the eye could reach instantaneously followed by a deafening sound. The earth seemed to rock and tremble as with the shock of an earthquake, and immediately afterward hundreds of shells would explode in the air and send their iron spray down far below the bridge. As the immense magazines of cartridges ignited, the rattle of thousands of musketry would follow, and then all was still for a moment, except the dull roar and crackle of the fast spreading fires," wrote Captain Clement Sulivane, who commanded the last Confederate force in the city.[8]

The concussions of the explosions would have been felt on Church Hill. Elizabeth listened to it all. The Union loyalist saw the hand of God in the scene below and noted the irony that the destruction wasn't caused by Federal forces but by Confederates. She wrote: "Square after square of stores, dwelling houses and factories, warehouses, hotels, banks and bridges, all wrapped in fire, filled the sky with clouds of smoke as incense from the land for its deliverance."[9]

Sulivane was charged with holding Mayo's Bridge until General Lee's rear guard crossed and destroying it after. While he waited, he watched the looting and torching of the city, mesmerized by the destruction while his men placed kerosene, tar, and pine knots on the last standing span of the James River. Finally, as dawn approached, the troops appeared, a Confederate cavalry unit who thundered across the bridge. After they passed, Sulivane lit the fuse and crossed ahead of the flames; and sending his command on its way, he turned to watch nearly the whole of the city south of Main Street blazing, smoke drifting above the skyline. Then the last Confederate soldier turned to go and left Richmond.

Sunrise brought no comfort. Instead, the extent of the destruction was revealed, and fires continued to rage. Reported the *Whig*, "At sunrise on Monday morning, Richmond presented a spectacle that we hope never to witness again. The last of the Confederate offices is gone, the air lurid with smoke and flame of hundreds of houses sweltering in a sea of fire." The blackened remains of furniture and household goods were trampled in the street. Twenty blocks of the city had been reduced to smoking ruins, brick rubble, blackened walls, and broken chimneys.

ACROSS THE NO-MAN'S-LAND OUTSIDE THE CITY'S PERIPHERY, FEDERAL forces had watched a red glow expand over the Richmond skyline early that morning. They could hear ordnance stores exploding. General Godfrey Weitzel of the Union forces, a young German civil engineer from Cincinnati, charged with bringing the city under control, had heard about the evacuation at 3:00 a.m. By 4:30, he informed Grant he would take the city. He ordered breakfast for his troops before proceeding into town, expecting that there might be fight left in the remaining citizenry of Richmond. There was not.

Weitzel first sent in a small contingent of forty of his headquarters' cavalry under Major A. H. Stevens and Major E. E. Graves to receive the surrender of the city. They were followed by the all-Black 25th Army Corps, the 24th Army Corps, and Weitzel's 5th Massachusetts Cavalry, each ordered to take different routes and to halt just outside the city. The infantry was set to follow.

After four years of furious fighting, the capital of the Confederacy quietly surrendered. Stevens's and Graves's men were met by Mayo outside the city gates, who handed them the following letter:

General, the Army of the Confederate Government having abandoned the City of Richmond, I respectfully request that you take possession of it with an organized force, to preserve order and protect women and children and property,

Respectfully, Joseph Mayo, Mayor.[10]

Stevens accepted the letter on behalf of Weitzel and set out for the city, entering it just before seven a.m., riding up Main Street and then into Capitol Square. His force's first piece of business was pulling down two Confederate flags and hoisting the Stars and Stripes. "We knew what that meant," wrote Richmond resident Nellie Grey. "The song 'On to Richmond!' was ended. Richmond was in the hands of the Federals. We covered our faces and cried aloud. All through the house was the sound of sobbing."[11]

"Richmond has fallen," wrote a despondent Mary Chesnut. "I have no heart to write about it. Grant broke through our lines. Sherman cut through them. Stoneman is this side of Danville. They are too many for us. Everything is lost in Richmond, even our archives. Blue-black is our horizon." [12]

The rest of the Union force followed, with Weitzel arriving at 8:15 a.m. to receive Mayo's letter of surrender. Standing atop the eastern porch of the Capitol, Weitzel and Mayo, surrounded by Union division commanders, made the transfer official. By 10:00 a.m., the city was teeming with blue uniforms.

At the Church Hill mansion that morning, Elizabeth's nieces Annie, who was just ten, and her younger sister, Eliza, had awakened early, running to the top floors of the house in their pajamas to see the city in flames. They dressed quickly and came downstairs, looking in on the escaped prisoners and Unionists in the parlor. As they seated themselves at the breakfast table, Annie recalled hearing music coming from outside the house. Someone was playing the tune "Yankee Doodle." "Sister and I ran to the bottom of the garden and were overjoyed to see the Yankees marching up Main Street," she wrote later. [13]

It's doubtful that Elizabeth had slept at all that night. She may have walked the rooms of the mansion, checking on her overnight guests, waiting for word of the Union army's entry into Richmond. But the morning brought joy. She and her family—in fact, the entire household—had survived, and what's more, at long last the city, her home, and the spy ring would be under the protection of the Union government. The fear of being dragged into one of the city's ghastly prisons or being hanged for her work as a spy—all of that was now lifted. She ran to her attic, pulling out the Union flag she had carefully hidden throughout the war, sewing in stars for each of the states admitted to the Union during those years. Elizabeth had worked so hard for this moment, and she was feeling more than simple relief. Richmond's fall was both a deliverance from threat and a vindication of her views. The forces of disunion, the fire-eaters, and the Rebels had been beat, and she had helped bring it all to fruition. Her hometown was in shambles, but the Union was preserved and slavery quashed. She ordered the flag raised in her front yard. How wonderful at last to be able to display this standard!

Outside, a crowd of neighbors assembled, watching the Stars and Stripes, a hated symbol, rising above their homes. Having lost so much, they felt this last insult to be too much. The rabble turned menacing as one of the neighbors threatened to set the mansion on fire. Elizabeth, filled with a winner's confidence and conviction, went out onto her front porch, anger flashing in her eyes, and told the crowd, "Lower that flag or hurt one bit of this property and I'll see that General Butler pays you back in kind—every one of you!"[14] The small woman's upraised fist dispersed the crowd.

Meanwhile, on the streets of Richmond, Union soldiers set about quenching the fire that had consumed so much of the city. As the firefighting equipment had been rendered useless by the night's rioting, Union soldiers and the few able-bodied Richmond men remaining created a break between the fire and untouched buildings, tearing down walls and destroying other buildings.

Weitzel would be one of the first Union commanders to run Richmond, but he would do so for just ten days. He was relieved after his administration of the issue of a prayer in Episcopal churches sparked controversy among Union officials. Apparently, the Episcopal ministers of the time prayed for the president of the Confederate States, not the president of the United States; and Weitzel failed to successfully resolve that problem. The city would not be free from military rule for another four years, not until January 28, 1870, when the commonwealth was readmitted to the Union. (The city's government was civilian during that period and retained many policies to clamp down on the Black population.)

That afternoon, Elizabeth, accompanied by Annie and her sister, went into the city, the three of them deliriously greeting Union soldiers on Main Street, and according to ten-year-old Annie's account, "we spoke to many of them, and even hugged the horses. I will never forget how she [Elizabeth] looked with that huge bonnet on which we thought was very fashionable."[15]

And just as some wept at the site of the Yankees in their city, others celebrated. Elizabeth recounted "wild bursts of welcome from the negroes and many whites as they poured in. In an incredibly short space of time, as by magic, every part of the city was under the most kind and respected of guards."[16] Elizabeth regarded the destruction of the city with the eye of someone who not only loved her hometown but had been a member of a class responsible for its expansion and development. "The loss of public and private property was immense. Our beautiful flour mills, the largest in the world and the pride of our city, were destroyed. Square after square of stores, dwelling houses and factories, warehouses, banks, hotels, bridges, all wrapped in fire, filled the sky with clouds of smoke as incense from the land for its deliverance."

Not until four p.m. that day were the fires finally quenched. In total, twenty city blocks and as many as a thousand buildings were lost to the conflagration. That night a Union curfew was ordered, and those who could not return to their homes camped in Capitol Square.

Early the following morning, Sheridan reported the capture of 1,200 Confederate troops and a massive trail of munitions and supplies left by the retreating Army of Northern Virginia. In Richmond, repairs were already under way. Newly emancipated freedmen began building a new span across the James and clearing up debris. Relief organizations arrived to care for the homeless and hungry.

And that afternoon, Richmond residents witnessed a spectacle they probably never thought they would see. At three o'clock, President Lincoln, who had been at City Point, came to Richmond with his son Tad. Getting to the city, however, was a trial for the president. A grand entry had been planned by Rear Admiral David Dixon Porter and the beginning went well enough. Aboard Porter's flagship, the *Malvern,* the president sailed by cheering sailors and Union gunboats, but in short order, problems arose. Confederate boats sunk in the river made passage by the steamer impossible. Lincoln was transferred to a barge, which was tugged upstream, but again Confederate obstructions blocked passage. Finally, the president was rowed onto Rocketts Landing, where only a small group of sailors and Porter were on hand to protect him. They were still two miles from Capitol Square, and nearly immediately the tall form of the president was recognized and surrounded.

"No electric wire could have carried the news of the President's arrival sooner than it was circulated through Richmond. As far as the eye could see, the streets were alive with negroes and poor whites rushing in our direction, and the crowd increased so fast that I had to surround the President with sailors with fixed bayonets to keep them off . . . They all wanted to shake hands with Mr. Lincoln or his coat tail or even to kneel and kiss his boots."[17] But the president himself shook them off, saying it was inappropriate for them to kneel to anyone other than God. He continued walking, making his way to Capitol Square. With each step, more Blacks joined him. When he reached the Confederate White House, he turned to the ebullient crowd and bowed, a respectful gesture thanking the loyal Union people and particularly Blacks, who had done so much to bring about the result they were celebrating that day, the fall of the capital of the Confederacy.

Carl Sandburg foreshadowed events only days away now, writing this: "Any one of many kinds of fools could have taken a potshot at Lincoln." [18]

A military escort was eventually found and accompanied the president inside the Confederate White House, which had become the site of Union military headquarters. Lincoln was immediately approached by a delegation of Southerners who wanted to discuss a negotiated peace settlement, but the president said that was impossible until the Confederate army laid down its weapons. Lincoln apparently had that discussion from Davis's office, sitting in his chair.

From there, the president toured the city, visiting Libby Prison, for which Elizabeth had so eloquently argued for relief, and the State Capitol. Weitzel asked the president how he was to treat the conquered Southern citizens. Said Lincoln, "If I were in your place, I'd let 'em up easy." By nightfall he was back at Porter's steamer, much to the relief of Union military officials. Four days later, Robert E. Lee surrendered.

For Elizabeth, the days were a validation of her work that she had reason to believe she might not live to see. "What a moment! Avenging wrath appeased in flames! The chains, the shackles fell from thousands of captives . . . Civilization advanced a century."[19]

STOUT MEN CRIED

After Richmond fell, Elizabeth's social position changed dramatically. Suddenly a long line of gentlemen callers made their way to the mansion on horseback, their blue uniforms making their allegiances perfectly clear. The best known was Colonel Ely S. Parker, a member of the Seneca tribe and a key staff officer for General Grant who drafted Lee's surrender. His younger brother, Colonel D. B. Parker, also a member of Grant's staff, came by as well. Major General Marsena Patrick, who would soon run Richmond as provost marshal, paid his respects to the spymaster, too. Elizabeth also got to meet face-to-face for the first time her Union secret service boss, George Sharpe. Grant, grateful for Elizabeth's work for him during the war, ordered a cordon of security guards be placed around the Church Hill mansion and instructed his staff to supply all her needs.

The house was full of Unionists. Members of her spy ring congregated in the halls, laughing and reminiscing, while her close associate F.W.E. Lohmann recovered in one of the mansion's bedrooms from wounds he had received as a prisoner in Castle Thunder. The notorious Libby Prison clerk Erasmus Ross, his cover now intentionally blown, was on hand. Friends and fellow travelers came from all over the city to congratulate Elizabeth. After all, her hard work had prevented many of them from being arrested, tortured, or worse. They may also have ventured to Church Hill to get a look at the new guard who would be in charge of the city for five long years.

The house they saw may not have resembled the mansion they had known in its antebellum years. Elizabeth and her mother had given away much of what they owned—not just money, but also household goods, for as the war ground on, even common items like blankets became difficult to come by. The rooms may have been somewhat bare as a result. No doubt the Confederate flag Elizabeth had hung in the massive eighteen-foot entry hall had long ago been taken down. There was no need to disguise her allegiances now.

There was just one visitor who had yet to cross the Church Hill threshold, General Grant. Elizabeth was eager to meet face-to-face with the man whom she had come to respect and admire over the many months of working for him. Also, she wanted to plead the case for supplying the needs of fellow Unionist spies who had given so much during the war. Elizabeth herself was near destitute.

Then one afternoon just before the general was leaving the city, he and Julia Grant came to the mansion for tea and dinner. How happy and proud Elizabeth must have been to receive them. The petite Elizabeth would have been one of the few people that Grant would have towered over. Social customs of the time may have prevented a warm embrace, but they may have ignored those strictures. Grant may have simply taken her hands in his and thanked her heartily for her work, his bright blue eyes shining directly into hers.

What followed was a party. According to Lohmann family lore, twenty-five people attended the dinner, sitting at Elizabeth's dining table, where her best china had been laid out to welcome visitors. Lohmann and his younger brother John were there, as was William Rowley, other members of the spy ring, and even General Weitzel, who was a friend of Grant's. Mary Richards was no doubt in attendance. Members of the underground who had unearthed Ulric Dahlgren from his grave and serenaded his body with hymns sat with Grant and considered their good fortune over glasses of champagne poured into Elizabeth's finest crystal glasses. (It's not likely Grant partook of the champagne.) A bowl of cut-up fruit drew surprised gasps. Most had not seen fresh fruit in months. Despite the privations of Richmond, the meal Elizabeth served was a feast. The menu included beef, turkey, mashed potatoes with butter, corn, squash, and string beans. Apple pie and coffee came after the meal. Grant may well have stood to toast Elizabeth and her ring of spies, thanking them for their courage and sacrifice, sharing that their contributions were critical to the Union's success.[1]

The general and his wife stayed overnight, no doubt sleeping in Elizabeth's best guest room. The next morning, over cups of tea served on the porch, Grant reassured Elizabeth he would see to getting the government to reimburse her and her ring for their losses, and outlined the steps they would need to take to file claims.[2]

And then they were gone. Elizabeth and her mother must have shared a quiet moment of reflection and satisfaction. The spymaster snapped up the calling card Grant left behind and held on to it for the rest of her life.[3]

But Elizabeth did not consider her work done. In fact, even as the Union army doused the flames of the fire that consumed Richmond and cleared the streets of debris and litter, she headed to the State Capitol and took historical documents that she worried might go missing. Some could implicate members of her ring, whom she hoped to keep safe, but she also grabbed the papers of John Brown, which had been seized before the war.

Beyond her doorstep, the city's residents grieved their personal losses and pondered their futures. The depth of Elizabeth's betrayal was clear. Her success stood in contrast to Richmond's ruin. The capital city, once the pride of the South, had been reduced to broken buildings and rubble, Confederate stragglers and occupying soldiers. The few ladies of Richmond left behind were shell-shocked by the sight of blue-suited soldiers and cavalry on their city streets. Union artillery dashing up Broad Street were pulled by well-fed horses so stout that one woman wrote it was the first time she truly understood what Rebel armies had been up against.

Just as Elizabeth was celebrating in a city that mourned, Booth was in Washington, nursing his hatred, disconsolate against a backdrop of public celebrations and euphoria. The atmosphere in Washington was Richmond's opposite in nearly every way. At dawn the day after Lee's surrender, as an early morning mist still enveloped the city, its streets reverberated with a huge boom. A 500-gun salute ordered by Secretary of War Stanton to celebrate the laying down of arms shattered windows in Lafayette Square as the concussion rolled through the city's neighborhoods. Government workers were furloughed for the day and celebratory bonfires were lit throughout town. The Stars and Stripes were proudly displayed from Georgetown to Capitol Hill. Children chanted and cheered. Men and women once bowed with worry danced in the streets, hooted, and hollered. Many wept.[4]

That night the capital was bathed in the light of thousands of flickering candles, celebrating victory. Washingtonians walked through the streets listening to the sounds of bands and firecrackers exploding. The new iron dome of the capitol had finally been erected. The natural place for the crowd to gather was the White House. "Speech, speech!" yelled the onlookers, demanding Lincoln come and address them. But the president didn't want to give a speech that night. In fact, he was preparing an address for another night that might not satisfy this celebratory crowd. He wanted to talk about what should happen after the war.

Even so, the president appeared at a second-story window, where he was met with exuberant cheers from the thousands that gathered. People threw their hats in the air and ladies waved their handkerchiefs. Instead of a ponderous speech, Lincoln greeted the crowds and then requested that the band play the Southern anthem "Dixie."

"I have always thought 'Dixie' one of the best tunes I have ever heard," the president said, adding that though the South had appropriated the song, he believed it to be the North's "lawful prize." The crowd roared its approval.

The speech Lincoln yearned to give was delivered two nights later as another massive crowd gathered in candlelight streaming from the windows of the White House. Rain falling onto the crowd's umbrellas set up a steady thrumming as they waited. The skies were inky dark. Lit from behind, Lincoln appeared silhouetted when he finally moved into the second-story window at the front of the building, a golden glow surrounding his form. Waves of applause poured from the audience.

In his hand he held the pages of a speech, written down to make sure his words would be delivered as planned. A taper held by a journalist named Noah Brooks illuminated the carefully chosen words. At the president's feet, his son, Tad, collected the pages as his father dropped them one by one after reading.

The speech contained none of the soaring rhetorical flourishes that Lincoln had become known for. Instead, it was a policy tract, and a plea that the country award voting rights to Blacks, especially literate Blacks who had "served our cause as soldiers."[5] Nearly 200,000 Black men had served in the Union army, representing 10 percent of total Union forces. They had fought in some of the bloodiest engagements of the war. Three regiments of the United States Colored Troops had participated in the Battle of Cold Harbor. It was a thank-you that was overdue.

John Wilkes Booth was in the crowd that night, standing with his co-conspirators, Lewis Powell and David Herold. Booth begged Powell to shoot the president when he first appeared at the window. Powell demurred and strode off. Booth listened to the speech, his anger growing as the president implored the country to give Blacks the vote. Turning to Herold, he muttered, "Now by God! I will put him through." Later that night he forecast that the speech was the last Lincoln would ever make. An idea nagging at Booth's brain for months grew more urgent. It was too late to abduct the president, he decided. Assassination was the only way forward. His conspirators would take some convincing of the change of plan.[6] He would hound and badger them into complying with his dark vision.

In the days before the speech, Lincoln had been obsessed by his own dark thoughts. He shared with Mary and his bodyguard Ward Lamon a dream that had disturbed him. In it, he arose from his bed in the middle of the night to the sounds of sobbing. Walking to find the source of the weeping, he moved from room to room. Finally, on entering the White House's East Room, he saw an open casket, where a corpse rested. When Lincoln asked one of the guards who was in the coffin, the guard said the president had been killed by an assassin. Mary was aghast at the dream, and Lincoln attempted to reassure her and Lamon, explaining that some "other fellow" was killed, not himself. [7]

Lincoln shook off his grim dream and spent the morning of Good Friday, April 14, attending the regularly scheduled cabinet meeting in which members discussed how to reestablish law and order in the Southern states. Lincoln favored a lenient approach to the men who had led the rebellion. Enough lives, he said, had already been sacrificed. He found time to give advice to his son Robert, suggesting he leave the military and finish his education. Lincoln met with friends and even took a carriage ride with Mary, just the two of them. By all accounts he was cheerful and happy.

Meanwhile, Booth spent the morning writing a letter to his mother about the previous night's festivities, describing another "grand illumination," which he said was "bright and splendid." With a fellow guest at the National he had been less restrained, saying he wished the city had been burned down. [8]

By midday, Booth headed over to Ford's Theatre to pick up his mail. The theater, located just five blocks from the White House, was a home away from home for the actor. He had performed there many times and was friends with the owner's son, Harry Ford. Most of the staff was familiar with his political sentiments. Booth wasn't the only Confederate at the theater. Actor Harry Hawke said Southern sympathies at Ford's were common. "Behind the scenes, they were all secech," he commented, describing how even late in the war secessionist sentiment was still common. [9]

Ford, a longtime friend, had news for Booth that the actor had been pestering him about for weeks. The White House had called just that morning to reserve the state box to see *Our American Cousin*. Both the Lincolns and the Grants planned to be in attendance. A mischievous Ford added that the foursome was bringing along General Lee as a prisoner to the performance. Booth erupted, not recognizing that the theater manager was teasing him. "Never!" he exclaimed.[10]

Secretly, though, Booth was gleeful. Here was his opportunity to finally achieve the goal that had eluded him for months. And now his role would be assassin, not abductor. He rushed to prepare. Early that evening, he met with his band of conspirators, Herold, Powell, and Atzerodt, informing them of their new and more dangerous mission, assassinating the president, Secretary of State Seward, and Vice President Johnson. Abduction, he said, was too complicated for such a small band of conspirators, Booth said. Powell and Herold were to kill Seward at his home in Lafayette Square. Atzerodt would shoot the vice president in his hotel room at the Kirkwood. Booth, unsurprisingly, would take the lead role, murdering the president. Atzerodt balked. He hadn't agreed to murder. When did the plan change? Booth became enraged, threatening to shoot him then and there. As he had throughout their relationship, Atzerodt backed down, acceding to Booth's direction.

Booth had one more item to accomplish before the plan was set in motion. He wrote an earnest and long defense of the actions he was about to take with his associates. In the letter, which he gave to a friend for safekeeping, he wrote:

> For a long time, I have devoted my energies, my time, and money to the accomplishment of a certain end. I have been disappointed. Heartsick and disappointed, I turn from the path which I have been following into a bolder and more perilous one. Many will blame me for what I am about to do, but posterity, I am sure, will justify me.[11]

In fact, Booth believed future Americans would not merely justify his acts but celebrate them. He would become a hero, not on the stage for a few hours, but for all time.

Booth arrived at Ford Theatre, which was full but not packed, at 10:10 p.m. He carried his derringer, a .44-caliber single-shot pistol. So absorbed was he in his plans that as he mounted the steps to the dress circle, he passed several people he knew well but didn't acknowledge. Next he moved to the state box, where the president's valet sat. The actor handed Charles Forbes a card, the contents of which have never been determined, though some say it was a simple calling card. Forbes stepped aside. Now there was nothing between Booth and the president of the United States.

He stepped into the back of the box, a small, dark vestibule. He felt along the floor for a pine bar he had hidden there earlier that afternoon. It would serve as a brace for the door to prevent anyone from coming in behind the assassin. He pushed it in place as quietly as he could.

Two closed paneled wood doors led into the box where Lincoln and his party sat. Peering through a small peephole that Booth himself had put in the door only hours before, he could partly see the box's interior. The president was at the far left of the box. Mary sat to his right, and to her right sat a young couple, Mary Harris and Major Henry Rathbone.

Booth pulled the derringer and a hunting knife from his deep pockets. He waited. The actor knew the script well and waited for his cue, a line delivered by a single actor onstage that would send the audience into fits of laughter. He listened intently to the exchange that preceded the laugh line, opening the door and stepping inside the box. He was so close he could have tapped Lincoln's shoulder.

And then, as he knew it would, the line he was waiting for was delivered. Booth raised the derringer and aimed for the president's head. He squeezed the trigger.

LINCOLN DIED OFFICIALLY AT 7:22 ON THE MORNING OF APRIL 15, 1865, nine hours after Booth shot him, in a boardinghouse behind the Ford Theatre. The president was taken there because it would have been embarrassing and controversial for the American head of state to die in a common house of entertainment. Of the four assassins, only Booth was successful in his quest. Atzerodt changed his mind, leaving the Kirkwood House where Johnson was staying and disappearing into the night. Powell stabbed Seward repeatedly, but the secretary of state managed to survive his wounds. Initially spared from the news, the recovering Seward managed to deduce Lincoln's death himself when he glimpsed a flag at half-mast. Noah Brooks wrote that Seward then lay back onto the bed, "the great tears coursing down his gashed cheeks, and the dreadful truth sinking into his mind."[12]

It would have been easy to think that there was no more capacity for grief in the country after the death of three-quarters of a million Americans in the war. But the opposite was true. Across America, there was an eruption of emotion. Some people mourned privately, others at the hundreds of memorial church services held across the country. The fact that Lincoln's death occurred on Good Friday, two days before the Christian calendar's most holy day of the year, Easter, deepened the experience for many Americans.

"Stout men cried and trembled," one businessman wrote home to his wife. John W. Meath, an Irish immigrant and a Union soldier described the reaction among soldiers. "It went to their heart like an arrow. Every soldier here looked as though he had lost his nearest or best friend. In reality, we had."[13]

In Washington, Blacks gathered in front of the boardinghouse where Lincoln had died, and at the White House, some pressed their faces against the black iron gates. In Richmond, Blacks hung their mourning clothes on the outside of their homes and prayed, fearing the death of Lincoln might well lead to the loss of their newly found freedoms.

Not everyone was saddened by the news. On Hilton Head Island, a man was murdered for cheering the death of Lincoln. Even in some Union cities the news was welcomed. One New Jersey company privately celebrated the news, and one Bloomington, Indiana, woman organized an elaborate dinner to celebrate.[14]

In the South, the reaction was mixed, though many were sympathetic. Lincoln was widely recognized as the region's best opportunity for fair treatment in the years after the war. Davis disavowed the murder, as did many Confederate generals. Across the country, the overwhelming sentiment, however, was grief. The number of Americans who turned out to pay their respects to the slain president was unparalleled. The day before the president's funeral, 25,000 mourners filed through the White House. His hearse the next day was followed by 40,000 people marching on foot.

It's estimated a million Americans saw Lincoln's funeral train, which meandered 1,700 miles from Washington to Springfield, Ill. The route retraced the whistle stops the president had made just four years previous when he made his way from the Illinois capital to the national capital just before his inauguration. Lincoln's black mahogany coffin was placed in a fourteen-foot-long, fifteen-foot-high train car. Originally built to transport the living president, the carriage was transformed into a funeral car, draped in black cloth.

The casket was displayed open in ten cities, allowing mourners a look inside. The president's body had been preserved by embalming, a process developed during the war that allowed thousands of Union soldiers to be sent from Southern battlefields to their homes in the North.

Crowds were respectful for the most part, even in Baltimore, the city that had produced the first Lincoln assassination attempt. Grief-stricken Blacks and whites solemnly viewed the body together in the city that had been home to Booth for many years.

In New York, 125,000 people filed past the casket, which was displayed in the soaring rotunda at City Hall, where masses pushed and shoved to gain admittance. Neither four regiments of Union soldiers nor city police could calm the crowd, which became more disorderly after nightfall. At Philadelphia's Independence Hall, the crowds numbered 150,000. In the first of the cities the mobile cortege visited, Lincoln looked lifelike. As the trip progressed, however, his body decayed, his face appearing more and more sallow, his eyes sunken.

Americans crowded train stations and camped along the route to get a glimpse of the great man's casket. At West Point, a company of cavalry and two of cadets stood in formation as minute guns fired from the fort across the river. The train paused to take in the scene. As it passed Tarrytown, New York, twenty-four young women stood together, wearing white dresses and black rosettes. And at Sing Sing Prison in Ossining, New York, convicts stood in their black and white prison stripes, removing their caps as the train passed by. [15]

While Americans in Northern and Western states watched for Lincoln's train, thousands of enlisted soldiers and civilians joined the manhunt to find Booth. Stanton ran the operation, but in truth the government was caught flat-footed, preoccupied with the winding down of the war and celebration. The night of the assassination, Stanton made capture of Booth and his conspirators an immediate priority. He set up a three-man board of inquiry at the boardinghouse and interviewed every witness possible. Early on, he had decided that the Confederacy had a role in the assassination, and he was determined to find the links to Richmond.

In truth, the Confederacy's secret service did assist Booth. His days in Montreal yielded the support and contacts that he used to elude his trackers for twelve long days. Booth's original plan, abduction of the president, would have required significant support in the field to transport the president. But Booth used those same contacts to facilitate his own escape. Without the support of the Confederate secret service, it's not likely Booth would have attempted either an abduction or an assassination. While he was certain that Lincoln should die at his hand, his was never a suicide mission. He planned to escape and thrive in what he hoped would be a welcoming South.

The assassin's very first stop in his flight from Washington was a tavern owned by the family of John Surratt, a Confederate courier who ran messages for Davis, among others. Surratt was a Booth conspirator. Booth was introduced to Surratt by Dr. Samuel A. Mudd, a Confederate sympathizer and gentleman farmer whom the blockade runner Charles Martin connected him to six months prior in Montreal. Mudd's house was the first place he stayed overnight on his flight from Federal authorities. Mudd gave him medical care and his next field contacts: Samuel A. Cox, an unapologetic Rebel, who, in turn, connected Booth to Thomas Jones, a longtime Confederate agent and member of the Confederate secret service. Jones helped Booth cross the Potomac into Virginia, where they were to meet Thomas Harbin, a leading Confederate agent. These were the very stepping-stones that Booth had planned to use in transporting Lincoln away from Washington and to Richmond. Instead, he used them for his own flight.

Booth's ultimate destination was the Deep South or possibly Mexico. He expected grateful Southerners to celebrate him and help him make his escape, but the well-publicized dragnet closing in on him frightened the Rebels. Eager for public praise, the assassin sought out newspapers. Surely, he reasoned, the editorial writers of Southern papers would praise his action. He was appalled by his reviews. He believed his actions were brave. But editorial writers saw a traitor and a coward. And worse, from Booth's point of view, they wrote of Lincoln as a martyr. Though controversial in life, the sixteenth president was a hero in death, viciously attacked and murdered. The papers sang his praises. Even in the former capital of the Confederacy, the *Richmond Whig* called the assassination "the most deplorable calamity which has ever befallen the people of the United States." And to Booth's further surprise, the U.S. government kept functioning. He assumed that the government would seize up with the loss of leadership; that Congress would dissolve into fighting factions. But the opposite happened. Within hours, Johnson was sworn in as president at the very hotel where Atzerodt planned to kill him. The Union continued.

Booth met his end in a desperate and chaotic fashion. On April 25, 1865, troopers of the 16th New York Cavalry tracked him down at a farm near Port Royal, Virginia, where he was shot in the neck in a burning barn. His last words were these: "Tell Mother I die for my country."

A MUFF AND GUNPOWDER TEA

The savvy Elizabeth must have seen the irony in her situation the morning of March 19, 1869. She was, after all, a woman trained as a Southern belle to graciously host parties and perhaps dictate the family's dinner menu, never sullying her hands with work. But on that spring morning she began a nine-to-five job. Many in Southern (and Northern) society had assumed that women who had filled positions of power during the war when men were away on the battlefield would step back and allow men to continue running the show when the war ended. Elizabeth didn't share that view.

Neither did her former boss, Ulysses S. Grant. Now president, Grant rewarded his star spymaster for her war service by fulfilling her request to be named Richmond's postmaster. It was a role of incredible prestige and power. Now Elizabeth was a legitimate boss, no more hiding behind her lady manners. Only a couple of days after her appointment, she went to work, sweeping into Richmond's Custom House office building no doubt wearing her customary black silk dress. She may have paused at the threshold to consider the recent inhabitants of the imposing gray granite structure. During the war Jefferson Davis had maintained an office there on the third floor, and he was later tried for treason in a courtroom on the second floor. The offices were currently filled with federal government bureaucrats. There was the collector of customs, the internal revenue supervisor, the U.S. district attorney, and several judges. All, save Elizabeth, were men. The building, ancient by American standards, had managed to survive the war, forming a back-drop for Capitol Square, the statehouse, and the former White House for the Confederacy. There was a lot of Southern history in the Custom House, and Elizabeth wanted to make some of her own.

Already Elizabeth had become something of a celebrity in the North. Reporters scoured Southern towns and cities for stories of the valiant Union spies and agents, which were then run in the Northern papers. The national magazine *Harper's* praised Elizabeth and her mother in 1866. Writers of those early stories had a difficult time imagining her gritty role as spymaster. Instead, they celebrated Elizabeth and Eliza as the Florence Nightingales of the capital, tending Union soldiers. This was fine by Elizabeth. She preferred keeping her past as a spy secret. She refused to write an autobiography, even though the proceeds might have helped bail her out of debt. In those early days after the war, her public legacy was left to newspaper editors and advocates for women's suffrage, who became fans of the war-time spy. Activist Susan B. Anthony visited Elizabeth on Church Hill, describing herself as a "great admirer" of Elizabeth's. The Southern belle, ironically, was the "it girl" of suffragists. Strangely, Elizabeth was also cited as a positive role model by men who believed women shouldn't have the right to vote and could accomplish much without it.[1]

While the North applauded her appointment, Richmond simmered. The *Richmond Enquirer* and *Examiner* expressed disgust at her nomina-tion, asserting that "the delegation of a Federal spy to manage our post office is a deliberate insult to our people."[2] Another paper described her as a dried-up old maid, predicting she would spend her time in the office gossiping and drinking tea. Clearly, they didn't know her well.

Though Elizabeth was not the first female postmaster in the country, it was unusual for a woman to hold the position in a large city. In fact, post offices functioned as a place for men to gather and talk. Some post offices had a separate window for women to discourage them from lingering in this male bastion. This is what makes Elizabeth's appointment all that more impressive—post offices were a place where respectable women did not tarry, but in Richmond, at least, it was being run by one.

Richmond's anger was no surprise. The job was lucrative, with an excellent salary, and politically important. Her $4,000 salary would be equal to $90,000 to $100,000 today. The postmaster controlled scores of jobs that could be filled by loyalists. The role of postmaster was considered a launching pad to higher political office. In fact, Abraham Lincoln had once been a postmaster. Elizabeth did not seem to hold ambition for higher office, but her appointment blocked old-line Confederates from appointing one of their own.[3]

Had Elizabeth been anything but successful in her management of the post office, no doubt her tenure would have been ended quickly by her Richmond enemies. But she showed an incredible aptitude for running things, a facility she had developed administering her spy ring. Letters began arriving more quickly and in greater numbers under her management. Letter boxes popped up on major city streets, removing the need to walk to the post office. Letter deliveries increased sixfold under her management. Elizabeth was proud of her work, and its effective administration was critical to Richmond's social and economic functioning. That's because the postal service was the link connecting far-flung families. As the primary method of delivering payments via checks and money orders, it was essential to the orderly working of the economy. It was also the central presence of the federal government in small towns, rural outposts, and major cities across the country. Elizabeth took her responsibilities seriously and even published a guide to its workings.

While she excelled at running the post office, she was at a loss when it came to the politics of the job. In fact, she swore off politics, claiming to run the operation as nonpolitical to benefit everyone in Richmond. Her plan was naive yet admirable, and she might have yet succeeded if she hadn't had a way of unnecessarily provoking *both* parties. Her fellow

Republicans didn't like the fact that she didn't provide the favors they believed they deserved. She found herself caught in a feud between two competing factions of the party and charged alternatively with insubordination and the inability to successfully navigate political waters. Whether she was too forceful or not forceful enough, it's clear she was out of favor with her own party. They tried desperately to get her canned.

Conservatives were no fans of her, either. Elizabeth chose Black candidates to fill many of the positions in her post office, from the coveted job of mail carrier to clerkships. Some of her hires were former slaves from the Church Hill mansion; others were Black civic leaders. Under her stewardship, the postal service had become a center of power for Blacks. The fact that she pointed out unfair treatment of Blacks at the hands of Conservatives did not endear her to them. After one law made it illegal for a voter who has been charged with a petty crime to cast a ballot, large numbers of Black men were rounded up on bogus charges to keep them from voting. Elizabeth called this practice out publicly. She kept fighting for full enfranchisement for Blacks, starting a library for the city's Blacks filled with books donated by Richmond's well-to-do.

Given the backdrop of race relations during Grant's terms of office after the war, Elizabeth showed extreme courage in continuing to press for the rights of Blacks and hiring them in publicly visible jobs. Newspapers were full of stories of a vicious backlash in the Deep South against the 14th and 15th Constitutional Amendments guaranteeing Black citizenship and the right to vote. In the wake of the war, a number of freedmen and whites sympathetic to the cause of racial equality were elected to office. Organizations like the Ku Klux Klan, and later, the Red Shirts and the White League, arose to force them out of office. Those resentments exploded in the 1872 Louisiana election for governor. The Colfax Massacre of 1873 was one of the worst incidents of violence of the Reconstruction era. An armed group of white supremacists attacked a courthouse guarded by mostly Black militia units. One hundred and fifty people died, nearly all of them Black. But the Colfax Massacre was by no means the only violent uprising by whites who refused to give up power in the Reconstructionist South. There were many others. Grant, who was committed to supporting Black men who had fought on behalf of the Union, sent Federal troops to numerous Southern cities, attempting to enforce legal elections and put down violence against Blacks.

Like others who supported the rights of Blacks, Elizabeth received direct threats. A band of vigilantes calling themselves the White Caps left a frightening note for her. The paper featured the image of a skull and crossbones. Its message was direct. "White Caps are around town. They are coming at night! Look out! Look out! Your house is going at last. FIRE." The message so impressed Elizabeth that she saved it with her most important papers. [4]

Elizabeth served two terms as postal office chief, but her fate as a public servant was inextricably linked to Grant's. By the end of his second term, Reconstruction was on its final legs. The president was battling another foe, economic depression, with little success. He was out of his depth on economic issues, something that had become critical to the voting public. His civil rights agenda was in tatters. The civil rights bill he pushed through in 1875 guaranteeing equal rights in public accommodations and transportation for Blacks, which Elizabeth supported, was mostly ignored, especially in the South. Later, it would be declared unconstitutional by the Supreme Court. In Richmond, even Unionists began to decry Elizabeth's treatment of Blacks, and across the country, voters wanted to move on from the issues of race. A generation of soldiers who had fought in the Civil War grew misty-eyed about their service, and the commitment to equal treatment and opportunity for Blacks dissolved into a haze of the Myth of the Lost Cause, burying the war's real cause.

Even after Grant left office, Elizabeth didn't stop fighting to retain her lucrative perch at the post office, writing letters to party leaders and even traveling to Washington to make a case for her reinstatement directly to the new president, Rutherford B. Hayes. Again, Grant wrote her a letter of recommendation. Elizabeth's attempts to keep her job and the campaign against her became nasty and played out in the papers, where her critics described her as mentally unbalanced. She shot back, describing her critics as Northern carpetbaggers. Increasingly, she began to view herself as a victim, but in truth, across the country Hayes was replacing Grant loyalists with conservatives and Democrats. Hayes replaced Elizabeth with a former Confederate colonel.

Just as Grant's popularity had waned and his time on the national stage had ended, so, too, Elizabeth, who had been so connected to him, was also forced to retreat to private life. Battling both throat cancer and bankruptcy, Grant went off to a simple log cabin in the mountains of upstate New York to write his memoirs. During the last year of his life, he finished his two-volume autobiography describing his experiences in the Civil and Mexican-American Wars. There, sitting on the porch of his cabin, covered in a blanket and wearing a knit skullcap, he wrote at a ferocious pace, producing 25 to 50 pages a day. He was racked with pain from cancer. The books, published by Mark Twain, were a monumental success and saved his family from bankruptcy. But Grant could not beat the throat cancer caused by his years of chain-smoking cigars. He died on July 23, 1885.

Given time to consider Grant's legacy, the public embraced the general in death. It is estimated 1.5 million people attended his funeral procession in New York City that August. The column of mourners walking alongside his casket was seven miles long. One editorial writer, summing up the feeling of the time, said no monument needed to be built to honor Grant because the Union itself was his legacy. Fittingly, his pallbearers included both Confederate and Union generals.

While Grant's life was celebrated in New York, Elizabeth struggled to keep her small family afloat. When her mother had died in 1875, the family's status in Richmond was so low that they struggled to find enough pallbearers to carry her casket to her grave.

Without a regular source of income, the household was quickly sinking in debt. Elizabeth's brother, John, tried to reestablish the family's hardware business, but failed. Elizabeth put some of the family's land up for sale and even tried her hand at running a business, but none of it amounted to much. She even put the Church Hill house on the market, but received offers so low she found them insulting. She stayed put.[5]

The federal government would have been an obvious source of support. Federal soldiers, after all, were awarded pensions and in some cases land grants to recognize their contributions. Surely Elizabeth deserved as much. She did receive some recompense. During the war, the federal government allotted her expense money that covered a portion of her costs. Benjamin Butler had once sent her a muff and gunpowder tea, but that did little to help her pay her bills. After the war, Grant sent her $2,000. George Sharpe, her minder, appealed to Congress to give her $15,000. In a letter describing her contributions, he also noted how her extreme generosity to both Union soldiers and Richmond's "families of plain people" helped generate support for the federal government. "For a long, long time," he wrote, "she was all that was left of the power of the U.S. government in the city of Richmond."[6] Congress finally approved a payment of $5,000.[7] But that money, too, was soon spent, as Elizabeth's generosity to friends and family continued unabated.

Finally in 1883 she applied for a low-level clerkship in the post office department in Washington. With some trouble she was awarded the job, but it paid a fraction of what she had made in Richmond. What's more, her boss was argumentative and demoted her to the dead letter office. It was an omen. There was no reviving Elizabeth's career as a federal employee, so she resigned and went home after four years of hard work.

There on Grace Street, the old spymaster found her allies, friends, and acquaintances ebbing away. Many of the men she had hired and promoted at the Richmond post office died young, several from tuberculosis. Some fellow members of her ring moved to the North where they felt their opportunities would be better. Only F.W.E. Lohmann, the agent who had disinterred the Union colonel Dahlgren at her request, visited her on a regular basis. Over dinner at the mansion, the two would share stories of their work undercover for the Union. She refused to venture far from the house. John, the brother who had lived in the house with his family, moved miles away to a farm in Louisa County.

The women's rights activists who had been so enamored of Elizabeth's wartime contributions now found her views too extreme. A new generation of suffragists courted white support by playing the race card, arguing that white women should be awarded the vote in order to counter the votes of Black men. [8] Elizabeth found the logic detestable.

The Church Hill mansion was now inhabited by just her and her niece, Eliza. A handful of paid servants remained loyal to the old spymaster. Her friends in the Black community continued their support, but social Richmond snubbed her. Elizabeth recalled in a letter how one gentleman told her that Richmond society would never forget what she did to help the Union, nor would they forgive her.

The isolation took a heavy toll. Writing to a friend in Massachusetts— John H. Forbes, a former Union soldier who sent her money in her later years—she said: "No one will walk with us on the street. No one will go with us any where—and it becomes worse and worse, as those friends I had go . . . We are held so utterly as outcasts here."[9] At least one of her remaining friends advised her to move away, but she was set against it. She couldn't sell the Church Hill home, which she now described as an "elephant," because no one would buy it. Plus, Richmond was her home.

The year before, Richmond had erected a massive, sixty-foot statue of Robert E. Lee astride his horse. The monument sat in the middle of what would become a well-to-do neighborhood on a traffic circle at the corner of Monument and Allen Avenues. Ultimately, it would dwarf the homes built around it. One hundred thousand people gathered to see the statue unveiled on Memorial Day weekend 1890.

The statue was a physical manifestation of the national sentiment building among whites for reconciliation of the North and the South. This Lost Cause mythology cast the South and its heroes, like Lee, as just and heroic. Rebel soldiers, under this construction, nobly and courageously fought for states' rights, losing only because of the Union's overwhelming advantages in men and resources. The idea cast aside Reconstruction and the central issue of the conflict, slavery, and emancipation. For the nation, the mythology allowed both sides to claim they had fought with honor and thus promoted unity. Richmond was the center of the Lost Cause mythology. And much to Elizabeth's chagrin, it was here that the embers of Southern patriotism were warming.

Elizabeth grew thinner and thinner, her demeanor anxious and frail. Her graying hair was now white. A picture from this period shows her tiny frame perched on a settee in the yard of her home, her presence dwarfed by the mansion's massive columns. She is dressed in her perennial black silk. It's not surprising that her critics began describing her as a witch. Crazy Bet, they called her.

She grew more and more argumentative and bad-tempered. She arrived late to service at St. John's, noisily settling into a pew and annoying other congregants, who ultimately locked her out. And she complained about paying taxes to the city, attaching a note of "solemn protest," explaining it was unjust to tax someone who couldn't vote.[10]

People who knew her at the time said she was as sound in mind as ever and still an avid reader of the newspapers. She still loved discussing politics. She had sense enough to court fans of hers in Boston. The family of Colonel Paul J. Revere, whom Elizabeth had nursed during the war, sent her financial support and even set up a subscription fund to assist her.

Her losses continued in the last five years of her life. Her brother, John, died in 1895. Her sister, Anna, passed away not long later. But it was the death of her most important companion, Eliza, whom Elizabeth regarded as a daughter, that stung her the most. The two bickered frequently, and Eliza sometimes sent Elizabeth to the streets, where her aunt wandered for hours. When Eliza died unexpectedly in 1900, Elizabeth ordered that the Christmas decorations her niece had placed should never be removed.[11]

Elizabeth became ill several months later with dropsy or edema, an accumulation of fluid in the body's tissues that swells the extremities. As she lay dying, she told relatives about her diary, what she regarded as the true story of her life. When the pages were brought to her, she was shocked. Half of it was missing and never found. The remainder told little of her spying, but was filled with her thoughts on slavery and racism. Her cipher key for encoding reports was a part of the trove, as were letters, mementos, and Grant's calling card.

She died on September 25, 1900, at the age of eighty-one, and as was the custom, her family laid her to rest for a brief period in the drawing room of the mansion, where a life-size portrait of herself at age six looked down upon her. She was buried in Shockoe Cemetery across from her parents. But because of crowding in the cemetery, her casket was placed vertically. A service was attended by a small handful of people, mostly extended family members. Ten men bore her casket to her grave.

A memorial stone paid for by her Boston friends still marks her grave. It reads, "She risked everything that is dear to man—friends—fortune—comfort—health—life itself—all for the one absorbing desire of her heart—that slavery might be abolished and the Union preserved."

The story of her life was told in obituaries published across the country. Newspapers in New York and Boston recounted her work as a spy; the Richmond papers gave her grudging respect.

The Church Hill mansion went through many changes. A civic organization called the Virginia Club purchased it, and those who worked there claimed it was haunted. Some said they heard the ghost of Elizabeth walking about. Elizabeth's doctor, William H. Parker, converted the house into a sanatorium in 1908. Twelve years after Elizabeth's death, the building was marked by the city for demolition.

The son of F.W.E. Lohmann, Charles Lohmann, read of the plans to demolish the Church Hill mansion and headed to Richmond to see it. After his father had died in 1877, Charles had visited Elizabeth at the house several times. The two had reminisced about the war years, talking about how she and his father had fought the Confederacy. He enjoyed their visits and felt it brought him closer to his father. Charles drove his carriage to the corner of Grace Street where he had a good view of the house he had spent so much time in and watched as the destruction began. His eyes welled with tears. He was the only one crying. Some Richmond residents standing by cheered.

Eventually, the city built a school on the site. It does not bear Elizabeth's name.

EPILOGUE

It would have been difficult to predict the postwar fates of the characters presented here in *Lincoln's Lady Spymaster*. Some of the most well-known Confederates thrived. Varina Davis, the wife of Jefferson Davis, flourished, launching a successful career as a newspaper contributor for Joseph Pulitzer's *New York World* and living in New York after her husband's death. She became an advocate of reconciliation and friends with Julia Dent Grant, President Grant's wife. She died in her apartment overlooking the park in 1906 and was buried in Richmond, where her tombstone reads: *At Peace.*

There was no peace for Edmund Ruffin. The belligerent advocate for slavery and secession committed suicide in his son's home two months after Lee's surrender. He wrapped his body in a Confederate flag, put a rifle muzzle in his mouth and pulled the trigger with a forked stick. Still raging, his last diary entry proclaimed his "unmitigated hatred to Yankee rule." His wife and eight of his children died during the war.[1]

Elizabeth's ring of spies went their own ways after the war. Perhaps because they had lived under threat of death for so long, some, like William Rowley, returned to a quiet life. Rowley rebuilt his farm, using $1,850 from the federal government. The money was a reimbursement for the damage Union soldiers had done to his Henrico County home. They didn't know he was a Union spy.

Just as Elizabeth had gone to work for the federal government, so did many of her ring members, filling a variety of offices. F.W.E. Lohmann and his brother John were appointed as detectives in the office of Federal Provost Marshal Marsena Patrick. The two tracked down escaped convicts and searched for stolen goods. Likewise, Philip Cashmeyer, who had worked for the Confederates as a detective tracking Rebel traitors, also went to work for the federals hunting down criminals. Samuel Ruth, who manipulated train lines to assist the Union, fought to keep his job at the Richmond, Fredericksburg, and Potomac Railroad and fell into poverty. He eventually became a federal tax collector but died of a stroke at fifty-four. Erasmus Ross, Elizabeth's agent inside Libby Prison, survived the war, but barely. He died at the age of thirty in a Christmas Day fire at the Spotswood Hotel. Little is known of what happened to Abby Green, the woman who gave critical information to Libby Prison escapees, but the Black freedman Robert Ford, who worked with her to plan the escape, suffered for the rest of his life from the beating he received for cooperating with the Unionists. The violent prison commander Dick Turner gave him 500 lashes. Turner was himself imprisoned in the jail where he had presided over the misery of so many. Aided by a knife smuggled in by his wife, he escaped a cell in the cellar, possibly the only person to do so. He was recaptured and jailed but served only a single year. When he died in 1901, he was the Democratic party chairman of the southeast Virginia country where he lived.

Elizabeth's beloved servant Mary Jane Richards gained her freedom with the fall of the Confederacy at the tender age of twenty-three or twenty-four. After the war, she traveled north and began giving talks about her wartime experiences under an alias, still concerned she might attract reprisals. She also pursued a teaching career, working for the Freedmen's Bureau with a fierce dedication, continuing lessons with her Black students even when she was bedridden. When her students couldn't afford their books, she bought them using her own meager salary. The *Brooklyn Eagle* quoted her in one of her speeches as saying that Black people, not just men, should be given the right to vote, and that despite emancipation there was still a lack of equal treatment for Blacks in both the North and the South. In a final letter to Elizabeth, she appears to be turning down an offer to return to Richmond, saying she wanted to prove herself on her own.

John Minor Botts, Elizabeth's friend and an outspoken Unionist, died in 1869. He spent much of the war at his plantation in Culpepper County. Auburn, his whitewashed Southern mansion, still stands. Botts had moved there after his imprisonment in 1862, buying up land that had been marched across by both armies four different times. At Culpepper, Botts conducted endless negotiations with Union commanders to keep soldiers from stealing his livestock and horses and using his fence for firewood. He became a cantankerous but beloved figure. One Union officer said he would be happy to see him any time he had three hours to spare.

The Bureau of Military Information was closed for business after the war by a public eager to move on. But George Sharpe, BMI's talented chief, who was widely acknowledged as capable and trustworthy, was in demand. First, he was tasked with chasing down John Surratt, who had aided and abetted Booth in his escape but had managed to get away. Sharpe traveled all over Europe but failed to find Surratt, who had cleverly gone undercover as a papal guard for the Vatican. Sharpe's next gig would be more successful. Grant appointed the attorney to the post of U.S. marshal for the Southern District of New York, where he led the fight to end the rule of the corrupt Tammany Hall organization run by William "Boss" Tweed. He later became a New York state assemblyman and speaker. Sharpe also worked to extend the rights of Union veterans and was appointed to several diplomatic roles. Elizabeth's first boss, Benjamin Butler, also had a successful postwar career, serving as a U.S. congressman for Massachusetts and as governor of the Bay State.

Secretary of War Edwin Stanton, the man who may have authored the Dahlgren orders, remained in Andrew Johnson's cabinet after the war, but fought with Johnson due to his lenient treatment of formerly Southern states. And though Johnson attempted to have Stanton ousted twice, once forcing the cabinet officer to barricade himself in his office, the secretary of war remained due to his support from Congress. President Grant nominated Stanton to the U.S. Supreme Court, but he died only four days after the nomination.

The attack sustained by William Seward the night Lincoln was assassinated left the Secretary of State with permanent scars to his face, but he survived and continued to serve in Johnson's administration. Seward's true legacy, though it was commonly derided as "Seward's Folly" in his time, was helping to negotiate the purchase of Alaska from Russia in 1867.

Allan Pinkerton, the man who saved Lincoln from assassination before he took office and later worked for General George McClellan, went home to Chicago after the war and grew his detective agency into a national police force engaged in chasing Western train and bank bandits, like Jesse James. He was one of the few we have written about who got much in the way of recompense from the federal government, receiving $35,567 for his work with McClellan. But he didn't forget his loyal employees. He sat at Kate Warne's bedside as she was dying of pneumonia at age thirty-five. Unlike Elizabeth, Pinkerton sought publicity, producing eighteen books on his most famous cases and an entire volume on his exploits during the war. It is filled with exaggerations and outright fabrications.

The man Northern spies plotted against, Jefferson Davis, was never tried for treason. He lost his plantation in Mississippi, his wealth, and his U.S. citizenship due to an 1872 law that prevented high-ranking Rebels to run for office or vote. (His citizenship was restored posthumously by President Jimmy Carter.) He took his family to Britain and France to seek business opportunities. Finding none, he returned to the United States, where he eventually moved in with a widowed heiress, occupying a cottage on her plantation on the Mississippi Sound. There he wrote his memoir of the Confederacy, work that would consume him until his death from pneumonia in 1889.

Confederate spy Frank Stringfellow, who dressed as a woman to steal secrets at the Washington Ball in 1864, fled to Canada after the war to prevent being caught up in the dragnet of Booth conspirators. He came back to the United States to marry his sweetheart and was ordained as an Episcopalian priest. He wrote a letter to Grant, telling him that in 1864 he was close enough to shoot and kill the commanding officer of the Union army, but couldn't bring himself to do it. Grant responded kindly and offered to fulfill any reasonable request he might make. President William McKinley would make good on that offer in 1898, making Stringfellow a chaplain in the Spanish-American War.

Tom Hines, the Confederate operative who attempted to turn the war for the South in its waning days on Union soil, nearly died when a Detroit bar crowd turned abusive two days after the assassination of the president. The crowd mistook Hines for Booth. He survived by clubbing the men rushing him with the butt of his revolver. He ran for the ferry, holding the captain at gunpoint and forcing him to take him to the Canadian side of the lake. Andrew Johnson issued an amnesty proclamation that allowed him to return to the country. He eventually went back to his native Kentucky, where he became an attorney and later chief justice of Kentucky's court of appeals.

It's notable some Confederate leaders' loyalties changed in the years after the war. Anderson's rival at Sumter, P.G.T. Beauregard, was one. He tried to persuade Davis to concede in the war's waning days. In time, he advocated for a benevolent Reconstruction, speaking warmly of Lincoln. Even so, a monument of him on horseback was removed by his native New Orleans as part of a program to remove all Confederate figures in 2017. Lieutenant Bennett Young, who led the St. Albans raid, was another Confederate officer whose political views changed. After becoming a prominent lawyer in Louisville, he founded the first orphanage for Blacks in Louisville and a school for the blind, and did pro bono work for the poor. He represented former slave George Dinning in a case against the Ku Klux Klan.

Belle Boyd, one of the best-known Confederate women spies, married a Union naval officer after the war and went to England, where she was embraced as an actress, often portraying herself and her exploits during the war. She brought the act home, then married an Englishman who had fought for the Union army and gave birth to four children. She divorced him to marry an actor seventeen years her junior. She died in poverty at age fifty-six on tour in Wisconsin.

The leader of the Libby Prison breakout, Colonel Thomas E. Rose, stayed in military service for the duration of the war and then joined the regular army, never returning to the classroom. His headstone in Arlington National Cemetery notes his greatest achievement: *Engineered and executed the Libby Prison Tunnel.* Colonel Abel Streight, who escaped in the breakout with Rose and became an advocate for prisoners, went home to Indianapolis, where he served in the state senate. When he died in 1892, his wife, who had accompanied him on military missions during the war, had him buried in their front yard. "I never knew where he was in life," she said, adding, "But now I can find him."

Hugh Judson Kilpatrick, the leader of the failed Dahlgren raid, made an impressive rally after the war. He was just twenty-nine but received the second star of a major general. He was appointed the nation's envoy to Chile and moved there, enjoying a huge salary and getting married. When he returned home to New Jersey, he tried his hand at many things, becoming a popular dinner speaker, writing a play, and becoming a gentleman farmer.

He died in Chile on a second tour of duty in 1881. His West Point gravesite bears an impressive monument, paid for in part by his twin granddaughters, who continued his flamboyant legacy. One of the twins, Gloria Morgan, married Reginald Vanderbilt and gave birth to a daughter known as Little Gloria, a socialite and heiress and mother of cable television anchor Anderson Cooper. The other twin, Thelma Morgan, married the wealthy grandson of the founder of Bell Telegraph, then divorced him and married a British aristocrat. Soon after, she began an affair with the Prince of Wales. [2]

After three exhumations, Ulric Dahlgren finally received his funeral on November 1, 1865. An elaborate ceremony was held on this date in Philadelphia's Independence Hall, the same spot where Lincoln's funeral had been held six months earlier. Black crepe draped the room, strung from the central chandelier to the walls. The metal coffin was covered with a white cross made of white and yellow roses, the sweet smell of white tuberose filling the room. Reverend Henry Ward Beecher, brother of Harriet Beecher Stowe, delivered a stem-winder of a eulogy. "Dahlgren! As long as history lasts, Dahlgren shall mean truth, honor, bravery, and historic sacrifice," he said. There to listen were President Andrew Johnson, Secretary of War Edwin Stanton, and General George Meade, plus the nation's top military brass. Major newspapers covered the event. *The Philadelphia Inquirer* described him as a "martyred hero."

The young colonel's remains finally found a permanent home at Laurel Hill Cemetery outside Philadelphia, where his family lived before they moved to Washington. The headstone is simple, reading: *Col. Ulric Dahlgren, U.S. Army.*

ACKNOWLEDGMENTS

✥ ✥

I have a theory about women and how they learn. I believe we watch each other, eagle-eyed, warily gazing for clues on the best way to dress, or how to comfort a friend, watching for lessons both ordinary and profound. I've been watching other women since I was a small girl and studied my mother as she effortlessly prepared dinner, wrangled us to the table, and fielded work calls all at the same time.

So, when it came to understanding courage and leadership, I sought a woman to teach me. Elizabeth Van Lew was my subject in *Lincoln's Lady Spymaster*. Both courageous and intelligent, her leadership of a ring of spies was breathtaking in its ingenuity and resourcefulness. I was eager to do her justice, but desire was not enough. And, so, I studied women history writers, like the always compelling Doris Kearns Goodwin, the queen of American history authors. Stacy Schiff's stylish prose provided pure inspiration. I gleaned every possible fact from Elizabeth R. Varon's authoritative and excellent biography of Van Lew, *Southern Lady, Yankee Spy*. Sonia Purnell and her *A Woman of No Importance* provided a brilliant example of writing action with a woman at the center. Books by men were no less inspirational. Ron Chernow's *Grant* was a thrill, reconstructing my mental image of a figure I thought I already understood, though incorrectly as I learned. James L. Swanson's *Manhunt* was every bit as compelling as a spy novel and chock-full of incredible detail.

Terry Alford has done incredible work on John Wilkes Booth, finding the assassin shared a spiritualist with the 16th president. Truth is, anyone writing about the Civil War era stands on the shoulders of giants. My husband had to beg every night for the bedside table lamp to be put out as I turned page after page.

The folks at HarperCollins were amazing to work with and I greatly appreciate their efforts to make this book a reality. To Harper Influence publisher Lisa Sharkey, thank you for spotting the strength in my pitch. Eric Nelson, Broadside publisher, thank you for your insight and patience. And, finally, great thanks to my talented editor, Hannah Long, who managed me like a pro and is smart beyond her years. Much thanks as well to the artist who designed the beautiful cover for this book, Joanne O'Neill.

My employer, Fox, and the executives who run it create an environment where their employees can expand and try new things. I am grateful to Suzanne Scott, CEO, and President Jay Wallace. Fox Nation President Lauren Petterson is an amazing and tireless leader and EVP Kim Rosenburg has a mind that makes tacks look dull. Sharri Berg is a creative thinker who is transforming weather news. Amy Sohnen, an early supporter of this project, earns my gratitude. Thank you, Ralph Giordano, for your help and support at Fox Business over the many years we have worked together. Producers Sumner Park, Marc Smith, and Justin Freiman are producing pros who make me look good even when I am stressed by deadlines.

Thank you to my friends who listened with patience to my endless natterings about the book and cheered me when my energy flagged. To the Four Musketeers who kept my batteries charged—Jane Francisco, Beth Ann Kaminkow, Sarah Lubas, and Melanie Dadourian, thank you.

My family was a critical source of ideas and support. Thank you to my sister, Frankie Pryor, for supplying wisdom and energy in equal parts; to my brother, Steve Willis, for your grounding spirit. A big thanks to my nephew, Nate Willis, for serving as a tireless researcher! Working with you was more fun than I could have hoped for. And, to mom, Betty Jean, all the love in the world to you and thank you for everything.

No one was more essential to the production of this book than my husband and partner in everything, David Evans. He gave the idea support, the book its first edit, and calmed my endless anxieties about the project. I value his judgement more than I can say. Much love, honey. And, to my officemate, our toy poodle puppy, Rufus, thank you for being an adorable distraction. Treats are coming, I promise!

NOTES

INTRODUCTION

1. DeAnne Blanton and Lauren M. Cook, *They Fought Like Demons: Women Soldiers in the American Civil War* (Baton Rouge: Louisiana State University Press, 2002), 23.

CHAPTER 1: A KINDRED SPIRIT

1. Elizabeth R. Varon, *Southern Lady, Yankee Spy: The True Story of Elizabeth Van Lew, a Union Agent in the Heart of the Confederacy* (New York: Oxford University Press, 2003), 257.
2. Nancy Roberts, *Civil War Ghosts and Legends* (Columbia, SC: University of South Carolina Press, 1992), 103.
3. Edwin C. Fishel, *The Secret War for the Union: The Untold Story of Military Intelligence in the Civil War* (Boston: Houghton Mifflin Co., 1996), 551.

CHAPTER 2: SOUTHERN BELLES

1. Elizabeth L. Van Lew, *A Yankee Spy in Richmond: The Civil War Diary of "Crazy Bet" Van Lew,* edited by David D. Ryan (Mechanicsburg, PA: Stackpole Books, 1996), 27.
2. Elizabeth R. Varon, *Southern Lady, Yankee Spy: The True Story of Elizabeth Van Lew, a Union Agent in the Heart of the Confederacy* (New York: Oxford University Press, 2003), 32.
3. Varon, *Southern Lady, Yankee Spy,* 17.
4. Gregg D. Kimball, *American City, Southern Place: A Cultural History of Antebellum Richmond* (Athens: University of Georgia Press, 2000), 70.
5. Ryan, *A Yankee Spy in Richmond,* 33.
6. Varon, *Southern Lady, Yankee Spy,* 16.

7. Kimball, *American City, Southern Place,* 156.

8. University of Richmond Digital Scholarship Lab, "Hidden Patterns of the Civil War: Mapping Richmond's Slave Market," University of Richmond, https://dsl.richmond.edu/civilwar/slavemarket.html#redirect; Abigail Tucker, "Digging Up the Past at a Richmond Jail," *Smithsonian Magazine,* March 2009, https://www.smithsonianmag.com/history /digging-up-the-past-at-a-richmond-jail-50642859/.

9. Matthew R. Laird, *Archaeological Data Recovery Investigation of the Lumpkin's Slave Jail Site (44HE1053), Richmond, Virginia,* research report prepared for the Richmond City Council Slave Trail Commission, James River Institute for Archaeology, August 2010, 12–16, 23–25, https://www.dhr.virginia.gov/pdf_files/SpecialCollections /Lumpkin's%20Jail%20data%20recovery%20report%20vol.%201%20 (research).pdf.

10. Laird, *Archaeological Data Recovery Investigation,* 21.

11. Laird, *Archaeological Data Recovery Investigation,* 17–20.

CHAPTER 3: PEACE, PEACE, BUT THERE IS NO PEACE

1. Terry Alford, *Fortune's Fool: The Life of John Wilkes Booth* (New York: Oxford University Press, 2015), 69–70.

2. Stephen B. Oates, *To Purge This Land with Blood* (Brattleboro, VT: Echo Point Books, 1984), 196.

3. Oates, *To Purge This Land with Blood,* 400.

4. Oates, *To Purge This Land with Blood,* 446.

5. Henry Ward Beecher, "The Nation's Duty to Slavery," www.digitalhistory .Uh.edu/active_learning/explorations/brown/public_beecher.fm.

6. Elizabeth L. Van Lew, *A Yankee Spy in Richmond: The Civil War Diary of "Crazy Bet" Van Lew,* edited by David D. Ryan (Mechanicsburg, PA: Stackpole Books, 1996), 28.

7. Oates, *To Purge This Land with Blood,* 77.

8. Oates, *To Purge This Land with Blood,* 80.

CHAPTER 4: ELIZABETH VS. THE FIRE-EATERS

1. Abraham Lincoln, "Cooper Union Address," New York, February 27, 1860, Abraham Lincoln Online Speeches and Writings, AbrahamLincolnOnline.org/lincoln/speeches/cooper.htm.

2. John J. Hennessy, "Scourge of the Confederacy," *Civil War Monitor* 7, no. 1 (Spring 2017), 34.

3. James McPherson, *Battle Cry of Freedom: The Civil War Era* (New York: Oxford University Press, 1988), 223.

4. Elizabeth R. Varon, *Southern Lady, Yankee Spy: The True Story of Elizabeth Van Lew, a Union Agent in the Heart of the Confederacy* (New York: Oxford University Press, 2003), 39.

5. McPherson, *Battle Cry of Freedom*, 223.

6. "The Union Is Dissolved!" *Charleston Mercury*, December 20, 1860, Gilderlehrman.org/history-resources/spotlight-primary-source /union-dissolved-1860.

7. McPherson, *Battle Cry of Freedom*, 234.

CHAPTER 5: THE KNIGHTS OF THE GOLDEN CIRCLE

1. Samuel M. Felton, "Narrative of Samuel M. Felton," letter in William Schouler, *A History of Massachusetts in the Civil War*, vol. 2 (Boston: Dutton, 1868), 59.

2. Schouler, *A History of Massachusetts in the Civil War*, vol. 2, 62.

3. David C. Keehn, "Avowed Enemies of the Country," Historynet, February 24, 2017. https://www.historynet.com/avowed-enemies -country-knights-golden-circle; David Keehn, *Knights of the Golden Circle: Secret Empire, Southern Secession, Civil War* (Baton Rouge: Louisiana State University Press, 2013), 110–11.

4. Brad Meltzer and Josh Mensch, *The Lincoln Conspiracy: The Secret Plot to Kill America's 16th President—and Why It Failed* (New York: Flatiron Books, 2020), 311.

5. Erik Larson, *Demon of Unrest: Saga of Hubris, Heartbreak, and Heroism at the Dawn of the Civil War* (New York: Crown, 2024), 193.

6. Henry Adams, *The Education of Henry Adams* (New York: Modern Library, 1931; originally published in 1907), 104.

7. Elizabeth R. Varon, *Southern Lady, Yankee Spy: The True Story of Elizabeth Van Lew, a Union Agent in the Heart of the Confederacy* (New York: Oxford University Press, 2003), 42.

8. "Initial Problems at Forts Pickens & Sumter," Tulane University, https://www2.tulane.edu/~sumter/InitialProb/Mar5.html.

9. "Initial Problems at Forts Pickens & Sumter," www2.tulane .edu/~sumter/InitialProb/Mar5.html.

10. Bruce Chadwick, *The Cannons Roar: Fort Sumter and the Start of the Civil War* (New York: Pegasus Books, 2023), 235.

11. James McPherson, *Battle Cry of Freedom: The Civil War Era* (New York: Oxford University Press, 1988), 269.

12. Chadwick, *The Cannons Roar*, 241.

13. McPherson, *Battle Cry of Freedom*, 272.

14. Elizabeth Brown Pryor, *Reading the Man: A Portrait of Robert E. Lee Through His Private Letters* (New York: Penguin, 2008), 291.

15. William O. Stoddard, *Abraham Lincoln: The Man and the War President* (New York: Fords, Howard & Hulbert, 1888), 265.

16. Douglas Waller, *Lincoln's Spies* (New York: Simon & Schuster, 2019), 39.

17. Waller, *Lincoln's Spies*, 108

18. *Richmond Enquirer*, March 15, 1861.

19. Doris Kearns Goodwin, *Team of Rivals: The Political Genius of Abraham Lincoln* (New York: Simon & Schuster, 2006), 352.

20. Elizabeth L. Van Lew, *A Yankee Spy in Richmond: The Civil War Diary of "Crazy Bet" Van Lew,* edited by David D. Ryan (Mechanicsburg, PA: Stackpole Books, 1996), 32.

CHAPTER 6: AIDING AND GIVING COMFORT . . . TO THE ENEMY

1. "Rose O'Neal Greenhow," American Battlefield Trust, Battlefields.org /learn/biographies/rose-oneal-greenhow; intelligence.gov /evolution-of-espionage/civil-war/confederate-espionage/rose-greenhow.

2. Elizabeth L. Van Lew, *A Yankee Spy in Richmond: The Civil War Diary of "Crazy Bet" Van Lew,* edited by David D. Ryan (Mechanicsburg, PA: Stackpole Books, 1996), 34.

3. James McPherson, *Battle Cry of Freedom: The Civil War Era* (New York: Oxford University Press, 1988), 336.

4. Ann Blackman, *Wild Rose* (New York: Random House, 2005), 5–6.

5. Mary Boykin Miller Chesnut, *Mary Chesnut's Civil War,* edited by C. Vann Woodward (New Haven, CT: Yale University Press, 1981), 105.

6. Richard H. Abbott, *Cobbler in Congress: Life of Henry Wilson, 1812–1875,* vol. 2 (Madison: University of Wisconsin, 1965), 115–21, https://archive.org/details/cobblerincongres0000abbo/page/116 /mode/2up?q=%22Winfield+Scott%22&view=theater.

7. Van Lew, *A Yankee Spy in Richmond,* 35.

8. Van Lew, *A Yankee Spy in Richmond,* 34.

9. Van Lew, *A Yankee Spy in Richmond*, 35.
10. Elizabeth R. Varon, *Southern Lady, Yankee Spy: The True Story of Elizabeth Van Lew, a Union Agent in the Heart of the Confederacy* (New York: Oxford University Press, 2003), 59.
11. Van Lew, *A Yankee Spy in Richmond*, 60.
12. Varon, *Southern Lady, Yankee Spy*, 64.
13. Van Lew, *A Yankee Spy in Richmond*, 8–9.
14. Van Lew, *A Yankee Spy in Richmond*, 39.
15. "Seward was under a great deal of stress in 1861; both Greenhow and sources far more favorable to Seward attest that he was drinking rather heavily during this period and that alcohol caused him to speak more freely than was perhaps wise." Emily Lapsardi, "BookChat: Rose Greenhow's 'My Imprisonment,'" interviewed by Chris Mackowski, Emerging Civil War, October 25, 2022, https://emergingcivilwar.com/2022/10/25/bookchat-rose-greenhows-my-imprisonment-edited-by-emily-lapisardi/.

CHAPTER 7: IN THE CONFEDERATE WHITE HOUSE

1. Tour of the Confederate White House, April 2023.
2. Elizabeth R. Varon, *Southern Lady, Yankee Spy: The True Story of Elizabeth Van Lew, a Union Agent in the Heart of the Confederacy* (New York: Oxford University Press, 2003), 30.
3. Varon, *Southern Lady, Yankee Spy*, 30–31.
4. Lois Leveen, "Mary Richards Bowser," Encyclopedia Virginia, https://encyclopediavirginia.org/entries/bowser-mary-richards-fl-1846-1867/.
5. Leveen, "Mary Richards Bowser."
6. Tour of the Confederate White House, April 2023.

CHAPTER 8: INSIDE JOB

1. Lonnie R. Speer, *Portals to Hell: Military Prisons of the Civil War* (Mechanicsburg, PA: Stackpole Books, 1997), 91.
2. Douglas C. Waller, *Lincoln's Spies* (New York: Simon & Schuster, 2019), 127.
3. Elizabeth L. Van Lew, *A Yankee Spy in Richmond: The Civil War Diary of "Crazy Bet" Van Lew*, edited by David D. Ryan (Mechanicsburg, PA: Stackpole Books, 1996), 43.

4. Waller, *Lincoln's Spies,* 129.

5. John Nicolay, letter to Assistant Secretary of State Frederick Seward, May 22, 1861.

6. Christopher L. Kolakowski, *The Virginia Campaigns, March–August 1862,* Center of Military History, U.S. Army, 2016, 34, https://www .govinfo.gov/content/pkg/GOVPUB-D114-PURL-gpo72995/pdf/ GOVPUB-D114-PURL-gpo72995.pdf.

7. Van Lew, *A Yankee Spy in Richmond,* 43.

8. Van Lew, *A Yankee Spy in Richmond,* 44.

9. Elizabeth R. Varon, *Southern Lady, Yankee Spy: The True Story of Elizabeth Van Lew, a Union Agent in the Heart of the Confederacy* (New York: Oxford University Press, 2003), 96.

10. William B. Feis, *Grant's Secret Service: The Intelligence War from Belmont to Appomattox* (Lincoln: University of Nebraska Press, 2002), 88.

11. Waller, *Lincoln's Spies,* 99.

12. Waller, *Lincoln's Spies,* 178.

13. Varon, *Southern Lady, Yankee Spy,* 75.

14. Van Lew, *A Yankee Spy in Richmond,* 45.

15. Edwin C. Fishel, *The Secret War for the Union: The Untold Story of Military Intelligence in the Civil War* (Boston: Houghton Mifflin, 1996), 164.

16. Waller, *Lincoln's Spies,* 40.

17. Katharine M. Jones, *Ladies of Richmond, Confederate Capital* (Indianapolis: Bobbs-Merrill, 1962), 221.

18. Sara Agnes Rice Pryor, *Reminiscences of Peace and War, by Mrs. Roger A. Pryor* (New York: Macmillan, 1905), 188.

19. David B. Parker, *A Chautauqua Boy in '61 and Afterward* (Boston: Small, Maynard, 1912), 56.

20. Van Lew, *A Yankee Spy in Richmond,* 42.

21. Parker, *A Chautauqua Boy in '61 and Afterward,* 56.

22. Van Lew, *A Yankee Spy in Richmond,* 27.

CHAPTER 9: THE MAKING OF AN ASSASSIN

1. Amanda Zimmerman, "From Captivity to Capsized: Wild Rose O'Neal Greenhow," *Bibliomania* (blog), September 7, 2023, https://blogs.loc.gov/bibliomania/2023/09/07 /from-captivity-to-capsized-wild-rose-oneal-greenhow/.

2. Terry Alford, *Fortune's Fool: The Life of John Wilkes Booth* (Oxford: Oxford University Press, 2015), 133.

3. Alford, *Fortune's Fool*, 142.

4. *Boston Transcript,* May 9, 1862.

5. Alford, *Fortune's Fool*, 131.

6. Alford, *Fortune's Fool*, 163.

7. Alford, *Fortune's Fool*, 147.

8. Alford, *Fortune's Fool*, 166.

9. Alford, *Fortune's Fool*, 139.

10. Alford, *Fortune's Fool*, 140.

11. *Chicago Times,* April 20, 1865.

12. Terry Alford, *In the Houses of Their Dead: The Lincolns, the Booths, and the Spirits* (New York: Liveright Publishing, 2022), 181.

13. Asia Booth Clarke, *John Wilkes Booth: A Sister's Memoir,* edited and with an introduction by Terry Alford (Jackson: University Press of Mississippi, 1996), 104.

CHAPTER 10: GLORIOUS CHARGES AND YELLOW RIBBONS

1. National Park Service, "Financial Ruin at White Haven: The Panic of 1857 Comes to White Haven," ND, https://www.nps.gov/articles/000/financial-ruin-at-white-haven-the-panic-of-1857-comes-to-white-haven.htm.

2. National Park Service, "Financial Ruin at White Haven."

3. Stephen Z. Starr, *The Union Cavalry in the Civil War* (Baton Rouge: Louisiana State University Press, 1979–1985), preface.

4. Starr, *The Union Cavalry in the Civil War,* preface.

5. John Adolphus Bernard Dahlgren, *Memoir of Ulric Dahlgren. By His Father, Rear-Admiral Dahlgren* (Philadelphia: J. B. Lippincott, 1872), 225.

6. Ron Chernow, *Grant* (New York: Penguin Press, 2017), 55.

7. National Park Service, "Sample Letters from Ulysses S. Grant to Julia Dent Grant," https://www.nps.gov/articles/000/ulsg-sample-letters.htm.

8. Chernow, *Grant,* 47.

9. Chernow, *Grant,* 87.

10. "Ulysses S. Grant," A House Divided: America in the Age of Lincoln, https://www.digitalhistory.uh.edu/exhibits/ahd/civilwar27.html.

11. Edwin C. Fishel, *The Secret War for the Union: The Untold Story of Military Intelligence in the Civil War* (Boston: Houghton Mifflin, 1996), 3.

12. Fishel, *The Secret War for the Union*, 123.
13. Fishel, *The Secret War for the Union*, 5.
14. Edward G. Longacre, "Was Grant a Drunk?" History News Network, September 9, 2007, https://www.hnn.us/article/was-grant-a -drunk#sthash.52YT4xs2.dpuf.

CHAPTER 11: BEGGING FOR BREAD

1. U.S. Army Continental Commands, Record Group 393, entry 3980.
2. Stephen V. Ash, *Rebel Richmond: Life and Death in the Confederate Capital* (Chapel Hill, NC; University of North Carolina Press, 2019), 58–61, 71.
3. Elizabeth L. Van Lew, *A Yankee Spy in Richmond: The Civil War Diary of "Crazy Bet" Van Lew*, edited by David D. Ryan (Mechanicsburg, PA: Stackpole Books, 1996), 54.
4. Katharine M. Jones, *Ladies of Richmond, Confederate Capital* (Indianapolis: Bobbs-Merrill, 1962), 155.
5. Elizabeth R. Varon, *Southern Lady, Yankee Spy: The True Story of Elizabeth Van Lew, a Union Agent in the Heart of the Confederacy* (New York: Oxford University Press, 2003), 102; "Bread Riot, Richmond," Encyclopedia of Virginia, https://encyclopediavirginia.org/entries /bread-riot-richmond/.
6. "Speculation During the Civil War," Encyclopedia of Virginia, https:// encyclopediavirginia.org/entries/speculation-during-the-civil-war/.
7. "Speculation During the Civil War," Encyclopedia of Virginia.
8. Van Lew, *A Yankee Spy in Richmond*, 49.
9. Varon, *Southern Lady, Yankee Spy*, 104.
10. *Richmond Examiner*, April 4, 1863.
11. Varon, *Southern Lady, Yankee Spy*, 105.

CHAPTER 12: TOO CLOSE FOR COMFORT

1. Elizabeth R. Varon, *Southern Lady, Yankee Spy: The True Story of Elizabeth Van Lew, a Union Agent in the Heart of the Confederacy* (New York: Oxford University Press, 2003), 168.
2. Varon, *Southern Lady, Yankee Spy*, 74.
3. Elizabeth D. Leonard, *Benjamin Franklin Butler: A Noisy, Fearless Life* (Chapel Hill: University of North Carolina Press, 2022), 168.

4. Benjamin F. Butler, *Butler's Book: Autobiography and Personal Reminiscences of Major-General Benjamin Butler* (Boston: A.M. Thayer & Co., 1892), 415–19, 617; *Richmond Dispatch,* January 28, 1864.

5. Varon, *Southern Lady, Yankee Spy,* 111.

6. Varon, *Southern Lady, Yankee Spy,* 151.

7. Varon, *Southern Lady, Yankee Spy,* 149.

8. Elizabeth L. Van Lew, *A Yankee Spy in Richmond: The Civil War Diary of "Crazy Bet" Van Lew,* edited by David D. Ryan (Mechanicsburg, PA: Stackpole Books, 1996), 55.

9. National Archives, Record Group 393, Entry 3980.

CHAPTER 13: THE JOURNEY THROUGH RAT HELL

1. Lonnie M. Speer, *Portals to Hell: Military Prisons of the Civil War* (Mechanicsburg, PA: Stackpole Books, 1997), 224.

2. Speer, *Portals to Hell,* 53.

3. Speer, *Portals to Hell,* 20.

4. Joseph Wheelan, *Libby Prison Breakout: The Daring Escape from the Notorious Civil War Prison* (New York: Public Affairs, 2010), 37.

5. Wheelan, *Libby Prison Breakout,* 105.

6. Douglas C. Waller, *Lincoln's Spies* (New York: Simon & Schuster, 2019), 124; Wheelan, *Libby Prison Breakout,* 125.

CHAPTER 14: THE UNDERTAKING IS A DESPERATE ONE

1. Duane P. Schultz, *The Dahlgren Affair: Terror and Conspiracy in the Civil War* (New York: W. W. Norton, 1998), 85.

2. Virginia Lohmann Nodhturft, *F.W.E. Lohmann, Elizabeth Van Lew's Civil War Spy* (Outskirts Press, 2019), 108–109.

3. *The New York Times,* November 28, 1863.

4. James Harvey Kidd, *A Cavalryman with Custer: Custer's Michigan Cavalry Brigade in the Civil War* (Skyhorse, 2018), 93–95.

5. Charles S. Wainright, *A Diary of Battle: The Personal Journals of Col. Charles S. Wainwright, 1861–65,* edited by Allan Nevins (New York: Da Capo Press, 1998), 265.

6. E. B. Long, *The Civil War Day by Day; An Almanac, 1861–1865* (New York: Doubleday, 1971), 462.

7. Margaret Leech, *Reveille in Washington: 1860–1865* (Garden City, NY: Garden City Publishing Co., 1941), 5.

8. John Adolphus Bernard Dahlgren, *Memoir of Ulric Dahlgren. By His Father, Rear-Admiral Dahlgren* (Philadelphia: J. B. Lippincott, 1872), 211.

9. The Civil War News & Views Open Discussion Forum, "Sherman's Thoughts on Southerners," http://history-sites.com/cgi-bin/bbs62x /nvcwmb/webbbs_config.pl?md=read;id=73379.

10. Nodhturft, *F.W.E. Lohmann, Elizabeth Van Lew's Civil War Spy,* 108.

11. Schultz, *The Dahlgren Affair,* 88–89.

12. Schultz, *The Dahlgren Affair,* 80.

13. Schultz, *The Dahlgren Affair,* 127.

14. Elizabeth L. Van Lew, *A Yankee Spy in Richmond: The Civil War Diary of "Crazy Bet" Van Lew,* edited by David D. Ryan (Mechanicsburg, PA: Stackpole Books, 1996), 68.

15. Van Lew, *A Yankee Spy in Richmond,* 68.

16. Schultz, *The Dahlgren Affair,* 125.

17. Schultz, *The Dahlgren Affair,* 143.

CHAPTER 15: ULRIC THE HUN

1. Virgil Carrington Jones, *Eight Hours Before Richmond* (New York: Henry Holt, 1957), 148.

2. Duane P. Schultz, *The Dahlgren Affair: Terror and Conspiracy in the Civil War* (New York: W. W. Norton, 1998), 153.

3. Schultz, *The Dahlgren Affair,* 154.

4. *Richmond Sentinel,* March 5, 1864.

5. *Richmond Whig,* March 5, 1864.

6. *Richmond Examiner,* March 7, 1864.

7. Stephanie McCurry, *Women's War: Fighting and Surviving the American Civil War* (Cambridge, MA: Belknap Press, 2019), 15.

8. Stephen W. Sears, *Controversies and Commanders: Dispatches from the Army of the Potomac* (New York, Houghton Mifflin, 1999), 229.

9. Sears, *Controversies and Commanders,* 230.

10. *Richmond Examiner,* March 5, 1864.

11. *The New York Times,* March 10, 1864.

12. Elizabeth L. Van Lew, *A Yankee Spy in Richmond: The Civil War Diary of "Crazy Bet" Van Lew,* edited by David D. Ryan (Mechanicsburg, PA: Stackpole Books, 1996), 73–74.

13. Sears, *Controversies and Commanders,* 245.

14. Sears, *Controversies and Commanders,* 244.

15. Sears, *Controversies and Commanders,* 246.

16. Jerry Keenan, *Wilson's Cavalry Corps: Union Campaigns in the Western Theatre, October 1864 Through Spring 1865* (Jefferson, NC: McFarland, 1998), 15.

17. *New York Herald,* September 18, 1863.

18. *Richmond Sentinel,* March 6, 1864.

CHAPTER 16: TOTAL WAR

1. William A. Tidwell, *Come Retribution: The Confederate Secret Service and the Assassination of Lincoln* (Jackson: University Press of Mississippi, 1988), 149.

2. Tidwell, *Come Retribution,* 39.

3. Tidwell, *Come Retribution,* 49.

4. Edward Steers Jr., *Blood on the Moon: The Assassination of Abraham Lincoln* (Lexington: University Press of Kentucky, 2001), 301.

5. Asia Booth Clarke, *John Wilkes Booth: A Sister's Memoir,* edited and with an introduction by Terry Alford (Jackson: University Press of Mississippi, 1996), 104.

6. Terry Alford, *Fortune's Fool: The Life of John Wilkes Booth* (Oxford: Oxford University Press, 2015), 186.

7. Steers Jr., *Blood on the Moon,* 301.

8. Alford, *Fortune's Fool,* 186–88; Steers Jr., *Blood on the Moon,* 72–73.

9. Duane P. Schultz, *The Dahlgren Affair: Terror and Conspiracy in the Civil War* (New York: W. W. Norton, 1998), 180.

10. Alford, *Fortune's Fool,* 193.

11. *Baltimore American,* December 7, 1902.

12. Alford, *Fortune's Fool,* 205.

13. Alford, *Fortune's Fool,* 199.

14. Alford, *Fortune's Fool,* 243.

CHAPTER 17: SWELTERING SEA OF FIRE

1. Elizabeth R. Varon, *Southern Lady, Yankee Spy: The True Story of Elizabeth Van Lew, a Union Agent in the Heart of the Confederacy* (New York: Oxford University Press, 2003), 171–74.

2. Varon, *Southern Lady, Yankee Spy*, 180.

3. E. B. Long, *The Civil War Day by Day; An Almanac, 1861–1865* (New York: Doubleday, 1971), 663.

4. Katharine M. Jones, *Ladies of Richmond, Confederate Capital* (Indianapolis: Bobbs-Merrill, 1962), 285.

5. "Five Forks," American Battlefield Trust, Battlefields.org/learn /civil-war/battles/five-forks.

6. Jones, *Ladies of Richmond*, 286–87.

7. Varon, *Southern Lady, Yankee Spy*, 192.

8. Ernest B. Furgurson, *Ashes of Glory: Richmond at War* (New York: Vintage Books, 1996), 335.

9. Elizabeth L. Van Lew, *A Yankee Spy in Richmond: The Civil War Diary of "Crazy Bet" Van Lew*, edited by David D. Ryan (Mechanicsburg, PA: Stackpole Books, 1996), 105.

10. Furgurson, *Ashes of Glory*, 333.

11. Jones, *Ladies of Richmond*, 281.

12. Mary Boykin Miller Chesnut, *Mary Chesnut's Civil War*, edited by C. Vann Woodward (New Haven: Yale University Press, 1981), 782.

13. Varon, *Southern Lady, Yankee Spy*, 193.

14. Waller, *Lincoln's Spies*, 392.

15. Varon, *Southern Lady, Yankee Spy*, 194.

16. Van Lew, *A Yankee Spy in Richmond*, 105.

17. Sarah Pruitt. "What Lincoln Said in His Final Speech," History Channel, https://www.history.com/news /what-lincoln-said-in-his-final-speech.

18. Carl Sandburg, *Abraham Lincoln: The War Years* (New York: Harcourt & Brace, 1939), 104.

19. Sandburg, *Abraham Lincoln: The War Years*, 105.

CHAPTER 18: STOUT MEN CRIED

1. Virginia Lohmann Nodhturft, *F.W.E. Lohmann, Elizabeth Van Lew's Civil War Spy* (Outskirts Press, 2019), 171.

2. Lohmann Nodhturft, *F.W.E. Lohmann*, 172.

3. Elizabeth R. Varon, *Southern Lady, Yankee Spy: The True Story of Elizabeth Van Lew, a Union Agent in the Heart of the Confederacy* (New York: Oxford University Press, 2003), 198.

4. Doris Kearns Goodwin, *Team of Rivals: The Political Genius of Abraham Lincoln* (New York: Simon & Schuster, 2005), 726; William A. Tidwell, *April '65: Confederate Covert Action in the American Civil War, April 1865* (Kent, OH: Kent State University Press, 1995), 203.

5. Goodwin, *Team of Rivals,* 729.

6. Terry Alford, *Fortune's Fool: The Life of John Wilkes Booth* (Oxford: Oxford University Press, 2015), 256.

7. Tidwell, *April '65: Confederate Covert Action,* 205.

8. Alford, *Fortune's Fool,* 259.

9. Alford, *Fortune's Fool,* 207.

10. Alford, *Fortune's Fool,* 259.

11. *Washington National Intelligencer,* July 18, 1867.

12. Goodwin, *Team of Rivals,* 745.

13. Michelle Miller and Christopher Wills, "'Stout Men Cried and Trembled'—A Nation Reacts to Lincoln's Assassination," Abraham Lincoln Presidential Library and Museum, April 13, 2023, https://presidentlincoln.illinois.gov/Blog/Posts/175/Abraham-Lincoln/2023/4/Stout-men-cried-and-trembled-a-nation-reacts-to-Lincolns-assassination/blog-post/).

14. Martha Hodes, *Mourning Lincoln* (New Haven: Yale University Press, 2015), 84.

15. *Philadelphia Inquirer,* April 26, 1865.

CHAPTER 19: A MUFF AND GUNPOWDER TEA

1. Elizabeth R. Varon, *Southern Lady, Yankee Spy: The True Story of Elizabeth Van Lew, a Union Agent in the Heart of the Confederacy* (New York: Oxford University Press, 2003), 219.

2. *Richmond Enquirer and Examiner,* March 23, 1869.

3. Varon, *Southern Lady, Yankee Spy,* 217.

4. Elizabeth Van Lew papers, New York Public Library.

5. Varon, *Southern Lady, Yankee Spy,* 238.

6. Elizabeth L. Van Lew, *A Yankee Spy in Richmond: The Civil War Diary of "Crazy Bet" Van Lew,* edited by David D. Ryan (Mechanicsburg, PA: Stackpole Books, 1996), 116.

7. Douglas C. Waller, *Lincoln's Spies* (New York: Simon & Schuster, 2019), 438.

8. Varon, *Southern Lady, Yankee Spy,* 243.

9. Van Lew, *A Yankee Spy in Richmond,* 131.

10. Varon, *Southern Lady, Yankee Spy,* 242.

11. Varon, *Southern Lady, Yankee Spy,* 250.

EPILOGUE

1. Eric H. Walther, *The Fire-Eaters* (Baton Rouge: Louisiana State University Press, 1992), 228.

2. Duane P. Schultz, *The Dahlgren Affair: Terror and Conspiracy in the Civil War* (New York: W. W. Norton, 1998), 263.

ABOUT THE AUTHOR

❧ ❧

GERRI WILLIS has extensive experience reporting and anchoring business news and personal finance topics for cable news outlets. She is a correspondent and anchor at Fox Business and appears frequently on *Fox News*. She contributes to a variety of the company's platforms, hosting the *Real Tough Women* series on Fox Nation, and the *Fearless & Proud* podcast for Fox Radio.

Her writing career as a magazine and newspaper reporter spanned three decades. Her award-winning work has appeared in *SmartMoney* magazine, *Money* magazine, Crain's *New York Business,* and *USA Today*.

Her nightly hour-long show at Fox Business, *The Willis Report,* aired for five years, and featured coverage of a range of economic and political topics. Prior to that, she anchored a half-hour personal finance show on Saturday mornings on CNN, first called *Open House* and then *Your Bottom Line*. While there, she also wrote a monthly column for *Money* magazine.

She is an outspoken advocate for breast cancer awareness. She tested positive for Stage 3 lobular breast cancer in 2016 and was treated with two surgeries, including a mastectomy, chemotherapy, and radiation therapy. In 2019, she was awarded the Susan G. Komen Image Award. She later joined the Komen board where she served for two years.

Willis studied economics and finance at Columbia Business School as a Knight Bagehot Fellow in 1991–1992.

She and her husband, David Evans, live in Westchester, New York, where they spend an inordinate amount of time spoiling their toy poodle puppy, Rufus.